The Corporate Practice of Me

California/Milbank Series on Health and the Public

The Corporate Practice of Medicine

Competition and Innovation in Health Care

James C. Robinson

A Copublication with
the Milbank Memorial Fund

University of California Press
Berkeley·Los Angeles·London

A copublication with
the Milbank Memorial Fund

University of California Press
Berkeley and Los Angeles, California

University of California Press, Ltd.
London, England

Library of Congress Cataloging-in-Publication Data

Robinson, James C., 1953–.

The corporate practice of medicine : competition
and innovation in health care / James C. Robinson.
        p.   cm.
    "A copublication with the
    Milbank Memorial Fund."
    Includes bibliographical references and index.
    ISBN 0-520-22075-7 (alk. paper).—ISBN 0-520-
22076-5 (pbk. : alk paper)
    1. Medical corporations—United States.   I.
Title.
R728.2.R63   1999
610'.65—dc21   99-14072
                                                CIP

Manufactured in the United States of America

08 07 06 05 04 03 02 01 00 99
10 9 8 7 6 5 4 3 2 1

The paper used in this publication meets the minimum requirements of ANSI/NISO Z39.48-1992
(R 1997) (Permanence of Paper). ∞

Contents

Foreword

The Milbank Memorial Fund is an endowed national foundation that supports nonpartisan analysis, study, research and communication on significant issues in health care and public health. The Fund makes available the results of its work in meetings with decision makers, reports, articles and books.

The Fund's publishing partnership with the University of California Press encourages the synthesis and communication of findings from research that could contribute to more effective health policy. James Robinson's book is an exemplary beginning for the California/Milbank Series on Health and the Public. Robinson, an economist, studied the methods and findings of adjacent disciplines and then talked to hundreds of persons who have firsthand knowledge about recent changes in medical practice. This book builds on research he has reported in articles in major journals of medicine and health policy.

The Fund and the Press solicited reviews of Robinson's manuscript from physician executives, lawyers, regulators, purchasers, consumer advocates and social scientists, and then convened many of these reviewers to discuss the manuscript with the author. Robinson's book is designed to contribute to public understanding of the history and prospects of the contemporary corporate practice of medicine and to enhance discussion about appropriate policy that assures accountability to both purchasers and patients.

Daniel M. Fox   *Samuel L. Milbank*
President   Chairman

Preface

It is customary in the preface for the author to acknowledge those who provided the material and intellectual sustenance for the work at hand. Here the list must be longer than usual, since this book builds on over 400 formal interviews and countless informal conversations with physicians and physician leaders, medical group directors and hospital administrators, insurance executives and benefit managers, investment analysts and corporate consultants, association presidents and industry critics, consumer advocates and newspaper reporters, brokers and agents, lawyers and lobbyists, professors and pundits. Its ideas have been tempered in dozens of presentations to professional societies, corporate boards, policy roundtables, legislative committees, university seminars, regulatory agencies, and industry conferences. Statistical data and company documents have been supplied by medical groups, health plans, corporate purchasers, and investment analysts. I feel a great personal and professional debt to the many individuals and organizations who have given generously of their time.

The research underlying this book was supported in large part by the Robert Wood Johnson Foundation through its Investigator Awards in Health Policy Research, a program conceptualized by Steve Schroeder M.D., Jim Knickman, and Bob Hughes as an opportunity for scholars to break out of their disciplines and bring new ways of thinking to the health care system. The research applied case study methods to multispecialty medical groups and independent practice associations and to the contractual relationships between these physician organizations and hospitals, health insurers, large public and private purchasers, and the ultimate consumers of care. In this I have been fortunate to have the sustained commitment of numerous health care leaders, many of whom engaged in a series of day-long discussions on the structure, strategy, and challenges of physician organization. Participants in these roundtables, whose contribution cannot be overemphasized, included (in random order) Al Barnett M.D., Bob Margolis M.D., Michael Abel M.D., Andy Adams M.D., Darryl Cardoza, Jay Crosson M.D., Bob Jamplis M.D., Kurt Sligar M.D., Pat Kapsner, Steve Posar M.D., Tom Waltz M.D., Peter Grant, Ron Lossett, Jim Hillman, Gloria Mayer, Arnie Millstein M.D., Barbara Shaw, Elliot Sternberg M.D., Mark Wagar, Ed Geehr M.D., and Leo Lopez M.D. These roundtables and the related discussions were partially cosponsored by the Pacific Business Group on Health, with active participation from Pat Powers, Tanya Bednarski, Paul Fearer, Robin Wythe, Suzanne Mercure, Cheryl Damberg, Tracy Rodriquez, Margaret Stanley, Tom Davies, John Ramey, and Margaret Jordan, and included colleagues of mine such as Oliver Williamson of the University of California at Berkeley and Alain Enthoven of Stanford University.

Despite their obvious importance for the research underlying this book, the industry roundtables constituted just the visible tip of a much larger set of interviews, meetings, and debates with physician leaders, administrators, clinicians, and critics. Other medical group leaders who have been particularly helpful at one or more points during the process include Walter Mullikin M.D., John McDonald, Steve McDermott, Steven Aharonian M.D., Shelley Horwitz, Ira Davidoff M.D., Lori Hack, Mathew Mazdyasni, Joe O'Heier, Marc Moser, Jack Lewin M.D., Daniel Temianka M.D., David Druker M.D., Gary Groves M.D., Norm Vinn D.O., Trudi Carter M.D., Dick Ferreira M.D., Richard Dixon M.D., Jim Selevan, Ken Brin M.D., Don Balfour M.D., Victor Corsiglia M.D., and Rob Filuk M.D.

Under the growing pressures of competition and consolidation, many physician organizations have sought affiliations with hospital systems, physician practice management companies, or other large entities that offer a new set of challenges. The original study of medical groups naturally led to involvement with hospital systems that seek stronger relationships with physicians and physician organizations. The work on physician practice management was built around a project sponsored jointly by the California HealthCare Foundation and the policy journal *Health Affairs*. Particular appreciation for their contributions to this dimension of the work is owed to Terry Hartshorn, Derril Reeves, Ron Loeppke M.D., Kevin Ellis D.O., Mike Linn, Larry Marsh, Jerry Coil, John Austin, Jim Yoshioka, Cliff Ossorio M.D., Robbie Rygg, Ray Fernandez M.D., Jonathan Fuchs, Steve Rosenthal, Dave Hoskinson, Rick Lanman M.D., Bob Fraschetti, and Larry Wellikson M.D.

It is impossible to analyze physician organizations without analyzing the health insurance plans with which they are bound in a relationship of continual cooperation and conflict. My understanding of medical markets and organizations has benefited from extended discussions with many health plan leaders, both through firm-specific case studies and through a variety of board meetings, strategy retreats, and industry conferences to which I was invited to contribute. My thinking has been influenced by Artie Southam M.D., Leonard Schaeffer, David Lawrence M.D., Jay Gellert, George Halverson, Wayne Moon, Bruce Bodaken, Henry Loubet, Andy Allocco, David Pockell, Jeff Folik, Mark Hyde, Linda Lyons M.D., Joe Criscione, Roger Greaves, Ron Williams, Steve Zatkin, Rick Badger, Sam Ho M.D., Gordon Norman M.D., Howie Arkans M.D., Jeff Kamil M.D., Ferial Bahremand, and Curtis Terry. Other individuals who have been particularly helpful to my understanding of relationships between purchasers, health plans, and physician organizations include Peggy O'Kane, Bob Galvin M.D., Nancy Oswald, Beau Carter, Don Fisher, and Alan Zwerner M.D.

But in the end all this wealth of interview notes, company documents, statistical reports, and investment banking analyses had to come together into a book manuscript. The lonely process of pressing recalcitrant reality into orderly text was relieved by the unflagging personal support from Larry Casalino M.D., my friend and colleague with whom I worked on many of the case studies and roundtables; John Iglehart, whose editorial review process at *Health Affairs* tightened my thinking on many of the ideas presented here; Dan Fox, who steadfastly supported the application of institutional economic theory to the health care sector; Mark Smith M.D., for whom organizational innovation is one of the great untold stories of contemporary medicine; and Barbara Krimgold, whose personal mission was to see that the Investigator Award projects fulfilled their promise. The first draft was transformed as the consequence of a day-long review sponsored by the Milbank Memorial Fund and the University of California Press. Dan Fox, Lynne Withey, Suzanne Samuel, Peter Grant, Clark Kerr, Bob Leibenluft, Nancy Oswald, Pat Powers, Mark Peterson, Jeff Rideout M.D., Bill Sage, Rosemary Stevens, Carl Volpe, and Bart Wald M.D. read the entire manuscript, contributed detailed suggestions, and collectively created one of those rare events in which we can step back and reflect on what the creative chaos of the moment means for the future of medicine.

These many fine people agree on many issues but disagree on many others, and hence could never be held accountable for the final form of any one book. They are therefore exonerated from responsibility but thanked again for their ideas, their enthusiasm, and their energies devoted to building a better system of health care.

CHAPTER I

Introduction

America had declared anathema on the corporate practice of medicine. Insurers and hospitals were prohibited from employing physicians, who were to remain in independent practice. Investor ownership of hospitals was discouraged by philanthropic donations and tax subsidies to non-profit organizations. Insurers adopted an arms-length approach to the health care delivery system, reimbursing costs as incurred without questioning clinical appropriateness. The ban on corporate practice also played a larger, more symbolic role. It drew a clear line demarcating medicine, where financial incentives, private capital, and the entrepreneurial ethos were disdained, from the commercial sector, where they were tolerated and even acclaimed. The delivery of health care was seen to be different. It promoted health, which is fundamental to all other endeavors. The unequal distribution of income and illness engendered insurance mechanisms that divorced the patient receiving the service from the citizen paying the tab. Americans might talk about their consumer preferences for videos and automobiles, but they insisted on their needs for vaccines and angioplasties. They sought to substitute cooperation for competition, trust for contract, moral exhortation for economic incentive, and professionalism for business organization.

In the waning decades of the twentieth century, however, the basic structures of the health care system began to lose their uniqueness and came to resemble those in the mainstream of the economy. Insurance plans and hospital chains were the first to adopt corporate strategies and structures, integrating vertically and horizontally, seeking economies of scale and scope, financing growth through the stock and bond markets, and competing ever more aggressively on price and service. The tumult of change initially appeared to be passing the physician by, with solo practice and fee-for-service payment remaining the dominant forms of organization and payment. But suddenly in the 1990s the storm of change broke upon the profession, sweeping away the illusion of continuity along with unquestioned clinical autonomy, unconstrained practice income, and unparalleled cultural authority. Now the medical marketplace is a maelstrom of primary care and multispecialty medical groups, independent practice associations and single-specialty networks, physician practice management firms and physician-hospital systems, open-access provider panels and tightly integrated prepaid plans. The emerging forms of physician organization vary across geographic regions, influenced by local demographics, economics, and politics. But the change convulsing health care is national in scope, with turbulence everywhere replacing stability, innovation replacing inertia, and risk replacing security.

The physician is the central figure in health care, the individual who must translate scientific knowledge into clinical technique, accommodate epidemiological patterns to local idiosyncrasies, balance patient preferences with professional precepts, and live daily with both urgency and uncertainty. The organizational form of physician practice is central to the health care system, more important ultimately than the fate of insurance plans and hospital chains. In seeking to understand the changing structures of physician organization, it is imperative to maintain a dual focus on the external pressures that impinge on the profession and on the internal responses to those pressures. A single-minded focus on context would miss the internal dynamism of physician organization, the ability to experiment, learn from mistakes, emulate examples from other sectors, and rise again from the ashes of failure. A single-minded focus on internal organization would further the illusion that the profession is master of its own destiny.

The dominant force exerting itself on the medical profession, to which all other forces are subsidiary, derives from the conflicting pressures between expenditure-increasing technological change, on the one hand, and revenue-constraining resistance by taxpayers, employers, and individual purchasers on the other. The twentieth century produced an ever-growing range of new clinical interventions in response to deeper scientific understanding, rising social wealth, and a cultural emphasis on the longevity and quality of life. Some new technologies have reduced

expenditures by replacing cruder and costlier interventions or by preventing illnesses altogether. Most, however, have raised overall costs by
allowing physicians to intervene in previously hopeless cases, palliate
what formerly was endured, or raise expectations about the possibilities
available at each stage of life. The medical profession responded with
alacrity to the loosening of social purse strings through the spread of public and private health insurance. The extension of insurance coverage
stimulated further growth in utilization and expenditure. Between 1960
and 1970 medical spending increased from $27 billion to $73 billion, or
from 5.1 percent to 7.1 percent of the economy. By 1980 it had increased
to $247 billion, by 1990 it reached $700 billion, and by the end of the century had surpassed one trillion dollars.[1] Yet obviously the system could
not continue to grow at the accustomed rate. The rise from 5 percent to
almost 15 percent of the economy cut deeply into consumer income, fueled the flames of taxpayer revolt, and made insurance unaffordable to
40 million citizens. A continued rise from 15 percent to 25 percent of total spending would exert intolerable pressures on other social priorities.
Payers and purchasers are now thoroughly aroused, demanding restraint
in health insurance premiums and health care prices, in income taxes and
payroll deductions, in fringe benefit programs and out-of-pocket contributions. Expenditures will continue to rise, given the underlying technological, economic, and cultural conditions, but henceforth at a much
more constrained rate. The health care environment is a tightening vise,
with rising costs pushing against constrained revenues, exerting ever
greater pressures and inflicting ever greater pain on the profession.

The imagery of pressure and pain, of increasing social conflicts and
heartrending personal choices, emphasizes only one of the two dynamics in health care. The second, more optimistic, dynamic is propelled by
innovation in forms of physician organization, financial payment, and
clinical practice. As in all economic sectors, the pressures from rising
costs and constrained revenues create opportunities for individuals and
organizations that can offer the same services at lower cost or better services at the same cost. Challenge is the spur to change, to new ways of
thinking and new ways of acting, to individual initiative and cooperative
venture. Most experiments fail, and system-wide innovation is a close
cousin to chaos. But the record of the modern economy, which combines
market competition with corporate organization, is that ingenuity tends
to outrun constraints. The health care sector generally, and the physician profession specifically, now manifest an extraordinary proclivity toward experimentation. Of particular importance are the legacies of the

multispecialty medical group, as embodied most clearly in the Mayo Clinic, and of the prepaid group practice, as embodied most clearly in the Permanente Medical Group. These organizations established the possibility that innovation could simultaneously improve quality and efficiency, uphold professional standards and accommodate market realities, gain physician commitment and retain patient loyalty. The emerging forms of physician organization do not mimic Mayo and Permanente in their specifics. Large, prepaid, multispecialty clinics remain the exception to a rule of smaller groups and individual practices coordinated by nonexclusive contractual affiliations, reimbursed by diverse financial mechanisms, and relating in numerous ways to insurance and hospital organizations. Yet the principle and promise of organizational innovation is firmly established in the historical record and in the contemporary marketplace.

ENVIRONMENTAL PRESSURES: REGULATION, PURCHASING, AND INSURANCE

Throughout most of the twentieth century the organization of health care differed in striking ways from organizational forms typical of other industries. Most physicians practiced in solo or small group settings, with informal referral linkages within the guild and between physicians and hospitals. Advertising and fee discounting were frowned upon, and for many years professional collusion to prevent competition was sanctioned by governmental authorities. Modern medicine was a capital-intensive industry but most of the expensive technology was concentrated in nonprofit hospitals governed by community leaders with little expertise in corporate finance. Insurance and payment were coordinated by a mix of public, nonprofit, and commercial entities that paid higher revenues to providers who incurred higher costs and reimbursed higher claims for patients who chose more expensive settings. The bills were paid in the first instance by employers and governmental programs and in the last instance by individual employees and taxpayers. No one questioned the price and quality of the services purchased, employers on the principle of not interfering with personal medical decisions and employees under the impression that they were spending someone else's money. Fragmented, powerful supply combined with fragmented, powerless demand to create the system of professional dominance.[2]

The unusual economic features of medicine were defended by physician and hospital leaders, celebrated by scholars, and accepted by policymakers as organizational adaptations to the unique features of illness and medicine. Over time, however, the relentless expansion of the system nurtured a vocal chorus of critics. The most obvious symptom of malfunction was the inflation in expenditures, which undermined wage growth and fueled the fires of taxpayer revolt. Insurance coverage spread from the war years until the 1970s and then began to recede as cost inflation drove premiums beyond the reach of low income workers and their families. By the end of the century, over 40 million Americans were uninsured at least part of the year; over three-fourths of these were the families of working people. Epidemiologists have documented dramatic variations in health care utilization across geographic regions and an only tenuous association between economic investments and health status improvements. Residents of the Boston metropolitan area, which is dominated by the Harvard medical establishment, incur hospital expenditures 80 percent higher than residents of New Haven, dominated by the Yale medical establishment, even though the demographic characteristics of the communities are almost identical.[3] Doctors in Miami spend over twice as much on each patient as do doctors in San Francisco.[4] Not even the most enthusiastic apologist claims that patients in Boston and Miami are getting better quality care than patients in New Haven and San Francisco.

Most nations use regulatory means to counter the inherently expansionistic tendencies of modern medicine. National health insurance programs have tended to leave the organizational structure of the profession intact, with solo practice and fee-for-service payment continuing to dominate in Canada and many European nations; instead, they control costs by upstream limits on physician supply and specialization, technology diffusion, capital expenditures, hospital budgets, and professional fees. The United States made numerous forays in the direction of public financing and control, but always in the face of determined resistance from the medical profession, other vested interests, and a broad-based popular skepticism of governmental authority. The most important initiatives sought to extend the principles of utility regulation from the transportation, communication, energy, and finance industries to hospitals and ultimately to the whole of health care. Had these initiatives succeeded, the subsequent changes in the structure of the profession would have been precluded. But the attempt to apply utility regulation to health care occurred at precisely the time when analogous controls were being dismantled elsewhere. Utility deregulation was itself only one symptom of a global disenchantment with centralized economic authority, which manifested itself even more dramatically in the collapse of state socialism in eastern Europe, the privatization of infrastructure industries in western Europe, and the opening of economies everywhere to greater trade and rivalry. Moreover, the American flirtation with regulatory strategies in health care was accompanied by simultaneous but logically incompatible initiatives to increase competition. After decades of exemption, the medical profession was brought within the purview of the antitrust statutes, which interpreted many guild practices as collusion and regulatory controls as barriers to entry. The simultaneous pursuit of regulation and antitrust was schizophrenic but not unprecedented in American economic history, having prominent though dubious precedents during the Progressive era, the New Deal, and the Great Society. But the antitrust agencies did much to undermine the organizational structures of professional dominance and to forestall incipient regulatory oversight.

In direct contrast to utility regulation, the managed competition approach to health care reform favored thoroughgoing change in the basic organizational and payment structures of the profession. It embraced the tradition of prepaid group practice as the core of a new professional paradigm, relying on multispecialty cooperation among physicians who would accept budgetary and clinical responsibility for a defined population of patients. The efficiency of prepaid group practice would be ensured by offering choices to individual consumers, thereby forcing providers to structure and price their services in a manner attractive to the patient. Given the potential for adverse selection, inadequate information on quality, and other market failures, competition among prepaid groups would be managed by large public and private alliances. These sponsors would use purchasing strategies to reward performance and enforce a framework of rules that included standardized benefits, open enrollment, and information disclosure. Some policy entrepreneurs emphasized the management aspect of managed competition, with mandatory participation in purchasing alliances and governmentally enforced budgets, while others emphasized the competitive aspect, with voluntary participation and consumer-driven pricing. But all variants embraced the sponsor and thus all suffered the same fate when neither the political process nor the private sector spawned more than a few purchasing alliances.

The organization of physician practice and the performance of the broader health care system have always been heavily dependent on the structure of health insurance and finance. The traditional framework of solo practice was initially supported and ultimately undermined by the indemnity structure of the Blue Cross, commercial, and Medicare insurance plans, which passively reimbursed costs as incurred and claims as filed until the taxpayers and purchasers rebelled. Many indemnity carriers have exited the marketplace and those that remain have re-engineered themselves into managed care plans that offer preferred provider, point-of-service, and related managed care products. The staff- and group-model Health Maintenance Organizations (HMOs), which combine finance and delivery within one integrated system, also have mutated in response to market exigencies and no longer play the central role that their proponents envisaged. With a few salient exceptions, HMOs have divested their exclusive provider relationships and now contract with networks of independent physicians, medical groups, and hospital systems. The evolution of indemnity carriers and HMOs into multiproduct health plans plays a central role in explaining the competition and cooperation, fragmentation and consolidation, acquisitions and divestitures to which physician organizations has been subjected. Health plans are diversified into multiple benefit designs, provider networks, distribution channels, and geographic markets. Physician organizations, in response, are developing nonexclusive relationships with health plans and with the insurance products offered by each plan. The emerging insurance framework now occupies a middle ground between the extremes of arms-length indemnity insurance and of vertically integrated HMOs. Virtual integration between insurance and delivery parallels similar changes elsewhere and reflects new understandings of how to balance independence and interdependence in a dynamic economy. It contributes to the promise of the emerging health care system, to its flexibility, dynamism, and innovation, but also to the perils of that system, to its fragmentation, conflict, and confusion.

ORGANIZATIONAL INNOVATION: MEDICAL GROUPS, IPAs, PRACTICE MANAGEMENT, HOSPITAL SYSTEMS

Physicians, physician organizations, and the medical profession have responded to the pressures for cost control with both backward-looking defenses and forward-looking strategies. Professional societies have used their fading political power in favor of any-willing-provider statutes, mandated benefits, balance-billing provisions, and other attempts to frustrate limits on prices and prerogatives. Physicians in some communities have boycotted health plans that seek lower fees or utilization oversight, although the antitrust agencies have curtailed blatant collu-

sion. But the most important responses, from a larger and longer perspective, have been those where physicians have developed, joined, or
affiliated with new forms of organization that promise better clinical
coordination, scale economies in administration, advanced computer information systems, aligned incentives for generalists and specialists, partnerships with hospital systems and health plans, and more committed
relationships with patients and purchasers. These new forms of organizations pose a new set of problems, since most seek stronger bargaining
power as well as enhanced efficiency. But in this respect medical groups
and physician networks resemble all economic organizations, which invariably pursue higher revenues as well as lower costs and are kept in line
only by marketplace pressures from rivals, purchasers, and suppliers.

Innovations in physician organization vary across regions at any one
point in time and within particular regions across different points in time.
They respond to the environmental context within which they find themselves, which leads to divergence and dissimilarities, but also observe
and imitate each other, which leads to convergence and similarities. No
one book can capture the breadth of experiments across the nation, and
none confidently can predict which will spread and which will languish.
This book will focus on four major forms of physician organization,
each of which had precursors in earlier decades but all of which came to
national prominence in the last years of the twentieth century. Multispecialty medical groups, independent practice associations, physician
practice management firms, and physician-hospital organizations respond in different ways to the changing clinical, economic, and cultural
pressures on American medicine. They are presented not with the claim
that they alone represent the future, although the future of physician organization certainly will be built on their foundations, but rather to support the broader assertion that environmental pressures on health care
costs lead to organizational innovations if not prevented by overly restrictive regulation.

Multispecialty medical groups have a long and distinguished history
in American medicine, beginning with the Mayo Clinic and diffusing
throughout much of the South and West. Some multispecialty groups
have remained focused on fee-for-service reimbursement, but most have
become deeply involved with prospective payment and managed care.
The prepaid group practice moved from the margins to the mainstream
of American health policy with the HMO Act of 1973 but remained peripheral to most local communities until the 1990s. I focus on the organizational evolution in California, North Carolina, and New Jersey to

highlight the salient features that distinguish contemporary group practices from their antecedents. Large group practices enjoy a competitive advantage within the otherwise fragmented cottage industry in matching financial resources to population needs, in monitoring the process of care using epidemiological methods, and in incubating a professional culture that supports cooperation among individual physicians. In local markets with high HMO penetration, multispecialty groups are accepting capitation payment and delegation of utilization management. In communities without extensive managed care, multispecialty groups nevertheless are trendsetters in adapting to new methods of payment and quality monitoring. As part and parcel of this managed care orientation, many multispecialty groups are evolving away from their historical dominance by physician specialists and toward greater participation by primary care physicians. These changes toward capitation payment, utilization management, and primary care are accelerating most rapidly in regions where multiple groups compete and copy each other's innovations. Competition is the greatest spur to performance in the larger economy, and the medical group sector is no exception to the rule. In some regions, prepaid group practices remain in exclusive relationships with particular HMOs, for whom they function as the delivery system and provider network. In most communities, however, medical groups are retaining their independence and contracting on a nonexclusive basis with multiple health plans. This vertical disintegration of relationships between plans and providers contributes to the turbulence of the contemporary marketplace, but also to its creative energy. Successful collaborative ventures between one plan and one medical group diffuse rapidly throughout the contractually promiscuous system to other health plans and provider organizations.

Despite their advantages, multispecialty medical groups suffer from structural defects that limit their growth and explain why most American physicians remain in small practices. Multispecialty groups harbor multiple constituencies with different trainings, technologies, and cultures. Primary care, for example, is a high volume but low margin business reliant on a steady patient flow and severe attention to the details of practice efficiency. Many forms of specialty care, on the other hand, are low volume but high margin businesses reliant on irregular referrals, expensive technology, and close cooperation with hospitals. The heterogeneity of the multispecialty medical group is conducive to internal politics of influence that impede decision making, aggravate tensions, and may foreclose pursuit of a unified strategy. Large groups are bedeviled by low physician productivity, compared to small practices, since the individual members are paid by salaries and gain personally only a small fraction of the group's aggregate profits. Finally and most importantly, multispecialty medical groups are hindered by a scarcity of physician leaders able to guide their partners through the difficult challenges facing the organizations. The multitude of small independent practices has less need for leadership, since physicians in those practices are their own boss and do not need to coordinate closely with their neighbors.

The virtues of multispecialty clinics in capitation and delegation and the vices of those clinics in politics and productivity give new life and significant market opportunity to the Independent Practice Association (IPA). The IPA emerged originally as a defensive response by solo practitioners to competition from prepaid group practice, but has proven itself a flexible form of organization that often balances better than the multispecialty clinic the needs for independence and interdependence in physician practice. The IPA unites its physician members to perform the contracting and oversight functions of managed care but leaves them as owners and operators of their individual businesses. IPA physicians cooperate with each other in attracting HMO patients and compete with each other in attracting indemnity patients. They have pioneered new forms of physician payment, since financial incentives are the principal link between the individual and the organization. Over time, the leading IPAs develop primary care panels, specialty departments, and quality committees that mimic the organizational infrastructure of the multispecialty clinics. IPAs suffer from their own characteristic weaknesses, however, with physicians looking first to the success of their own individual practice and only secondarily to the success of the group. More generally, IPAs must struggle against the entropy of energy and initiative that afflicts all network forms of organization.

Multispecialty medical groups and IPAs are discovering that even they lack the scale and sophistication to succeed in the ever more competitive environment. They feel the need to satisfy consumer demands for broader geographic coverage, to spread the insurance risk of capitation payment across larger patient populations, and to develop more cost-effective patterns of clinical practice. This growth offers potential advantages but requires significant capital investments. Banks once were willing to make short-term loans to individual physicians, often on no more security than a medical license, but have become concerned about default. Most medical groups have no retained earnings to use as seed capital, since they pay out net revenues to physician partners to avoid corporate taxation. Many medical groups also need investments of intellectual capital, in better ways of contracting, coordinating, measuring, and motivating. Individual clinics and IPAs are continually experimenting in these matters, but some mechanism is needed to identify, validate, and disseminate the most successful changes to the broader population of physician organizations. Many medical groups and IPAs are turning to nonphysician entities and larger corporate organizations as potential partners in their business ventures. Those who are first learn many a bitter lesson but those who hang back often find that they have missed the opportunity to lead and now must follow.

The most obvious sources of investment capital in health care are the local hospitals, now increasingly consolidated into chains of inpatient, outpatient, and subacute facilities. Many hospital systems have deep capital pockets built up over years of cost-based and fee-for-service payment and have fared well even under Medicare's prospective payment system. Their expansion-oriented managers see affiliation with physician practices as essential to their long-term strategy. Leading hospitals have reconceptualized themselves as integrated delivery systems that coordinate the full spectrum of clinical services; some hope ultimately to integrate forward into insurance, squeezing out the health plans and marketing their services directly to purchasers and consumers. Ownership of physician practices offers the potential for aligning economic incentives, reducing duplication of outpatient services, and promoting commitment and cooperation among all participants. The first generation of Physician-Hospital Organizations (PHOs) has fallen far short of these optimistic expectations, as acrimonious disputes develop between the physician and institutional components and among the various clinical specialties. Hospitals have resisted the painful imperative to reduce excess capacity despite the decline in patient admissions and length of stay, and have interpreted physician employment as a means of guaranteeing high occupancy. Managed care is shifting revenues from specialty care and inpatient services to primary care and outpatient services, forcing readjustments in status and income that magnify tensions within large bureaucratic organizations. The greatest difficulty, perhaps, derives from the cultural differences between medical groups and hospital institutions, the former being for-profit and entrepreneurial and the latter being nonprofit and risk-averse. The medical profession fought capture and control by hospitals throughout the twentieth century, as symbolized in the statutory prohibition on corporate practice of medicine, and is not eager to capitulate now.

A quite different but equally problematic source of capital for physician organization is to be found in the public equity markets. Venture capital firms, corporate underwriters, institutional investors such as pharmaceutical and device manufacturers, and individual stockholders are eager to invest in a major growth industry. Through the procedures they perform, the tests they order, and the drugs they prescribe, physicians control 80 percent of a trillion-dollar industry. Whoever manages the physician organization stands at the center of the health care system. Because of the enormous transformation at hand, the stock market is particularly attractive, since equity investors can finance firms with few assets but great expectations. The public capital markets are very demanding, however, since the boundaries of the physician services industry are unclear and the identity of the long-term players is uncertain. The public markets have funded numerous start-up organizations that seek to consolidate primary care and specialty practices, multispecialty clinics, and IPAs into large corporate entities. Physician Practice Management (PPM) firms have diversified across services and markets, accepting global capitation from HMOs and fee-for-service from indemnity insurers, supplying emergency room service to hospitals, and managing clinical trials for pharmaceutical manufacturers. Some focus on a single facility or disease, while others bring together generalists, specialists, and subspecialists to assume responsibility for the care of defined populations. They enjoyed a meteoric rise and suffered an even more spectacular fall as leading firms reached too far, too fast, acquiring numerous medical groups and merging with erstwhile rivals at a rate that far outstripped their ability to operate their far-flung empires. Rapid growth in physician affiliations, patient services, and managed care revenues heightened expectations among investors for accelerated growth, thereby driving up share prices, enriching a generation of entrepreneurs, but culminating in a cascade of earnings shortfalls, investor disenchantment, collapsing share prices, and organizational crises.

Despite potential efficiencies and bargaining leverage, both PHOs and PPMs have experienced enormous difficulties. The advantages of consolidation will accrue only over time, if integrated systems can reduce excess capacity, align internal incentives, develop unified cultures, and coordinate clinical services. The disadvantages of consolidation are most severe in the short term, however, as large organizations struggle with duplicative facilities, conflicting goals and expectations, individualistic subcultures, and inconsistent practice styles. This book examines physician-hospital organizations and physician practice management firms in New York, California, and on the national level as they struggle to transcend traditional product and geographic boundaries. It evokes their strengths and documents their weaknesses to highlight the challenges that face corporate forms of organization in what remains a highly personal and strongly professionalized consumer services industry. Neither the physician-hospital nor the practice management organization will continue in their present form. Yet their experiences are not to be disregarded, since they embody unparalleled efforts to disseminate the legacy of multispecialty medical groups and IPAs. Some form of organization is needed to coordinate the diversity and complexity of health care, whether it be through multispecialty clinics or networks of small practices, with ownership or contractual alliances with hospital systems, reimbursed through capitation or fee schedules, and financed through publicly traded equity or tax-exempt debt.

THE CONCEPT OF CORPORATE PRACTICE

The "corporate practice of medicine" historically has been a term of vilification in health policy and health care organization. In the narrow sense, the corporate practice of medicine denoted the employment of physicians by hospitals, insurance plans, and other nonphysician entities that might have objectives different than those embodied in the individual doctor-patient relationship. Most states responded to these concerns by legislating statutory prohibitions on corporate practice, albeit with the result of fostering creative evasions by health care lawyers. In the broad sense, the corporation and corporate practice have echoed the American populist heritage, with its distrust of railroad monopolies, manufacturing conglomerates, Wall Street finance, and concentrated economic power. This heritage was embodied in antitrust statutes, utility commissions, and limitations on vertical integration, product diversification, and multistate expansion affecting many industries. More recently, the language of corporatism has come to be applied to the turbulent changes in health care, including the privatization of formerly public functions, hospital conversions from nonprofit to for-profit ownership, and the emergence of multistate, multiproduct insurance plans.

The language of corporation and corporate practice is used throughout this book in both conventional and unconventional ways. Sometimes it is used narrowly to denote physician employment, but at other times it evokes more diffuse meanings, some ancient and some perhaps quite new. A very old and etymologically correct use of the term "corporation," now much neglected in health policy debates, is that of the group, the collectivity, or the association of individuals joined by a common purpose and often endowed with special rights or privileges. The profession of medicine was a classic example of the corporation in this sense. This generic sense of the term is important for the purposes of this book, which examines forms of physician organization that sustain shared purposes in the contemporary context. In an analogous use of the term this book will refer to "corporate practice" as the endeavor to bring together, not individual physicians into medical groups, but medical groups into larger health care systems. Physician practice management firms that span multiple markets, physician-hospital organizations that combine multiple facilities, and health plans that design multiple products seek to coordinate physicians in economically more efficient, clinically more effective, or at least financially more profitable ways. These systems are adopting forms of organization, governance, finance, compensation, and marketing from the larger corporate sector into medicine.

The language and imagery of the corporation also is employed in a symbolic sense, in a manner similar to but with a different connotation than the conventional usage. This book pursues comparisons between the social and political forces inside health care and those outside, between the rise of large, diversified organizations in medicine and the experience of large, diversified corporations elsewhere. It links the rise of competition in health care to the deregulation of the utility industries, the enforcement of antitrust in medicine to the enforcement of antitrust elsewhere, the fiscal crisis of health care entitlement programs to the broader revolt of the taxpayer, the evolution of health care purchasing to the erosion of corporate paternalism, and the riotous diversity in health insurance products to the broader idiosyncrasies of consumer preference. The profession of medicine is but part of an economic flotsam being swept along by currents of technology, demography, epidemiology, and ideas whose depth and direction we but dimly perceive. Medicine possesses special characteristics that require specific language, but in this it is similar to other industries that possess unique technological and organizational features. Understanding is impaired and initiative is frustrated if we seek a wholly new language and set of rules for each sector.

The concept of the corporation, evocative as it is of large scale, broad scope, and conglomerate structure, receives an ambivalent treatment in economic theory and public policy. Some view the corporation as the engine of technological invention, economic growth, and social wealth, while others view it as an imperial bureaucracy that tramples individual rights, impedes efficiency, and concentrates power. The treatment of corporate ownership and finance in health care has been uniformly negative, as many historically agreed that something smaller, closer, and more intimate was preferable. The corporate practice of medicine, the penetration to the heart of health care of the strategies and structures from the larger economy, continues to arouse deep anxieties. But if understanding is to guide initiative, if we are not to limp through the new century hindered by the rhetoric of the old, the corporate practice of medicine must become a multivalent concept that encompasses efficiency and innovation as well as hierarchy and rigidity. There is no going back to professional dominance, to the organizationally fragmented and fiscally irresponsible era from which we have emerged. Nor is regulation of every price, procedure, and practitioner a likely scenario in an information economy and an ever more individualistic society. The future of health care will be defined by new methods of practice and payment, new concepts of oversight and accountability, and new forms of ownership and governance, by innovations in market contracting and corporate organization that have proven their mettle in global manufacturing, deregulated utilities, and consumer services. It is with these complementary and perhaps contradictory meanings that the corporate practice of medicine is evoked, excoriated, and embraced in this book.

CHAPTER 2

Unregulated Professionalism

Medicine is the embodiment of the learned profession. A strong scientific foundation and long clinical apprenticeship make medicine esoteric for the ordinary citizen and create an asymmetry of information and authority between the physician and the patient. The personal one-on-one delivery of medical services requires trust, confidentiality, and a service orientation not found in purely technical endeavors. Historically, this combination of science and service generated a social framework that granted unique rights and imposed unique responsibilities on the profession. Physicians were ceded control over licensure, entry into the profession, standards of training, and criteria for demonstrating competency. They dominated ancillary providers such as nurses and pharmacists and exerted a decisive if often implicit oversight over hospitals, insurers, and pharmaceutical manufacturers. They could expect deference to their clinical opinions and cooperation with their therapeutic recommendations. Individual physicians were responsible for ensuring the well-being of their patients, maintaining their own clinical skills, providing charity care to the indigent, and staying with the sick in their time of greatest need. The profession was responsible for self-regulation through the upgrading of clinical standards, the unmasking of quackery, and the expulsion of members with deficient expertise or ethics.

Medicine also has been the embodiment of the small entrepreneurial business. Historically practicing physicians have been self-employed or members of a small partnership, free from direct managerial oversight and responding only to the dictates of the guild. They owned most of the tools of their trade and found the remainder in philanthropic hospitals that offered free access without imposing an employment relation. Fee-for-service payment bound physicians intimately to their clientele, ensuring a direct responsiveness to patient concerns without interference from third parties. The cottage industry of solo practitioners and small proprietors resonated well with the American culture of economic and political democracy, and was protected from corporate consolidation by a dense web of restrictive legislation.

The salience of small-scale professional structures in an economy otherwise characterized by large organizations is celebrated by many and criticized by a few, but ultimately these traditional forms of medical practice have been undermined by their own contradictions. The guild structure imposes no budgetary discipline on the profession and has facilitated rapid growth in utilization and expenditure, driving health care beyond the reach of citizens with modest means. Epidemiological studies document extensive variations in styles of care across geographic regions and organizational settings, with better patient outcomes not consistently associated with greater resource investments. Accelerating costs and decelerating benefits raise demands for macroeconomic budgets and microeconomic incentives. Other nations have preserved guild structures while keeping cost inflation within politically acceptable limits by regulating hospital capacity and operating budgets, physician specialization and fee schedules, and technology development and diffusion. The United States flirted with regulatory controls in the 1960s and 1970s. Hospitals were subjected to limits on capital investments and operating expenditures under the assumption that they suffered from insufficient or perhaps excessive competition. Regulatory enthusiasts dallied with the notion of extending fee schedules and expenditure guidelines to the physician sector. These controls were modeled partly on the health care systems of other nations but mostly built on American experiments in utility regulation of the transportation, communication, energy, and finance industries. But by 1980 the sun was setting on New Deal economics, which had deviated from the long-run trend in American social policy in distrusting markets and trusting government. Liberals and conservatives came to agree that utility regulation was inefficient and subject to capture by the regulated industries. Attempts to extend entry barriers and rate regulation to health care at the moment they were being abolished elsewhere were doomed from the start, enacted without great hopes and enforced without great enthusiasm. The more significant policy interventions came with the enforcement of antitrust statutes, which derived from the contrary premise that competition rather than regulation stimulates economic efficiency. In the short run, half-hearted regulatory controls over capacity and prices failed to humble the medical profession. In the longer run, the abandonment of utility regulation and enforcement of antitrust law undermined professional dominance. Faced with a continuing imperative to staunch the budgetary hemorrhage and lacking public support for governmental controls, the American health care system was exposed to the marketplace.

THE PROFESSION OF MEDICINE

The central figure in the traditional health care system was the individual physician, practicing solo or with one or two like-minded partners.[1] The profession was coordinated by informal referral networks between generalists and specialists and by loose medical staff relations between physicians and hospitals. Physician fees and hospital charges were reimbursed on a fee-for-service basis by public and private insurers, with significant patient contributions through deductibles and coinsurance. Insurance premiums were passed on to employers and governmental programs, who in turn passed them on to employees through foregone wages and to the citizenry through higher taxes. Patients had free choice of physician and physicians had free choice of procedure, without oversight from insurers and regulators.[2]

The dispersion of physicians into numerous practices organizationally independent of one another initially benefited both patients and physicians. Primary care offices could be located in the neighborhoods where the patients lived, reducing travel times and facilitating closer match between the physicians' and the patients' ethnicity, language, and personal style. Small offices avoided the bureaucratic feel of hospitals and multispecialty clinics, encouraged the staff and the clientele to become personally acquainted, and permitted a flexible response to the unpredictable incidence of disease. The intimate organizational setting reflected the personal relationship between the individual physician and the individual patient, supporting the physician's sense of responsibility and the patient's need for trust.

Coordination among independent physician practices was achieved through the referral network. Patients selected their physician based on recommendations from friends and family, geographic proximity, and their own personal experiences. The difficulty in evaluating clinical quality made the choice depend more on the doctor's personal style and bedside manner than on technical expertise, but this disadvantage was mitigated by the relatively frequent interactions between patients and primary care physicians. Patients had less frequent interactions with clinical specialists, however, and were less able to evaluate the technical quality of the care they provided. The professional system relied on the primary care physician as the patient's guide to specialty care. Patients did not directly seek specialty treatment but followed the recommendations of their personal physician as to when to seek specialty consultation. The specialist was dependent on the generalist for referrals and hence was responsive to the generalist's evaluation of quality and service. The specialist knew that future referrals depended on a pattern of good clinical outcomes and satisfied patient reports. The relationship was embodied in the professional protocol that required the specialist to refer the patient back to the generalist as soon as the requested services had been delivered. It was symbolized in the ritual by which the generalist preceded the specialist into the patient's room and followed the specialist out of the room, thereby ensuring that the patient's faith in the referring physician's competency would not be undermined by to the specialist.

In the early twentieth century medicine was practiced in the patient's home or the physician's office, itself often part of the physician's domicile. The tools of the trade were simple and could be carried in a black bag. With the growth of diagnostic and therapeutic technologies, however, physicians required complex and expensive equipment. Some built their own clinics and hospitals, but most physicians found it cheaper to allow private philanthropists and public agencies to organize hospitals.[3] These institutions brought many patients together into one location, thereby economizing on the physician's travel time, and maintained operating suites and other clinical facilities, thereby economizing on the physician's capital expenditures. Hospitals provided important sites for hands-on medical education, and were increasingly supported by universities as they extended classroom and laboratory pedagogy into clinical apprenticeships.

The physician and the hospital maintained a relationship of mutual dependence without formal contract. The physician was not an employee of the hospital nor was the hospital owned by the physician. There were always some exceptions to this pattern, as when government hospitals hired salaried physicians or when entrepreneurial physicians purchased their own facility. But in the mainstream of medicine the independence of the physician and the hospital was enshrined as a mark of the physician's dedication to the patient rather than to any institution. The vulnerability of the independent physician was evidenced in the profession's long struggle against hospital employment, embodied in the "corporate practice of medicine" statutes that prohibit the employment of physicians by hospitals and other nonphysician entities.[4]

Hospitals were controlled initially by public agencies and private philanthropists, who often interpreted their mission more in social or religious than in medical terms. As improved clinical techniques brought in more middle class patients and made hospital revenues dependent on patient fees, however, the authority of the philanthropists declined. In this context, physicians held the strings to the hospital purse, since they influenced the patient's choice of facility. Together with the heightened status that inevitably accompanied new miracle drugs and procedures, this financial power made the medical staff the preeminent force in the community hospital, relegating the board of directors to a supportive role. The combination of organizational independence and clinical interdependence between physician and hospital was formalized in the dual structure of authority. Governance was split into separate administrative and clinical lines of control within each institution. The hospital superintendent was responsible for the physical facilities, the nonphysician personnel, and the capital budget. The medical staff was responsible for all clinical decisions, including admission, treatment, and discharge. This dual structure of authority was replicated in the dual structure of payment. Individual physicians would bill their patients directly for the clinical services performed in the hospital, rather than allow the hospital to bundle the professional and institutional components into one charge and pay the physician subsequently. Patients typically received one bill from the hospital and one from each physician who participated in the course of treatment, including the attending physician, the consultant specialists, the surgeon and surgeon's assistants, and in some cases the anesthesiologist, radiologist, and pathologist. The ability to use hospital facilities and to direct the activities of nurses and technicians without investing their own capital placed the physicians in a possibly unique organizational relationship to the hospital, which aptly came to be known as the doctor's workshop.[5]

The dominance of the health care system by the medical profession was cemented by the structure of financing and insurance coverage. Prior to 1933 almost all health care services were paid out of pocket by patients or subsidized by philanthropic hospitals. There was very little insurance in the sense of third-party reimbursement for costs incurred by patients choosing their own providers. A few hospitals and physician clinics developed prepayment plans that assured a defined set of services in exchange for a fixed monthly payment. The key feature of prepayment was that it covered only services provided by the sponsoring organizations, thereby stimulating each major provider to develop its own plan.[6] Plans began to compete with each other on the basis of price, which created cost control pressures on the physician and hospital sponsors. Incipient price competition and the stress of the economic depression stirred hospital and medical associations to pioneer a new form of health insurance, which came to be embodied in the Blue Cross and Blue Shield plans.

The Blue plans differed from their prepayment predecessors in covering services provided by any accredited or licensed provider, rather than limiting coverage to one sponsoring provider organization.[7] The fact that different providers maintained different practice styles and charged different fees for each service was not reflected in the cost to the patient, who received the same coverage regardless of which physician was chosen. Moreover, the insurers made no attempt to use their purchasing power to extract price reductions or quality enhancements from the participating providers. Indeed, given their commitment to equal treatment of all licensed providers, the insurers had no purchasing power, since they could not exclude recalcitrant physicians or channel volume to those charging low prices. Physicians and hospitals competed with one another in nonprice dimensions, including location, convenience, and bedside manner, but not through fee discounting. Price competition was disavowed as unbefitting a learned profession and as inappropriate for a vital service.

The rapid growth of the Blue Cross and Blue Shield plans stimulated entry into the market by commercial carriers with experience in property, casualty, and other lines of insurance. These carriers had avoided health benefits under the assumption that consumers anticipating extensive use of services would purchase coverage while their healthier counterparts would not. The appeal of health insurance as a fringe benefit of employment, which was stimulated by the exemption of insurance from the wartime wage and price controls, provided a solution to this adverse selection. Employment groups included healthy as well as sick members, thereby ensuring a large pool of nonusers whose premiums could subsidize the costs of care incurred by the ill. Moreover, the sickest citizens were excluded from employment-based insurance since they were too ill to work. Sale of health insurance to employers rather than directly to employees reduced the administrative costs of marketing, enrollment, and collections. The Blue Cross and commercial insurers competed with one another on the price of their administrative services for marketing and claims processing, but not on the basis of the prices they paid to physicians. Physician payment was structured on a retrospective, fee-for-service basis with higher revenues being earned by physicians who provided more extensive and more complex services. Each visit, each test, and each procedure generated a new claim. In the absence of any independent measure of the appropriate price for each service, the insurers paid physicians on the basis of their usual charges, subject to ceilings that depended on the prevalent fees in the community. As increases in charges billed in one year contributed to a raising of the fee ceiling in the next year, physician prices escalated rapidly and were eventually subjected to fee schedules, but the basic principle of paying physicians for each individual service was retained.[8] Fee-for-service was comfortable for physicians and well adapted to the context of independent practice, in which physicians received payments from many sources.

With the rise of Blue Cross and indemnity insurance, the burden of paying for health care shifted to employers, who interpreted premium contributions as an element in their overall compensation systems. Employers often found that an additional dollar devoted to insurance benefits earned a greater return in attracting, retaining, and motivating conscientious employees than an additional dollar devoted to cash wages. These insurance premiums were shifted partly onto the general population, since employer contributions were excluded from the taxable income of their employees. The tax exclusion was a major public subsidy for private insurance, since it implied that a dollar of benefit to the employee required less than a dollar of expenditure to the employer.[9] The tax exclusion was economically regressive, providing greater subsidy for high income than for low income workers, but played the socially important role of encouraging healthy workers to purchase insurance and thereby offset the potential for adverse selection.[10]

The percent of the population covered by health insurance increased rapidly during the 1940s and 1950s but was limited mostly to workers and their families. Elderly citizens, the unemployed, and the disabled were least likely to be covered despite having the greatest needs. Even retirees who could afford premiums often found it impossible to purchase insurance, as carriers feared adverse selection and refused coverage to individuals with any history of illness. The passage of the Medicare and Medicaid statutes in 1965 solved the worst of the access problems by entitling the majority of the elderly and poor to public health insurance, spreading the costs widely through payroll and income taxes. Medicare and Medicaid were modeled explicitly on the Blue Cross plans, offering unrestricted choice of provider and paying physicians on the basis of their usual and customary fees.[11] Most observers believed that the remaining holes in the health insurance safety net would soon be filled. But the inflationary dynamic unleashed by new clinical technologies and broader insurance reversed rather than accelerated the trend toward universal coverage.

THE MEDICAL ARMS RACE

The framework of medical professionalism created a spiral of expanding capacity, technology, utilization, and cost. Fee-for-service payment to physicians and cost-based reimbursement to hospitals rewarded extensive and complex care. Physicians recommended more visits, more tests, and more procedures. Prices for particular services increased as physicians exploited the inflationary potential in the usual and customary payment methods, but played a secondary role to the expansion in quantity and complexity of services. Governmental policy overcompensated for the decline in physician and hospital supply during the depression years of the 1930s by legislating massive subsidies for medical schools, residency programs, and hospital construction. Widespread insurance protected most consumers from the cost of care, stimulating patient demand for ambulatory services and accommodating physician decisions to refer to specialty consultation. The quality of care increased rapidly as insurers reimbursed the capital and operating costs of new equipment, new drugs, and new surgical techniques. The 1970s and 1980s were in many ways the golden era of the medical profession, based on solo practice, fee-for-service payment, insulation from price competition, and generous public subsidy.

The Achilles' heel of the professional system was the lack of financial controls. Physicians and hospitals were motivated to provide ever more and better services, since higher costs generated higher revenues. Patients were motivated to demand more and better services since the costs were shifted onto insurers and thence to employers and taxpayers. Employers were motivated to expand the breadth and generosity of insured benefits to capture the tax subsidy. Medicare and Medicaid viewed their covered services as a statutory entitlement for beneficiaries, the capstone in the New Deal edifice of social security, and were eager to accommodate physician interests so as to mitigate the traditional hostility of organized medicine.[12] Everyone was saying yes and no one was saying no to the expansion of utilization, specialization, and expenditure.

In most economic sectors a rise in price is accompanied by a reduction in quantity sold, as consumers shift their purchases to other services and producers shift their focus in response. The rise in health care costs, however, stimulated a contrary shift toward greater volume of services and greater demand for insurance coverage. The self-correcting tendencies of supply and demand seemed to be confounded by a supplier-induced demand for physician services, a medical arms race among hospitals, and an expectation of continual insurance expansions by employees and beneficiaries. Rather than settling into an economic equilibrium, the health care system manifested a spiral of increasing demand, increasing supply, and further increasing demand.

By themselves, physicians would have faced sharp limits in expanding services since there are only so many hours in the work day and only so many services that can be provided in the outpatient setting. The hospital sector, however, opened up new avenues for expanding the volume and complexity of care. Hospitals seemed to operate on the principles that came to be known as Roemer's Law, according to which a built bed is a filled bed.[13] Physicians were willing to increase admissions, tests, surgeries, and other interventions if the hospitals increased the range of clinical technologies they maintained. Patients acquiesced under the assumption that more care was better care. Insurers paid the bill under the assumption that all services provided by licensed physicians were of equal value. Rates of hospitalization and surgery varied widely across geographic regions, with the best predictor being the number of hospital beds and practicing physicians; the prevalence of disease was not consistently associated with the frequency and intensity of care.[14]

Competition among hospitals stimulated a cost-increasing rather than cost-decreasing response. Hospitals depended on physician staff affiliations for their patient admissions, yet did not employ the doctors and could not compensate them directly for channeling patients to particular facilities. Physicians often maintained admitting privileges at multiple hospitals, particularly in large urban areas. Hospitals thus competed for patient volume by competing for physician loyalty. This was done in part through amenities such as convenient parking, subsidized office suites, and comfortable doctors' lounges. The more important dimension of competition occurred, however, through the accumulation of state-of-the-art clinical technologies and maintenance of excess hospital capacity.[15] New technologies allowed physicians to expand their services and increase their incomes by offering more and better care. Excess capacity reduced the potential that any particular physician would have to delay admitting nonemergency cases until incumbent patients were discharged.[16] As one hospital expanded capacity and added new technologies, nearby facilities felt compelled to do the same, generating a spiral of inflationary investments aptly described as a medical arms race. Whereas in most economic sectors local markets with many competing producers exhibit low prices and low costs, the reverse was observed in health care. Communities with many hospitals exhibited greater excess capacity, a duplication of clinical technologies, and higher costs than otherwise similar communities with fewer hospitals.[17] These higher costs resulted in higher prices, as the hospitals were reimbursed by Blue Cross, commercial carriers, Medicare, and Medicaid on a retrospective, cost-plus basis.[18]

The rise in capacity, utilization, and expenditure was due in part to the prevalence of insurance, which reduced patient resistance to higher costs. Rather than stimulate demands for reductions in insurance coverage to defuse the inflationary dynamic, however, the rise in health care costs produced demands for further extensions in that coverage.[19] Patients found themselves paying more in deductibles, coinsurance, and for noncovered services. They demanded better insurance, including first-dollar coverage that eliminated the deductible, removal of ceilings on hospital days, and extension of coverage to mental health, outpatient drugs, medical equipment, and other services not previously included in insurance contracts. Medicare beneficiaries found their public insurance covering only half of their health care costs, and eagerly sought private Medigap coverage to fill in the holes. The health care system seemed to be in permanent disequilibrium, unable to control itself, and in need of outside intervention. Analogous dynamics in other industrial nations had resulted in a sharing of authority between the medical profession and the government, with the former maintaining clinical autonomy and the latter ensuring budgetary discipline through controls on capacity, technology, and fees. This route might have been followed in the United States but for the crisis in social legitimacy that afflicted both the physicians and the regulators during the waning years of professional dominance.

THE PROFESSION AS MONOPOLY

A major source of strength for the professional organization of health care was its social legitimacy, which derived from the traditional role of the physician as counselor on matters of life and death but which received reinforcement from the dramatic improvements in clinical technique over the course of the century. The cultural authority of the physician reached its apogee in the 1950s and 1960s, as the nation celebrated the mastery over polio and smallpox and as the average American became habituated to the notion of regular checkups, surgical removal of inflamed tonsils, and antibiotic treatment of even passing infections. But this legitimacy began to erode under increasingly severe criticism that interpreted the medical establishment less as a scientifically based benevolent society and more as a self-interested economic monopoly. The profession always had been badgered by skeptics, from Molière to George Bernard Shaw, but these had based their attacks ultimately on exposure of the iatrogenic therapeutic regimens of their times.[20] Ironically, the revival of skepticism coincided with the era of continual breakthroughs in understanding of pathological processes and in methods of treatment. The 1960s and 1970s were distinguished by simultaneous condemnations of professional authority and demands for universal access.[21]

The various critiques were incompatible on logical grounds but mutually reinforcing in undermining the legitimacy of professional dominance. The scientific objection to the exalted status of medicine derived from the evidence that health improvements were due principally to advances in public health rather than advances in clinical treatment.[22] The more radical critics viewed the medical profession as not merely irrelevant to public health, but as a negative factor in community well-being. The profession was interpreted as imperialistic, continually seeking to interpret spiritual, cultural, and political problems as biomedical pathologies. Problems of social deviance and control, including mental illness, crime, learning disabilities, alcoholism, and drug addiction, were sliding under the authority of the profession.[23] The practical implications of the cultural critique were illusive at best, since few of the skeptics pursued the logic of their analysis to the curtailment of public subsidies.[24] Most advocated vague reforms such as informed consent and community control while continuing to adhere to the liberal tenets of national health insurance. A much more important threat stemmed from the administrative agencies and courts charged with enforcing antitrust laws, who shared the skepticism of professional monopoly and were better armed to intervene in professional practices.

The fundamental axiom of market economies is that competition rewards innovation, stimulates operating efficiency, improves quality, and

thus benefits the consumer. Producers should be prevented from colluding to block entry of new competitors, raise prices, or restrict access to
information on alternatives. But professionalism as an economic system
operates on contrary principles. Cooperation rather than competition is
viewed as the means to stimulate innovation, efficiency, and quality. In
the professional paradigm, physicians are selected and socialized to be
altruistic, and aberrant instances of self-interest can be controlled by formal and informal sanctions. Price competition should be resisted because
it is seen as encouraging quality shading. Price discrimination through
higher fees for the rich is seen as a socially desirable means of subsidizing services for the poor. Bans on advertising are designed to limit quackery and the promotion of nostrums. Patients are expected to rely on trust
in professional benevolence rather than in skeptical comparisons of price
and quality. For many years the paradigm was sanctified through the exemption of the learned professions from antitrust law, which serves as
the cornerstone of public policy in the mainstream of the economy.

The indictment of professional organization as anticompetitive
emerged in the 1940s in response to efforts to control licensure, medical
education, hospital residency programs, specialty certification, and insurance practices. Several of the profession's most cherished endeavors
appeared to outsiders as blatant examples of anticompetitive behavior.[25]
The century-long efforts to enforce licensure and prohibit the practice of
medicine by midwives, osteopaths, and homeopaths were interpreted as
efforts to restrict supply and raise price. This interpretation was bolstered by the profession's control over the number of medical schools in
the early decades of the century. While presented as a disinterested effort
to eliminate poor-quality care, the Flexner report and its aftermath had
led to a dramatic reduction in the number of physicians during the
1920s, 1930s, and 1940s.[26] Physicians who reduced fees and advertised
their services could be excluded from the local medical societies, which
as voluntary entities were under no obligation to admit all physicians.
These private societies wielded, however, very public powers over the
ability of physicians to practice medicine. Membership in the local society often was required to obtain admitting privileges at the local hospital and in order to take the examinations for specialty certification. Local and state medical societies used the boycott threat against hospitals
that allowed nonmember physicians to admit patients. The national
medical association could deny recalcitrant hospitals accreditation for
purposes of residency training, which deprived them of the ability to em-

ploy low-cost medical interns and residents as backups to the attending physicians.

These formal controls constituted only the tip of a much larger iceberg of professional sanctions against rogue physicians who would reduce their fees, advertise their services, or accept prepayment. The whole structure of traditional medical organization facilitated informal sanctions. The solo practice of medicine, while conducive to independence and autonomy in some respects, made individual physicians dependent in other important respects on their peers. Reciprocal referral between generalist and specialist physicians and among the various specialties was ideally suited for isolating uncooperative individuals.[27] A physician who received few referrals could not long survive in the local community even if not denied admitting privileges at the hospital. The profession systematically refused to discuss or divulge quality concerns to nonphysicians. Specialists who recognized low-quality care among the referring generalists, generalists whose patients experienced bad outcomes upon referral, and surgeons who recognized preventable morbidity among patients in the hospital kept their concerns within the fraternity.[28]

The greatest battle fought by the profession, and the one whose defeat had the most enduring significance, was the struggle against prepaid group practice.[29] In 1929 the Ross-Loos Clinic agreed to provide comprehensive medical and hospital services to employees of the Los Angeles Department of Water and Power in exchange for a prepaid monthly sum. The physician leaders of the clinic, including the former president of the medical society, were expelled from the Los Angeles County Medical Association. They were readmitted to the society upon appeal but agreed not to pursue additional prepaid business. More severe sanctions, entailing greater national attention, were imposed by organized medicine on the Group Health Association in Washington, D.C., and the Group Health Cooperative of Puget Sound in Washington State, multispecialty physician practices sponsored by consumer and employee groups. The medical society of Washington, D.C., disciplined the physician members of the Group Health Association, preventing them from receiving referrals from nongroup physicians and organizing the medical staffs at local hospitals to deny admitting privileges. Since the District of Columbia was under direct supervision of federal law, the Department of Justice was able to prosecute the American Medical Association for criminal conspiracy under the Sherman antitrust act. The U.S. Supreme Court upheld the conviction of organized medicine in a landmark case that established the illegality of physician boycotts under federal law.[30] However, most activities of organized medicine against prepaid group practice fell under state law, and needed to be adjudicated on a state by state basis. The boycott of physicians affiliated with Group Health Cooperative ultimately was proscribed by the Washington State Supreme Court, and the attempt to legislate crippling mandates for the prepaid Health Insurance Plan (HIP) in New York City was unsuccessful in the state legislature.

For decades the activities of physicians, lawyers, and other professions had been exempted from the purview of antitrust enforcement attorneys at the Federal Trade Commission and the Department of Justice. This exemption was overturned in the case of collusive price-fixing among attorneys in 1975, and soon extended to the medical profession.[31] In 1981 the U.S. Supreme Court ruled that physician associations created solely for the purpose of negotiating fees with insurers were engaged in illegal price fixing. Only if physicians pooled their assets by creating multispecialty clinics or prepaid independent practice associations were they judged to be engaged in efficiency-enhancing forms of organizational integration and hence exempt from price-fixing charges. This ruling directly contradicts the structure of regulated professionalism in nations such as Canada, where fee schedules are negotiated between insurers and medical associations. In the succeeding years the federal antitrust agencies prosecuted attempts by physician organizations to ban advertising to consumers, to limit price competition through relative value scales, and to boycott reviews of questionable clinical practices. The practical importance of the antitrust initiatives was to hamstring guild resistance to prepaid group practice, managed care, and the spread of competition in health care markets. The symbolic importance was to formalize a rejection of the profession's worldview. The dominant premise of the medical profession is that physicians are not self-interested and that competition is not necessary for furthering informed choice, cost control, and other health policy goals. Antitrust doctrine rejects the premise that any producer group can arbitrate price and quality and insists that such matters be decided by consumers themselves through choice among competing providers.[32] The antitrust critique ultimately contributed to the breaking up of the guild. But the competitive solution almost was precluded by an alternative response to the failures of guild professionalism, which would have substituted centralized regulatory for decentralized market oversight.

HEALTH CARE AS A PUBLIC UTILITY

Most industrialized nations have responded to the inflationary potential of comprehensive insurance, fee-for-service payment, and technological dynamism by developing a system of regulated professionalism: top-down planning for hospital capacity, physician supply, and technology diffusion; prospectively determined budgets for hospital expenditures; and fee schedules for physician services.[33] As cost pressures increased and the legitimacy of professional dominance eroded in the United States, the European and Canadian models became appealing to some American policymakers. Centralized budgeting and oversight was consistent with the tradition of public utility regulation, a legacy of the New Deal era. The ruling economic philosophy decreed that consumer choice and producer competition should be relied on whenever possible, but that competition should be replaced by regulation wherever the pursuit of private interests did not vicariously further the social good. The expansionistic philosophy of the public utility paradigm was reflected in its application to a wide range of industries.[34] Utility regulation had been prescribed for structurally concentrated industries that manifested "not enough" competition and for structurally unconcentrated industries that manifested "too much" competition.

The structurally concentrated industries, such as railroads, local telephone service, electric power, and natural gas transmission, manifest large fixed and small marginal costs, with the implication that a single supplier may provide the most efficient service. Competition among multiple suppliers within local markets might raise costs. To avoid exorbitant prices and excess profits in these natural monopolies, utility commissions were authorized to roll back rates that could not be justified due to efficient operation. The inherent difficulty in reviewing one dimension of performance in isolation from the others propelled the commissions ever further into the industries they regulated, leading to oversight of capital investments, frequency and quality of service, and the details of pricing such as time-of-day and seasonal variations.[35] The original concern for efficient performance broadened into a much wider regulatory agenda that included cross-subsidies for politically powerful constituencies.[36] Utility regulation also was imposed on industries that fit no one's definition of a natural monopoly but, rather, manifested the most vigorous forms of competition. Airlines, trucking, banking, stock brokering, taxis, and maritime shipping exhibit a tendency toward what came to be known as destructive competition: large numbers of firms, easy entry, aggressive advertising, and continually fluctuating prices. The logic of regulation was never clearly articulated for this sector, but public debates typically included references to competition imperiling service quality or infrastructure investments. Utility commissions created oligopoly by restricting entry into a regulated industry, putting floors on prices and ceilings on quality, allocating market shares, and establishing prices that sustained cross-subsidies.

Hospitals seemed ideal candidates for utility regulation since they exhibit the features of natural monopoly in small towns and of destructive competition in large cities. The cost-plus reimbursement principles developed by Blue Cross bore more than a casual resemblance to the allowable cost criteria used in electric power rate reviews. Roemer's Law that a built bed is a filled bed and the medical arms race for new clinical technologies suggested that health care competition needed to be tempered through cooperation and regionalization. Despite frequent references to the hospital as a natural monopoly, most efforts at utility regulation focused on dampening rather than stimulating competition. Early efforts were coordinated by Blue Cross plans and state hospital associations seeking to limit capacity and technology in the face of federal hospital construction grants, tax-exempt debt financing, Medicare's capital passthroughs, and indemnity insurance.[37] Voluntary private initiatives evolved into mandatory public requirements as the inflationary dynamic spilled over to state Medicaid programs. In the early 1970s many states imposed certificate-of-need (CON) barriers to entry, justified by Roemer's Law; these were authorized by federal statute in 1974.[38] CON statutes required firms seeking to build a new hospital or expand an existing facility to obtain prior regulatory approval. The abortive effort at wage and price controls in the early 1970s legitimized rate regulation in the hospital sector, initially for Medicaid and then for Blue Cross. Four states obtained federal authorization to include Medicare payments under their regulatory oversight, instituting price controls over both public and private forms of insurance.[39] The high water mark of utility regulation was reached in 1979 when President Carter proposed national limits on hospital rates, which would have extended all-payer controls from four states to fifty.

Unfortunately for advocates of regulated professionalism, the political heyday of the public utility was long past. Utility regulation had been subject to a sustained critique that by the early 1970s had achieved a new intellectual consensus. Rather than control monopoly, regulation creates monopoly; rather than promote the public interest, regulation rewards private interests; rather than encourage operating efficiency, regulation condones managerial slack; rather than reduce prices, regulation raises costs.[40] The balance of regulatory advantages and disadvantages had also been influenced by changes in technology and consumer demand. No one creating an Interstate Commerce Commission to regulate the railroads could have predicted the impact of trucking competition a half century later; the fledgling air transport firms dependent on the Civil Aeronautics Board had been replaced by huge airline companies scrambling for their share of escalating demand; electronic technologies undermined distinctions once maintained by the Federal Communications Commission between local telephone, long distance telephone, television, cable, and computer industries. The changed policy consensus created a wave of regulatory reform and deregulation that swept away the Civil Aeronautics Board and the Interstate Commerce Commission, broke up the telephone monopoly, opened maritime rates and Wall Street fees to discounting, and encouraged the vertical disintegration of the electric power industry into generators, wholesalers, and retailers.[41] It was an inauspicious time to initiate utility regulation of the health care sector.

THE EROSION OF PROFESSIONAL DOMINANCE

Against this backdrop, it is not surprising that utility regulation in health care was advocated unenthusiastically, legislated narrowly, enforced timidly, and abandoned quietly. Entry control and rate regulation in the hospital sector were the strongest initiatives; they produced few encouraging results and generated little political support.[42] Certificate-of-need as a control on destructive competition proved too little and too late, since the hospital industry already was veering toward excess capacity. Politically connected institutions rolled over understaffed health planning agencies to get their new facilities approved. Regulation of hospital charges had greater success, dampening the medical arms race in the largest metropolitan markets. The rate of growth in expenditures per admission and per patient day was lower in states with all-payer rate regulation than in unregulated states during the 1980s, which encouraged the policy analysts but alienated the regulated firms.[43] The hospital industry, which had evinced initial support for health planning, became disillusioned by controls on revenues that imposed no controls on physician fees, employee wages, and consumer demands. Hospitals rallied around a voluntary effort to control costs and defeated President Carter's proposal for mandatory controls, ending the national flirtation with utility regulation of a destructively competitive natural monopoly. Deregulation proceeded at the state level, as insurers and employers shifted their focus onto premium negotiations and price competition rather than uniform government-approved rates. By 1997, only Maryland maintained a commitment to utility regulation of the hospital industry.[44]

The physician services market, with hundreds of thousands of independent entrepreneurs, was never an obvious candidate for utility regulation. The political climate was less hospitable to regulation than in the hospital sector, with the American Medical Association continuing a century-long struggle against incursion by any third party into the physician-patient relationship. The fact that a licensed doctor was a busy doctor was viewed not as a variant of Roemer's Law but as a salutary diffusion of science's benefits to the citizenry at large. Physicians shifted equipment and services beyond the reach of hospital-centered regulatory controls. CT scanners and MRI units moved from institutional to freestanding centers, surgery migrated from inpatient to outpatient settings, postoperative recovery was transferred to subacute facilities and home health care, and Medicare's prospective payment system was evaded through upcoding of secondary diagnoses and unbundling of procedures.[45]

Utility regulation produced modest but ultimately transient respites from the inflationary dynamic, with one-time reductions in expenditures quickly subsumed into the succeeding year's cost acceleration.[46] The popular image of health care regulation was of a balloon squeezed at one end that bulged out at the other. Regulatory enthusiasts expanded their agenda to encompass comprehensive control over all aspects of the system, following the model of the neighbor to the north. The Canadian medical economy had closely resembled its American counterpart in costs and coverage until its national health insurance program was instituted in 1967, after which point the two medical systems diverged.[47] The Canadian model of upstream regulatory controls permitted an extension of comprehensive insurance coverage to all citizens while keeping medical cost inflation within politically acceptable levels. Moreover, and of great importance for subsequent cross-border comparisons, the taming of the financing beast was achieved without major disruption in the organization of care. Canadian physicians continued to practice in small group settings and to be paid on a fee-for-service basis, hospitals remained independent nonprofit facilities, and consumers enjoyed free choice of provider.[48] For advocates of single-payer financing of health care, regulated professionalism offered a squaring of the health policy circle.[49] But when given the chance to express their opinions in state ballot initiatives, the voters repeatedly turned back efforts to extend tax-based indemnity insurance and governmental price controls.

The failure of utility regulation spelled the demise of guild control in health care. Without top-down controls on capacity, technology, and prices, the inflationary dynamic continued unabated and purchasers' willingness to experiment with radical changes grew commensurably. Disaffected with professional dominance and disillusioned with utility regulation, the health care system lurched toward forms of organization and finance that prevailed in the economic mainstream. But for a moment it dallied with an intermediate position, an institutional framework that used competition to manage physicians and purchasing alliances to manage competition.

CHAPTER 3

Unmanaged Competition

Market economies rely on choice as the spur to efficiency and innovation. Informed and price-conscious consumers, spending their own money to suit their own preferences, stimulate rivalry among producers to reduce costs, improve quality, and enhance service. The traditional health care system, financed by indemnity insurance and serviced by many physicians with their small practices, offered free choice of provider to the patient and free choice of procedure to the provider, but undermined efficiency and impeded innovation. The consumer was spending someone else's money, was ill-informed about quality, and shopped off a menu truncated by provider collusion against price discounts, bans on selective contracting, boycotts of group practice, and prohibitions on the corporate practice of medicine. The professional guild fostered choice without competition, insurance without incentives, and entitlement without responsibility.

During the period when public attention focused on the epic struggle between the government and the medical establishment, between regulated and unregulated professionalism, a small but influential group of policy entrepreneurs was developing a market-oriented strategy to encourage efficiency by fostering an alternative form of choice. In contrast to the prevailing orthodoxy, these analysts insisted that achievement of health insurance goals required significant changes in the organizational structure of health care delivery. The system they envisaged would be based on multispecialty medical groups, which promised economies of

scale, coordination of patient care, and a culture of physician peer review. Incentives would be instilled through prospective payment on a per-
patient-per-month basis, thereby contrasting with the fee-for-service payments of traditional insurance. The nation already had several examples
of prepaid group practice, including the Kaiser Foundation Health Plan,
Group Health Cooperative of Puget Sound, and the Harvard Community
Health Plan. The performance of these group practices, renamed Health
Maintenance Organizations (HMOs), was to be stimulated by competition for price-sensitive and quality-conscious consumers. Private firms
and public programs would oversee market performance using purchasing power and market incentives rather than regulatory authority and bureaucratic controls. This was to be the system of "managed competition."

Managed competition proposed a balance of choice and efficiency
very different from that offered by indemnity insurance and the professional guild. Physicians would form multispecialty medical groups with
linkages to local hospitals, thereby facilitating cost-conscious practice
styles. Provider systems would integrate forward into marketing, pricing, and insurance risk bearing. Public agencies and private firms would
amalgamate into purchasing alliances to contract for low premiums,
standardized benefits, and measurable improvements in quality. Individual consumers would choose among competing plans based on price,
quality, and convenience. Market rivalry among large organizations
would minimize the need for governmental regulation of small practices.

By the early 1990s, managed competition appeared to have replaced
regulated professionalism as the inevitable future of the U.S. health care
system. The 1992 presidential election was interpreted widely as a mandate for health care reform, and the pursuit of social goals through market means was hailed as the politically most attractive strategy. The relevant choice seemed to be between the centralized, public sector variant
espoused by the Clinton administration and the decentralized, private
sector variant espoused by legislative moderates. At first blush, managed
competition appeared as a bridge to compromise, offering universal coverage to liberals, market-based cost control to conservatives, and richer
benefit coverage to almost every political constituency. Indemnity insurance companies had nothing to gain and everything to lose, however.
They organized against the Clinton initiative and found ready allies in the
business community that feared tax increases and coverage mandates.
Acrimony among the competing sects of policy reformers and only tepid
support from the intended beneficiaries crippled the initiative. Individual pieces of the managed competition edifice, including medical groups,

prepayment, and organized purchasing, would continue to play a role in the health care system, but without the universal insurance coverage, uniform benefits, and income-related subsidies that national legislation may have ensured.

The failure of managed competition has created the context for a different balancing of choice and efficiency. The essential feature of the health care market is the heterogeneity among consumers in what they are willing to buy and the heterogeneity among providers in what they are willing to sell. Managed competition sought to homogenize demand by specifying a uniform benefit package, premium contribution, quality monitoring mechanism, and distribution system. It sought to homogenize supply by consolidating insurers, hospitals, and physicians into health plans that contract on a prepaid basis with purchasing alliances. But consumers differ in their incomes and preferences, in the tradeoffs they are willing to make between premiums, copayments, benefit coverage, network breadth, and style of utilization management. Providers differ in structure and culture, in their preferences and tradeoffs for solo versus group settings, self-employment versus salary, fee-for-service versus capitation, and coordinated versus autonomous practice styles.

In the absence of standardization by public or private purchasing alliances, this heterogeneity of demand and supply spurs innovation in provider networks, methods of distribution, and scope of geographic coverage. Rather than offer a uniform benefit package, health plans now are configuring coverage and copayments in myriad ways to accommodate myriad pocketbooks. They are developing network designs that incorporate solo practices, multispecialty clinics, and hospital systems in ever-changing ways. Health plans are tailoring their marketing and distribution mechanisms to the very different channel structures operated by small firms and insurance brokers, large corporate accounts, state Medicaid agencies, and the federal Medicare program. They are expanding through mergers and acquisitions across state lines and, in some cases, reaching toward national scope. The multiproduct, multimarket health plans perform many of the functions assigned to purchasing alliances in the framework of managed competition. They no longer resemble the single-product, single-market firms of yesteryear but offer a full range of products across a full range of markets. They structure networks and negotiate payment rates on behalf of consumers and structure benefits and enrollment mechanisms on behalf of providers. But health plans are not selfless sponsors managing competition for the social good. They wrestle with purchasers for higher revenues, with providers for lower costs, and with each other for brand name recognition, market dominance, and profit leadership. This is the system of unmanaged competition.

THE CONSUMER CHOICE HEALTH PLAN

The Great Society programs legislated in the 1960s ignored prepaid group practice in their rush to universalize indemnity insurance. Medicare and Medicaid were conceptualized as means for improving financial access to care, not as means for improving the efficiency and quality of care. Legislators and administrators explicitly forswore any attempt to move the U.S. health care system away from solo practice, fee-for-service payment, and informal referral networks. Within five years of the passage of the major health care statutes, however, the cost implications of facilitating citizen access to a fragmented and expansionary system had become clear. Medicare and Medicaid expenditures exceeded the sums projected at the time of enactment and were growing at a breathtaking rate. Many observers advocated a broadening of coverage through national health insurance, combined with utility regulation of hospital capacity, technology diffusion, and professional fees. A small minority of policy analysts sought a less regulatory means to achieve the same social goals of universal access. Paul Ellwood, a physician with a sympathy for prepaid group practice, caught the attention of the Nixon administration with his plan for a private sector, market-oriented approach to national health insurance.[1]

Ellwood was able to use the success of Kaiser and its sister organizations to argue for prepaid group practice over conventional methods of health care organization and finance. He offered an explanation for why prepaid group practice had not grown faster and diffused to more regions of the nation, including hostility from organized medicine, capital costs of new facilities, lack of familiarity among private purchasers, and the fact that indemnity insurance paid more to inefficient fragmented systems than to efficient coordinated ones. Health care providers who reduced the costs of their services found their revenues cut dollar for dollar, while providers who allowed costs to inflate were rewarded by commensurably higher payments. Patients who chose less costly forms of care were not rewarded through lower premiums or taxes. Ellwood coined the term "health maintenance organization," which focused attention on the potential for prepayment and group practice to encourage disease prevention and thereby limit medical costs. The term extended to prepaid organizations that were not based on integrated medical groups but, rather, on more loosely constructed independent practice associations. Ellwood viewed these IPAs as transitional organizational forms that would help physicians move incrementally to more tightly integrated groups.

President Nixon was eager for something to offer voters that would demonstrate his concern for health care access while remaining consistent with Republican principles of limited government. The result was the HMO Act of 1973.[2] This legislation overrode state bans on prepaid group practice that had been created at the behest of organized medicine, offered low interest loans to subsidize HMO start-ups, and mandated that large employers offer their employees choice of an HMO in addition to their conventional indemnity plans. The legislation was enacted with considerable fanfare but produced disappointing results. The amount of money actually appropriated to subsidize HMO capital expenditures was much lower than originally authorized. Plans that sought federal qualification in order to be eligible for the employer mandate found themselves burdened with requirements for costly new benefits, guaranteed issue of coverage to all citizens regardless of health status, and a uniform community-rated price structure. Traditional indemnity insurers, however, were permitted to offer thin benefit packages, deny coverage to the chronically ill, and charge each covered firm or consumer a different premium. The decade of the 1970s proved to be a period of slow growth for HMOs, a major shortfall from the enthusiastic projections. Nixon's support for HMOs proved transitory. The administration became preoccupied with general inflation and engaged in a spectacularly unsuccessful adventure with economy-wide wage and price controls. The presidency changed hands after the Watergate scandal and then in 1976 passed to the Democratic party, which retained high expectations for centralized health care regulation.

Proponents of prepaid group practice focused more and more on nongovernmental solutions to health care reform. Alain Enthoven, a policy analyst and consultant to the Department of Health, Education, and Welfare under President Carter, articulated a strategy to promote HMO growth by restructuring private decision making rather than by promulgating public subsidies and regulations. This "Consumer Choice Health Plan" laid out a framework in which large purchasers and individual patients would face economic incentives to choose efficient forms of health insurance.[3] A restructured financing system would reward integrated delivery organizations. Enthoven placed his faith in informed and cost-conscious consumer choice, rather than in government regulation, to motivate organizational reform and coordination of care.

The Consumer Choice Health Plan was designed to be consistent with any combination of employment-based and tax-funded financing. It diverged significantly from the conventional wisdom of the time, however, in divorcing the principle of governmental funding, which it supported, from governmental operation of an indemnity insurance program. Rather than pay individual physicians on a fee-for-service basis and individual hospitals on a cost-plus basis, the proposed financing system would contribute toward the premiums charged by competing HMOs. Individual consumers would be able to choose among prepaid group practices, IPAs, and other insurance plans, but would pay the extra premium if they selected the less efficient and higher priced plans. The federal government would subsidize the health care system through a refundable tax credit equal to 60 percent of the average premium charged by health plans in each area. In this respect Enthoven's proposal was modeled on the Federal Employees Health Benefits Program (FEHBP), which offered choice among competing health plans to 10 million governmental employees, dependents, and retirees. In sharp contrast to Medicare, the FEHBP did not operate its own indemnity plan, but contracted with private carriers as well as with prepaid group practices. It made a fixed contribution toward the premium of whichever plan the employee chose, thereby requiring beneficiaries who chose a high cost indemnity plan to pay more than those who chose a low cost HMO.

The Consumer Choice Health Plan embodied a quite different concept of choice than did the professional guild. In the traditional framework, choice was defined in terms of the patient's ability freely to choose a different physician at any time from among the full range of licensed clinicians. In this guild model of choice, every doctor was assumed to be equally proficient, in the sense that the ultimate payer had no interest in steering consumers to particular physicians within the larger system.[4] In the Enthoven framework, choice was defined in terms of the patient's ability freely to choose among coordinated systems of care and then to select among the individual physicians within the chosen system. Consumers who chose more efficient systems would obtain the usual market reward: lower prices. In the guild framework, patients who selected efficient physicians and hospitals received no reward and those who selected inefficient providers paid no penalty. In effect, those who chose low cost care subsidized those who chose high cost care.

While skeptical of governmental regulation, the Consumer Choice Health Plan was by no means a paean for laissez faire. Enthoven described at length the ever-threatening failures of health care markets. Health insurers segment local markets by geography and type of employer to save themselves from the rigors of competition. They seek healthy consumers and discourage enrollment by the chronically ill. If explicit underwriting is banned, as it was for federally qualified plans under the HMO Act, insurers use subtle means to attract a favorable patient risk mix. Individual consumers often are poorly informed concerning quality and are confused by the multitude of benefit packages. Unemployed persons and the working poor need premium subsidies if they are to enjoy a reasonable set of choices and not be confined to the cheapest plans. Persons with chronic illnesses require special financial support to cover their exceptional health care needs if they are not to face discrimination in the marketplace.

Enthoven proposed a set of interlocking reforms that would level the playing field for competing health plans. Choice among plans would occur on an annual basis to avoid opportunistic consumer enrollment in low-priced plans with thin benefits when healthy and switching to high-priced plans with generous benefits when sick. All plans, not merely federally qualified HMOs, would offer "open enrollment," accepting all applicants without regard to health status or history of medical care utilization. The package of benefits would be standardized in order to facilitate consumer comparisons and impede strategic manipulation of benefits to attract low risk enrollees. Each plan would charge a single community rate to all subscribers, adjusted for expected utilization by age and gender. The government's tax credit would be adjusted by actuarial category to ensure that individuals with higher utilization did not have to pay higher premiums. The philosophical principle underlying this mix of financial incentives and subsidies was that the individual consumer should be financially responsible for premium costs due to differences in health plan efficiency, since the consumer has the ability to choose among plans, but society should be responsible for premium costs due to differences in health status.

The Consumer Choice Health Plan embraced a domino theory of health care system reform.[5] Restructuring the governmental subsidy would encourage consumers to choose health plans that offer the lowest price and highest quality. The resulting changes in market shares would encourage health plans to develop tighter relationships with providers and to embrace a more cost-effective style of care. Organizational changes among insurers would encourage providers to form medical groups and other integrated organizations. Physicians and eventually hospitals would affiliate with a single health plan. Enthoven sought to overcome the dichotomy between insurance and delivery that was embodied in the indemnity and Blue Cross models. In his framework, consumer choice of health plan would imply consumer choice of delivery system. Integrated groups of physicians and hospitals would provide the scale economies, professional culture, and organizational coordination of the best multispecialty groups coupled with the budgetary discipline of prospective payment and market competition.

THE PRUDENT PURCHASER

During the 1980s health maintenance organizations shook off the torpor of the previous decade and grew at a rapid rate. Continual inflation in health benefit expenditures increased interest among employers in the principles of a fixed premium contribution within a framework of competing plans. Employees were attracted to the richer benefits and lower out-of-pocket payments that distinguished HMOs from indemnity insurance carriers. The industry itself was energized by investor ownership, as many nonprofit plans converted to for-profit status and as commercial insurers launched new HMOs. Enrollment reached 37 million by the end of the decade. Public programs such as Arizona Medicaid and federal Medicare experimented with consumer choice and capitation payment. Nevertheless, the transformation of the health care system through competition fell short of expectations. HMO premiums were lower than those charged by indemnity carriers, but appeared to increase at approximately the same annual rate, raising accusations of shadow-pricing.[6] Rather than compete through lower prices, HMOs were attracting new enrollees through richer benefits and lower copayments. This nonprice competition improved consumer access to services but did little to control costs.[7] There was a continuing debate over the extent to which HMOs benefited from favorable risk selection, since healthier patients with weaker ties to traditional providers were more willing to switch into a new system.[8] These problems in the market for insurance weakened the domino pressures on the market for health care delivery. While prepaid group practices continued to grow, most physicians remained in solo practice.

The complexity of managing competition among health care providers highlighted the need for active sponsors of health care consumers.

Entrepreneurial HMOs were overcoming the comfortable lethargy of traditional group practice, but also were abandoning their social mission. The increasingly competitive environment would push health plans to seek every element of advantage, including those generated by distorted incentives for risk selection and market segmentation. Creative entrepreneurs would be able to exploit every dip and bump in the supposedly level playing field. Supporters of market-oriented health care placed increasing emphasis on the role of public and private purchasers to counteract these undesirable behaviors. Purchasing sponsors could be as innovative as the health plans, seeking better ways to reward efficiency and penalize opportunism. They could use the tools of the private purchaser rather than those of the public regulator, seeking lower prices and better services for their beneficiaries rather than imposing a one-size-fits-all straightjacket on the system. In the purchasing context, the burden of proof for good performance is on the seller who wants to have its contract renewed; in the regulatory context, that burden is on the agency that wants to terminate the seller's right to participate. Uniform regulatory standards tend to fall to the lowest common denominator of performance in order to allow even the weakest providers to participate, whereas purchasers can reward above-average performance through increased market share. Most importantly, the multiplicity of purchasers diffuses the targets for the inevitable supplier backlash, whereas the concentration of governmental authority creates a single target for regulatory capture.[9]

The FEHBP continued to serve as a model for effective health care purchasing in the 1980s and was copied by large private corporations such as Xerox and GTE and by state programs such as the California Public Employees Retirement System.[10] Some metropolitan areas spawned coalitions of corporate purchasers, such as the Pacific Business Group on Health in California and the Buyers Health Care Action Group in Minnesota.[11] But most Americans were not covered by these large programs. The U.S. economy was continuing its transition from a manufacturing to a service focus, from large to small firms, from full-time to part-time jobs, and from lifetime to short-term employment. The principles of managed competition were slow to penetrate the small and midsized firms, to say nothing of the insurance market for self-employed individuals. Small firms lacked the sophistication to manage choice and incurred high administrative costs and adverse risk selection if they tried.[12] Most contracted with a single health plan, chosen with the help of an insurance broker. The brokers were often sympathetic to traditional indemnity carriers that paid high commissions. Staying with an indemnity plan was particularly attractive for firms too small to offer multiple plan choices, since it interfered least with their employees' choices of physician. Rather than switch to HMO coverage when the costs of indemnity coverage became exorbitant, many small firms simply dropped benefits altogether. By 1990, most Americans without health insurance were employed by small firms or were the children of small-firm employees.

Market-oriented policy analysts endeavored to expand the managed competition framework to ensure universal coverage in the small-group and individual insurance markets. The core of the evolving framework, dubbed the Jackson Hole Group after the Wyoming community where Ellwood sponsored policy roundtables, was the health insurance purchasing cooperative.[13] Small firms and self-employed individuals would join a local cooperative and pay a premium contribution, adjusted for the age mix of their covered employees and dependents. The cooperatives would be private, nonprofit organizations governed by boards responsive to the constituent firms and individuals. They would not be governmental entities or private monopolies. Each community could have multiple cooperatives, sponsored by consumer groups, business associations, and labor unions. Each cooperative would contract with health plans, offer open enrollment to beneficiaries, develop quality measures on each plan, contribute a risk-adjusted percentage of the premium, and require that individual consumers pay the remainder of the premium depending on the particular plan they chose. The cooperatives would not bargain over premiums, since health plans would be disciplined by loss of consumer enrollment if their prices were out of line. Contracts by purchasing cooperatives would only be extended to "accountable health plans" that integrated physicians and hospitals. Citizens would only be eligible for their refundable health insurance tax credit if they obtained coverage through one of these integrated plans.

The purchasing cooperatives for small firms and individuals were embedded by the Jackson Hole Group in a larger institutional framework to ensure public accountability. A national health board would establish and annually review the benefit package that all plans would be required to offer. A national standards board would develop methods for measuring and monitoring severity of illness, quality of care, and actuarial adjustments for capitation payment. Employers would be mandated to offer insurance coverage to their full-time employees and to pay a payroll tax to help the purchasing cooperatives finance coverage for part-time employees. Governmental tax subsidies and individual enrollee contributions would make up the difference. This "pay or play" principle had been developed by advocates of universal coverage in the indemnity context, but was easily adaptable to managed competition. Medicare, Medicaid, and corporate insurance programs would remain outside the purchasing cooperatives in order to maintain pluralism on the demand side of the health care market.

THE HEALTH SECURITY ACT

Bill Clinton was elected to the presidency in 1992 with a perceived mandate to implement universal insurance coverage using private markets and economic incentives rather than public ownership and top-down regulation. Managed competition seemed a perfect fit. Soon after the election President Clinton assembled a large working group of policy analysts from inside and outside the government to develop a detailed proposal. The main focus of the proposed legislation would be the health insurance purchasing cooperatives, renamed health alliances. These regional alliances would permit the squaring of the health policy circle, subjecting the organization of services to discipline in the private sector while ensuring universal insurance coverage through the public sector.

In President Clinton's Health Security Act, each state or region of the nation would develop a single organization for the purchasing of health insurance using the principles of standard benefits, multiple choice, open enrollment, and cost-conscious consumer choice.[14] Health alliances would contract with HMOs and indemnity plans, contributing 80 percent of the average premium. Individual consumers would contribute the remaining 20 percent, plus the full difference between the premiums of the low and high cost plans if they chose a more expensive option. The health alliances would ensure that consumers had choice among health plans regardless of their health status or medical history, using risk-adjusted payments to compensate plans that attracted the sickest enrollees. A national health board would standardize the benefits to which all Americans would be entitled. The health alliances would be funded through a pay-or-play mandate for employers and the self-employed. Employers would be required to offer coverage to full-time employees, contributing 80 percent of the average health plan premium, and to pay a payroll tax to cover their part-time and temporary employees. Self-employed individuals would be required to purchase insurance individually. Governmental subsidies would be available for small firms with low wage workers and for low income individuals. These subsidies would be supported through taxes on cigarettes and through savings in the Medicare and Medicaid budgets anticipated to result from the shift from indemnity to managed care.

President Clinton's proposed health alliances differed from the purchasing cooperatives espoused by the Jackson Hole Group in both pragmatic and philosophic dimensions. The Health Security Act envisaged a single alliance in each region that would enroll public and private employees, the self-employed, the unemployed, plus Medicare and Medicaid beneficiaries, and thereby would constitute a single payer for all health care services. This monopsony structure would facilitate cross-subsidies from high income to low income citizens, since the coverage mandates would impose higher costs on large, high wage firms than on small, low wage firms. Moreover, it would create the organizational platform for a global health care budget. Each year the Congress could decide on the total budget for the alliances by specifying the details of the tax rates, mandates, and covered benefits. The regional alliances would have to live within these externally determined budgets in the same sense that the provincial health insurance programs in Canada live within their tax-based budgets. If competition among health plans in any particular region did not hold premium inflation to a rate compatible with the centrally determined budget, the federal authorities were empowered to impose regulatory controls on the alliances, the health plans, and on health care providers. The Jackson Hole Group, in contrast, had envisaged a multiplicity of voluntary purchasing cooperatives in each region, none with the authority to regulate health plans and providers.

The arcane dispute between multiple and single sponsors for managed competition overlay deep philosophical differences concerning the appropriate role for private initiative and public oversight in the health care system. For the Jackson Hole Group, the purchasing cooperative provided organizational support for market competition to control costs, improve quality, and make health care responsive to consumer preferences. It was important, from this perspective, that the cooperatives not have the ability to act like regulators who impose centrally determined budgets on the market.[15] Markets work best when a multiplicity of buyers interact with a multiplicity of sellers, each with the option of switching partners if satisfactory terms cannot be negotiated. For the Clinton administration, on the other hand, the health alliance constituted a platform for achieving universal coverage and cost control in health care, which need not be pursued through market mechanisms. In the Health Security Act, competition was merely one strategy that the health alliances could adopt.[16] If competition among plans and providers did not achieve the desired results, the alliances could shift to regulation. Indeed, the proposed legislation required the alliances to shift from competition to regulation if specific goalposts in cost control were not achieved in the first years after implementation. The Health Security Act evoked the imagery of countervailing power between a single large buyer and a few large sellers rather than of freewheeling competition involving many buyers and many sellers.

The philosophic differences between the Clinton and Jackson Hole proposals were most evident in their opposed interpretations of the appropriate rate of spending for health care. For President Clinton and his advisors, targets for national health care spending were to be established using political means. Benchmarks would be formalized in the annual global budget and enforced through the regional health alliances by whatever combination of competition and regulation produced the desired results. For the Jackson Hole Group, the appropriate rate of health care spending would be determined from the bottom up rather than from the top down. The right amount of money for the nation to spend on health care would be the aggregate of the amounts spent by the individual citizens, once they faced appropriate economic incentives. There would be no governmentally determined global budget for health care any more than there was a global budget for transportation, housing, or entertainment.

The differences between the competing variants of managed competition were resolved in the political rather than the philosophic arena. The Health Security Act pleased none of its intended beneficiaries. Traditional liberals disliked the flirtation with markets and competition, and favored an extension of fee-for-service Medicare to the entire population.[17] Individual citizens without health insurance remained passive and confused by the policy cacophony. HMOs were leery of the drift toward regulation and top-down budgets. Large corporations were put off by the barely veiled enthusiasm for tax increases. Small firms proclaimed a holy war against governmental mandates to provide employee health insurance. They were joined by the endangered infrastructure of indemnity insurance, including commercial carriers, Blue Cross plans, brokers, and agents. Rarely had such an impressive piece of policy analysis, commissioned by an incumbent President with a Congressional majority, proven such an unimpressive platform for political initiative.[18]

President Clinton had interpreted the political climate as demanding both universal coverage, which pointed toward a centralized public sector solution, and competition, which pointed toward a decentralized private sector solution. The combination he chose reflected the center of gravity in health policy debates but was far left of center for the American political system. Congressional Republicans initially were favorable to compromise but gradually came to view policy gridlock as the opportunity for a major political realignment. They were able to brand the Health Security Act as a government takeover of health care, thereby capitalizing on the American populist tradition in a manner akin to that used in previous decades by the American Medical Association. The elections of 1994 proved the acuity of their insight. It was one of the political landslides of the century, granting to the Republicans both houses of Congress, the majority of state governorships, and a multitude of state legislatures. President Clinton's bridge to compromise, the combination of government entitlements with market mechanisms, was intended to define a new middle ground for American health policy and politics. Instead it almost destroyed the Democratic party.[19]

THE FRAGMENTATION OF SPONSORSHIP

The defeat of the Health Security Act buried the big bang theory of health care reform, the simultaneous pursuit of universal coverage and efficient delivery. Without federal legislation, it would be impossible to make serious reductions in the number of citizens without insurance, since the states lack the political will to address their problems individually. On first blush, however, the lack of national initiative need not have impeded the other aspects of managed competition, including purchasing alliances and integrated health plans, since these focus on economic efficiency rather than on income redistribution. The purchasing alliance, in particular, seems to offer such important benefits that employers and employees should join them without governmental impetus. Several prominent examples already existed, documenting the potential virtues of sponsorship for public agencies, large corporations, and small firms. In the years after the Clinton defeat, purchasing coalitions did extend their reach and several new ones were formed. But the most striking event was a non-event. Despite the gains promised by alliances and cooperatives, the purchasing of health care did not consolidate. This continued fragmentation of demand has important implications for efforts to overcome the fragmentation of health care supply.

The original metaphor for the health care purchasing alliance was the consumer or producer cooperative, a legacy of western populism and the depression years of the 1930s. The Jackson Hole Group evoked the image of the private cooperative as an alternative to the public regulatory agency.[20] Purchasing cooperatives were to be responsive to their constituent firms. This voluntarist imagery is difficult to reconcile with the involuntary aspects of managed competition, including employer mandates, community rating, the requirement that the alliance admit any firm, and adjustment of premiums for patient risk mix.[21] Each of these functions involves elements of income redistribution, which is not something that a consumer or producer cooperative is designed to accomplish.

The voluntary purchasing alliance suffers from two salient characteristics that limit its inception and growth. First and foremost, the citizenry has very heterogeneous needs and expected patterns of expenditures for medical care. The problems of risk selection that face provider systems and health plans reappear, with greater force, at the level of the purchasing alliance. The alliance pools the risk of its constituent members and is charged premiums by health plans based on expected enrollee expenditures. Alliances with large numbers of sick members are charged higher premiums than alliances with healthier constituents. Only a universal alliance in each geographic area, precisely Clinton's single sponsor, would avoid this feature. Firms with low risk employees are reluctant to join alliances and thereby pool risk with firms with sicker employees, to say nothing of alliances that include retirees, the permanently disabled, the chronically mentally ill, and others too sick to work. Most voluntary purchasing alliances, such as the industry-specific trust funds, limit membership to firms whose employees had passed some form of health screening. The small-firm alliance in California allowed any firm to join but charged each firm a rate based on the age mix and geographic locality of its employees; these demographic adjusters accounted for only a small portion of the total variance in expenses within the covered population, which resulted in some adverse selection for the alliance.[22] The Buyers Health Care Action Group in Minnesota required each member firm to pay the claims incurred by its employees, thereby forestalling any pooling of risk between the healthy and the sick.

The second limitation of the voluntary purchasing alliance derives from its ownership and governance. Entrepreneurial rewards are not available to individuals that assume the risks and devote their energies to health care purchasing alliances. Most alliances are nonprofit and distribute any gains to members through lower premiums. Most are governed by boards that value benefits for existing constituents over addition of new constituents; they are reluctant to divert a significant fraction of premium contributions to marketing and geographic expansion. The staff of the alliance receives salaries for their services but does not own the organization and cannot profit personally from increases in its scale and value. This differs strikingly from the incentive structure in the for-profit sector, where the principal rewards for entrepreneurship are reaped through ownership shares rather than salary payments. In this respect purchasing alliances resemble nonprofit HMOs, which, with a few salient exceptions, have failed to grow beyond their original communities. Most nonprofit plans distribute the benefits from prepaid and coordinated care to their members, rather than investing them in organizational growth. HMOs only moved from the margins to the mainstream of the health economy after a significant number of for-profit plans were created. Analogous conversion of ownership and incentives would be needed to spur a nationwide expansion of private purchasing alliances.

The advantages and disadvantages of health care purchasing alliances are starkly evident in the small-firm sector of the economy. Small firms are particularly ill suited to sponsor health benefits for their employees, since they lack the scale to spread administrative costs and the sophistication to negotiate complex contracts. The costs of marketing, underwriting, and administration consume 40 percent of the premium dollars spent by firms with less than five employees, compared to only 5 percent for firms with more than 10,000 employees.[23] The concept of the purchasing alliance was designed to overcome these handicaps, converting a large number of small purchasers into a small number of large purchasers. But while the potential advantages of alliances are greatest for small firms, so are the organizational deficits. The costs of identifying, billing, and managing open enrollment for small firms are daunting. Many small firms have only a transient existence, with high rates of bankruptcy plaguing efforts to stabilize enrollment. In the insurance market outside the cooperative structure, these functions of identifying, convincing, and servicing small firms are performed by legions of brokers and agents. Brokers and agents serve as the personnel offices for small employers, advising them on employment discrimination, pension plans, tax codes, fire, property, and casualty insurance, workers compensation, family leave requirements, accommodation of employees with disabilities, and the other complexities of doing business. Most small firms are not willing to cut their broker links for health insurance when they remain so dependent for other aspects of survival. The small-firm purchasing alliance in California, for example, found that three-fourths of its member firms continued to pay commissions to their brokers even after joining the alliance, where no broker services were required.[24]

The advantages from purchasing alliances are modest for large firms, who possess the scale to purchase health benefits on their own, but the disadvantages of joining also are less salient. Large corporations are more stable, more committed to offering health benefits, less likely to go bankrupt, and less beholden to insurance brokers than are small firms. In some metropolitan areas, corporate purchasers have formed alliances and developed innovative approaches to controlling costs. Most important among the corporate alliances are the Pacific Business Group on Health in California and the Buyers Health Care Action Group in Minnesota.[25] But most large firms have chosen to remain outside the alliance structure and to purchase insurance individually. In many cases, the apparently large size of the corporation is illusory, since its workforce is spread over many communities. Large firms who perceive their workforces to be younger and healthier than the average bargain with health plans for experience-rated premiums rather than allow their advantage to be diffused over a purchasing alliance. Health insurance purchasing in large firms exhibits its own strata of self-interested individuals, including the middle managers who run the benefit programs and the corporate consulting firms that play a role analogous to insurance brokers. These individuals could lose their jobs, status, and consulting fees if large firms were to pool premium contributions and delegate decision making to an alliance. Many large firms interpret their self-insured health programs as a contributor to employee productivity. They are loath to trade specialized benefit programs that enhance employee satisfaction for generic purchasing alliances that generate employee indifference.

The combination of adverse selection and weak governance places severe limits on the formation of health care purchasing alliances in the private sector, but could have stimulated a leadership role by public sector programs. Not coincidentally, many of the leading alliances are public purchasers. Governmental programs have a disciplined administrative infrastructure and the organizational scale to pool insurance risk. However, the public sector is subject to a dense web of constitutional, judicial, and cultural limitations on the exercise of its purchasing power. The repeated failure of attempts to legislate national health insurance bears eloquent testimony to the citizenry's willingness to tolerate inefficiency to forestall a centralization of governmental power.[26] The public sector, which accounts for 45 percent of all dollars spent on health care in the United States,[27] acts like an impotent Gulliver fettered by thousands of Lilliputian rules and requirements. The Medicare and Medicaid programs appear more solicitous of the physicians, hospitals, and nursing homes whose services they reimburse than of the taxpayers whose dollars they dispense. The formation of public purchasing alliances is opposed by health plans and provider organizations, by brokers and consultants, and by individual citizens whose experiences with public education, public housing, and public transit are less than delightful. All in all, the government had no more success jump-starting purchasing alliances in the 1990s than it had jump-starting HMOs in the 1970s.

DIVERSITY AND DIVERSIFICATION

The emerging health care system is driven by the heterogeneity in consumer preferences and incomes, on the one hand, and in provider scale and sophistication, on the other. Diversity among consumers creates demands for multiple provider networks and benefit packages and a willingness to pay different premiums and different deductibles. Diversity among providers engenders a supply of health care as heterogeneous as the demand. Health plans could respond by specializing in particular networks, benefit designs, distribution channels, and geographic markets. The strategy of focus is successful for firms in protected niches but spells disaster for firms in the most competitive markets, where health insurance is subject to significant economies of scale and scope. There the dominant strategy is full service diversification, the development of numerous networks and products sold through multiple channels and markets.

The diversification of networks, products, and distribution methods within the corporate health insurance sector contrasts with the emphasis in public policy circles on standardization and uniformity. The early Blue Cross plans defined standard benefit packages, charged uniform community rates, and offered one fee-for-service network within each geographic market. The Medicare and Medicaid programs developed analogously uniform benefits, enrollee contribution criteria, and provider networks. Advocates of managed competition proposed the formation of purchasing alliances to achieve the same goals, mandating that each contracting health plan offer standard benefits and a community-wide premium. The diversified health plans now are a private sector substitute for these public sector alliances, structuring consumer choice among networks and thereby generating incentives for providers to compete on the basis of price, service, and quality. Rather than join a purchasing alliance that offers multiple health plans, each with a single provider network, consumers increasingly join a health plan that offers multiple provider networks. With the privatization of the purchasing alliance, moreover, comes the abandonment of uniformity in coverage and cost, now replaced by a diversity of benefits, copayments, and premiums. The private sector accommodates itself to the heterogeneity of supply and demand rather than seek to standardize supply and homogenize demand.

DIVERSIFICATION AMONG BENEFIT DESIGNS

Each health insurance product is characterized by a particular benefit design, including the range of covered services and the consumer cost-sharing requirements, as well as a particular network structure. Most designs include the same core of physician and hospital services, but vary considerably in coverage of ancillary services. Cost-sharing provisions encompass deductibles that make the consumer responsible for all costs up to a defined threshold, percentage coinsurance rates the consumer must contribute after paying the deductible, flat dollar copayments required for particular services, and annual ceilings that limit the out-of-pocket payments under all deductible, coinsurance, and copayment provisions. Many of the early Blue Cross plans offered a single benefit package, single deductible and coinsurance level, and a community-rated premium to all customers. The principle of uniformity was enshrined in the HMO Act of 1973, which specified many details of coverage and required a uniform premium in a period when indemnity carriers were shifting toward benefit diversity and experience rating. Generous benefit designs and modest copayment provisions enabled HMOs to penetrate large firms and public employee programs but kept them out of the individual and small-group markets, where purchasers are willing to accept thinner benefits and higher cost-sharing in order to obtain lower premiums. It also disadvantaged HMOs seeking contracts from the largest corporate accounts, which demanded that benefits and premiums be tailored to their specifications and risk profiles. Indemnity insurers were more flexible in their benefit designs and dominated the small-group as well as the self-insured corporate segments.

Multiproduct health plans now combine benefit coverage and cost sharing in many ways, each of which generates a different cost and premium to be charged to the customer. The structure and level of cost-sharing provisions can be adapted to fit the budgetary capabilities of the sponsor and the preferences of the consumer. Indemnity and preferred provider insurers traditionally have relied on deductibles and percentage coinsurance provisions but have discovered that many enrollees prefer the simpler copayment structure pioneered by HMOs. Percentage co-insurance clauses create uncertainty as to what the patient ultimately will have to pay, whereas copayment clauses explicitly define the dollar amount for which the consumer is responsible. Deductible clauses are unattractive to employers seeking to purchase employee loyalty through health insurance, since the employee perceives no financial benefit until after the deductible threshold has been crossed. Preferred provider in-surance products now can be purchased with zero, modest, or substan-tial deductibles; with zero, modest, or substantial coinsurance rates; and with a range of copayment levels. Deductibles, coinsurance, and copay-ments can apply in different ways to different services. Preventive ser-vices, for example, can be exempted from any cost-sharing provisions; primary and specialty care visits can be subject to dollar copayments; hospital services can be subject to a deductible per admission plus per-centage coinsurance. HMOs are increasing cost-sharing requirements in order to minimize premium increases, especially in the individual and small-group market, where they compete for very price-conscious small firms and self-employed individuals. HMO products now can be pur-chased with deductible clauses covering all services, hospital services only, or a range of services, and with copayments that range from zero to substantial and differ for preventive, primary care, mental health, home health, and other services. Indemnity, preferred provider, and HMO insurance products combine variations in cost sharing in myriad ways with variations in coverage, including or excluding physical ther-apy, rehabilitation, mental health, ambulance, chiropractic, comple-mentary medicine, prescription drug, and durable medical services.

Design, actuarial evaluation, and pricing are core competencies es-sential for the development of multiple health insurance products. These skills were of little value in the now departed era of uniform benefit packages and community-rated premiums. But without governmental mandates or private purchasing alliances to standardize demand, health plans must tailor their offerings to the diverse preferences and incomes of their consumers. It is essential that the health plan be able to estimate accurately the expected cost of each element in the product design, so that it can accommodate a desired change in coverage or copayment by an actuarially equivalent change in premium and, conversely, find the least onerous changes in coverage or copayment necessary to accommodate a desired reduction in premium. Health plans with only one benefit design cannot accommodate the heterogeneity in consumer demand and either offer thick coverage whose premium is too costly for the budget-minded small firm or a low-priced product whose coverage is too thin for the generous sponsor. Preferences also change rapidly over time. Health plans that offer multiple products can respond to labile preferences with new designs priced at sustainable levels, while firms with only one product struggle to adapt their stable supply to the shifting demand.

DIVERSIFICATION AMONG DISTRIBUTION CHANNELS

Health care is bought and sold through four major distribution channels, including individuals and small groups, large corporate accounts, the federal Medicare program, and the various state Medicaid programs. The channels vary dramatically in terms of desired provider networks and benefit designs, geographic concentration, reliance on independent brokers and consultants, multiple versus single source contracting, and competitive versus regulatory approaches to premium setting. These differences originally fostered a specialization among health plans, with most focusing on one or two channels and ignoring the others. Blue Cross plans dominated the individual and small-group segment in most states and the large corporate accounts in some. The indemnity carriers focused on multistate employers who need broad geographic coverage. The HMOs found it easiest to penetrate unionized firms and public employee programs and then moved into the Medicare program. State Medicaid programs long remained apart from the mainstream, running their own fee-for-service programs that relied on voluntary hospitals, public clinics, and safety net providers. Over time, however, the leading health plans have begun to diversify their marketing and distribution in pursuit of greater enrollment.

The individual and small-group segment of the health insurance market poses special challenges since the differences in preferences and incomes among the participants is reflected in demands for different networks and product designs. In contrast, the heterogeneity among employees and beneficiaries who obtain insurance through large firms and governmental programs is muffled by the uniformity in purchasing imposed by their sponsoring organizations. Successful marketing to individuals and small groups requires health plans to supply diverse networks, benefit designs, and premium levels corresponding to the diversity in demand. Small firms contract with a single health plan to cover all their employees in order to eliminate the administrative headaches of multiple contracts, and are attracted to plans that offer multiple networks. Most importantly from the health plan perspective, distribution in the small-group market is dominated by brokers and agents. Small firms rely on brokers as their part-time personnel officers, handling insurance services and guiding them through the complex world of governmental regulation. While large corporations maintain human resources and regulatory compliance units dedicated to these activities, small firms use brokers to manage their pension plans, select their life insurance coverage, and facilitate compliance with equal opportunity, occupational safety, and family leave regulations. Successful marketing by health plans requires the development of benefit designs, marketing materials, and after-sale servicing that make the broker's life easier.

Large private corporations and public employee benefit programs pose quite different marketing challenges. These sponsors often pay higher wages than small firms and are willing to offer more generous health insurance programs, with richer benefits, less consumer cost sharing, and broader provider networks. They are difficult clients for the insurers, demanding tailored benefit designs and often relying on the plans merely to administer self-insured programs. Some corporations contract with a single health plan, but many embrace the principles of managed competition, contracting with multiple plans and forcing them to compete for individual employees during open enrollment season. Large purchasers are more quality conscious than their smaller counterparts, demanding health plan accreditation from the National Committee for Quality Assurance (NCQA) and compliance with a range of specialized performance criteria. Manufacturing and service corporations that compete in global markets have become accustomed to imposing stringent price and quality demands on their suppliers, and are imposing an analogous set of expectations on their health plans.

The federal Medicare program maintains its own fee-for-service program but has gradually offered beneficiaries the option to join private health plans. The Medicare benefit package is one of the least generous in the industry, requiring high deductibles and coinsurance and excluding prescription drugs altogether. This creates two quite distinct subgroups within the beneficiary population, with some enjoying supplementary insurance benefits from their former employers while others are forced to purchase additional coverage with their own funds. HMOs compete for Medicare enrollment principally by offering richer benefits and imposing lower cost-sharing requirements than the fee-for-service plan, which makes them especially attractive to beneficiaries not covered by retiree programs. In sharp contrast to the small-firm and corporate segments, benefits rather than price is the salient factor in the Medicare market and there is little cross-selling of nonhealth insurance products. Brokers and consultants play only a minor role. Successful penetration of the market relies on specialized sales teams that sponsor group events for senior citizens and follow up with kitchen-table presentations. Long-term involvement of private health plans in the public Medicare program depends on the heavily politicized budgetary goals and purchasing strategies. After years of linking HMO payment rates to the ever-rising costs of its indemnity program, Medicare has adopted more aggressive efforts to cap payment rates and stimulate competitive bidding. Despite the program's desire to broaden the range of network designs to include preferred provider and managed indemnity insurance, the regulatory requirements are daunting for any plan not built around a tightly capitated provider network. Even HMOs are finding it difficult to continue funding the supplementary benefits, especially prescription drugs, that they have offered to Medicare beneficiaries. Medicare HMOs are carefully targeting their efforts at local markets with high reimbursement rates and with physician organizations willing to manage the care.

The Medicaid market poses particularly difficult marketing challenges to private health plans since state programs are chronically underfunded. They pay rock-bottom rates to providers in their fee-for-service programs and to health plans in their managed care programs. They impose draconian restrictions on marketing methods out of concern that the health plans will misinform beneficiaries or discriminate against the chronically ill. Private health plans avoided the Medicaid market for many years, but eventually the enormous size of the covered populations could not be ignored. Profitability depends on negotiating low rates with providers, imposing stringent review of emergency room usage, and rapidly generating large enrollment. Marketing to Medicaid beneficiaries relies on none of the conventional techniques, since brokers, consultants, and in-house sales teams have virtually no contact with the Medicaid population. Special marketing units that work with safety net providers and community organizations need to be developed.

The economies of scope available to health plans diversifying across distribution channels are limited. Broad-spectrum advertising offers some benefits through the creation of brand name recognition. Individual consumers shift among the self-employed, small-firm, and large-firm segments depending on their job possibilities, and many Medicaid beneficiaries move in and out of employment. Most importantly, everyone ages over time and many health plans have created Medicare HMOs to hold onto just-retired enrollees. But the distribution mechanisms remain distinct, with the individual and small-group segment dominated by brokers, corporate accounts by human resource departments, Medicare by kitchen-table sales, and Medicaid by specialized outreach programs. Channel diversification is pursued by major health plans, however, as the key means for sustaining enrollment growth. It is driven by economies of scale in each of the health plans' networks, products, and geographic markets rather than by economies of scope. This is reflected in the internal structure of many health plans, which maintain distinct corporate units for each major distribution channel. PacifiCare, for example, built its success around the Secure Horizons medicare product, which it operates and markets in many states across the nation separately from the commercial HMO. WellPoint credited the decision to structure the firm by distribution channel, rather than by network design, for its rise from regional focus and economic bankruptcy in 1986 to national scope and enviable profitability a decade later.

DIVERSIFICATION AMONG GEOGRAPHIC MARKETS

Health insurance plans originally were concentrated in one state or metropolitan area. The Blue Cross and Blue Shield plans began in particular cities and expanded outward but, until the 1990s, each remained within the confines of the state in which it first was licensed. HMOs originally were controlled by consumer cooperatives, nonprofit organizations, or provider systems and remained in their communities of origin, extending only gradually into adjacent areas. Commercial carriers such as Aetna and CIGNA were the exceptions to this rule of geographic concentration, since they followed their corporate clients wherever there were employees eligible for benefits. As indemnity insurers, however, these plans had little grassroots presence in most communities, processing claims and adjudicating benefits from their regional corporate offices. Health care was a local service and health insurance largely a local business.

Several pressures now propel health plans into geographic diversification, offering economies of scope beyond those available in the fee-for-service era. The most obvious one derives from the ability to spread administrative overhead across a large enrollment base. Managed care imposes significantly greater start-up costs on health plans than does indemnity insurance, since HMOs must develop provider networks, oversee utilization and quality, and comply with public regulatory agencies and private accreditation bodies. Geographic expansion adds to these costs but at a rate slower than it adds to revenues. Core administrative functions such as network and benefit design, actuarial estimation and pricing, and in-house capabilities in capitation contracting and utilization review can be applied in multiple markets. Compliance with demands from the Health Care Financing Administration for Medicare enrollees, the Department of Defense for military dependents, and NCQA for corporate purchasers requires that health plans develop uniform, national quality assurance capabilities. Network, access, and quality standards for Medicaid programs vary state by state, however, discouraging multistate expansion of private Medicaid health plans.

Multimarket diversification by health plans does not contribute to better rates from medical groups and hospital systems concentrated in particular markets. There is no reason for a provider in one community to offer better rates to a multistate health plan than to a local rival, since patients will not move among metropolitan areas for their care. Even multimarket contracts with geographically diversified physician organizations usually allow rates to vary according to local conditions. It may be that financial reserves derived from multiple markets strengthen the diversified health plan's staying power in a contractual standoff, but these advantages are modest. The one significant contribution of geographic diversification to bargaining leverage derives from the enhanced ability of the multimarket health plan to enter and exit particular markets as windows of profitability open and then close. Geographic variability in corporate purchasing strategies, local labor markets, and Medicare's payment methods support very different premium levels in different regions. Consolidation by provider organizations creates cartels in some markets, limiting the health plans' ability to negotiate favorable capitation rates and fee schedules, while provider fragmentation sustains competition and price discounting elsewhere. Health plans with the capability to analyze potential revenues and costs at the regional and subregional level, to enter particular markets when conditions are favorable, and to exit when conditions are unfavorable, are able to pick their battles. The threat to leave a particular market unless premiums increase or costs decrease limits the bargaining power of corporate monopsonies and provider monopolies. At a minimum, the ability to exit allows a health plan to staunch its losses and escape provider demands that it transfer to cartelized markets the profits earned in competitive markets.

National health plans with subsidiaries in many states enjoy advantages over local rivals in marketing to multistate corporations and to mobile individuals. The commercial carriers traditionally dominated the Fortune 500 insurance segment due to their ability to process claims incurred in any location. As the superior cost performance of HMOs became evident, however, national purchasers began to contract with local plans. They soon found themselves with dozens, if not hundreds, of HMO relationships. It is difficult to manage myriad contracts, much less to evaluate them for adverse selection and clinical quality. Multistate buyers increasingly have turned to diversified health plans that offer benefits, networks, and quality accreditation in multiple states. Most of the indemnity carriers found themselves unable to develop HMO and preferred provider products and have sold out to companies that could. Multimarket presence also is important for marketing health insurance to individuals who travel frequently or live in different regions during different seasons. Many Medicare beneficiaries, for example, spend the summer months in their northern homes but winter in Florida or Arizona. They are interested only in health plans that offer good coverage in both locales.

Geographic expansion reduces the health plans' cost of capital by diversifying risks across markets with different demographics, business climates, and regulatory environments. Investors are sensitive to the fluctuations in health plan revenues and earnings caused by changes in the local markets in which they operate. A regional recession that reduces employment and fringe benefits can cut health plan enrollments and revenues very quickly without cutting overhead expenses. State legislatures can mandate new insurance benefits, prohibit capitation contracting, limit utilization review, or require networks to include any willing provider. Some states and metropolitan areas contain large purchasers of health care able to leverage lower rates than can the small firms that predominate elsewhere. Physician groups and hospital systems are highly integrated in some regions but quite fragmented elsewhere. Viewed from Wall Street, the idiosyncrasies and uncertainties of each medical marketplace increases the financial risks facing health plans whose eggs are all in one basket. Diversification reduces aggregate risk, since plans can balance a temporary setback or a permanent failure in one region with ongoing profitability and new opportunities elsewhere. Risk diversification is valued not as a purely financial strategy, since investors can diversify their risks by investing in firms in different regions. Rather, it provides the financial stability that insulates firms from excessive volatility and unpredictability, thereby permitting the pursuit of consistent strategies.

The long-term benefit of geographic expansion derives from the differences across regions in the penetration of managed care. Health plans that develop special managed care capabilities, including network contracting, marketing, product design, capitation, and quality accreditation, can earn substantial profits by applying these to markets where the homegrown plans still offer indemnity products. For a time they can shadow-price the incumbents, setting premiums below the local average to induce customer switching but above what they would be willing to accept if faced with sophisticated rivals. Diversified health plans face substantial start-up costs in each new market, since most purchasers and all providers are local, but do not need to reinvent each time the wheel of managed care. In some respects this resembles the economies of scope achieved by chain stores and franchised restaurants, who can replicate a successful formula in each new context. In other ways, however, multimarket expansion resembles technology transfer and innovation, since novel forms of clinical practice, product design, network management, and business organization are to be found in every market. A diversified health plan can improve corporate performance by benchmarking each region against the others, repatriating new ideas to the home office, and disseminating successful practices to all sites.

FROM MANAGED TO UNMANAGED COMPETITION

Managed competition relied wherever possible on voluntarism over regulation to achieve its goals. But health care is plagued with numerous centrifugal forces that press against efforts at universal coverage and coordinated delivery. Providers value unsupervised autonomy, consumers value unimpeded choice, and voters resist the taxation necessary to cover the poor. Managed competition placed fewer demands on American political culture than did reform proposals centered around utility regulation, but imposed more requirements than the system was willing to bear. The incremental version favored by the Jackson Hole Group inspired neither liberals nor conservatives and could not overcome the inertia of the political institutions. President Clinton adopted key features of the managed competition framework and was able to develop substantial initial momentum. But the President's supporters turned the managed competition framework into a legislative Christmas tree, rousing antiregulatory conservatives into a crusade against what had been designed as an alternative to regulation.

Without legislative support, the financing and organizational edifice of managed competition has crumbled. Without new tax subsidies or a mandate for employer-paid benefits, health insurance coverage is continuing to shrink. Without a national health board to standardize the benefit package, health plans are offering a spectrum of benefits and prices to accommodate the diversity in demand. Without an open enrollment mechanism to coordinate selection and switching, health plans target marketing in different ways to the self-employed, small-firm, corporate, state, and federal distribution channels. Without the mandate or the mission of local ownership, health plans are expanding across state lines toward regional or national scope. The most important form of corporate diversification in health insurance, the one that is stimulating radical changes in the organization and delivery of medical services, is the development of multiple provider networks. Without public or private purchasing alliances to sponsor consumer choice, insurers are themselves becoming multiproduct organizations that structure enrollee choice among provider networks. The leading health plans now contract on a capitated, noncapitated, and partially capitated basis with broad, narrow, and tiered networks under their HMO, preferred provider, and hybrid product designs. The one-size-fits-all contract linking the insurer to the provider is going the way of one-size-fits-all benefit design linking the insurer to the consumer. The professional guild enforced a uniform, any-willing-provider relationship between insurers and physicians. Managed competition proposed a uniform, vertically integrated relationship between HMOs and physician group practices. Unmanaged competition eschews uniformity and stimulates varied and continually changing relationships between insurers and providers. This is virtual integration in health care.

CHAPTER 4

Virtual Integration

Professional dominance facilitates consumer choice but undermines provider efficiency, while managed competition fosters efficiency but impedes choice. The professional guild was supported by indemnity health insurance plans that offered free choice of provider to patients, without limits on self-referral and switching, and free choice of therapy to providers, without utilization review or budgetary discipline. The system was inherently expansionary, however, and required external governmental controls if it were to remain an affordable means for coordinating health care services. Political limits on system capacity and fees could have sustained a system of regulated professionalism, but were stillborn in the face of provider resistance and a trend toward deregulation in the utility industries. Managed competition was based on prepaid group practices that emphasized primary care, close coordination with specialists, salaried employment, and a culture of cost-effectiveness. But the prepaid group practice required that patients defer to their physicians' choice of specialist and hospital rather than exercise independent preferences of their own, and to acquiesce in their physicians' conservative style of practice rather than act on a belief that more care is better care. Purchasing alliances could have sustained managed competition by offering choice between group practices and loosely structured physician networks, but foundered on consumer skepticism and provider antipathy.

Popular ambivalence and policy gridlock has defaulted to the marketplace the chore of balancing the competing virtues of choice and efficiency. Under pressures to control premiums, traditional insurance plans now discount physician fees, limit access to high cost procedures, and channel consumers into networks of preferred providers. Under pressures to facilitate choice, health maintenance organizations now contract on a nonexclusive basis with independent provider networks. The market manifests a plethora of relationships between health plans and providers, with continual experimentation in network designs, payment incentives, and methods of utilization management. One central theme stands out. All the emerging relationships between insurers and providers lie between the two extremes of indemnity insurance, which reimbursed any willing physician, and the staff-model HMO, which employed salaried physicians. In economic language, the new relationships are more committed than arms-length spot contracting but are more flexible than unified ownership and vertical integration. Let us call these new relationships virtual integration.

Spot contracting through indemnity insurance froze in place the guild of solo physician practice. Vertical integration through the staff-model HMO froze in place the system of salaried physician employment. Virtual integration permits, even requires, innovation in forms of physician organization. Multispecialty medical groups can contract nonexclusively with HMOs and grow through capitation and delegation of clinical responsibility. Independent Practice Associations (IPAs) can take over network management from health plans while allowing physicians to remain in their solo or small-group practices. Physician Practice Management (PPM) firms can consolidate multispecialty clinics and IPAs across geographic regions, signing multiproduct, multimarket contracts with national health insurers. Physician-Hospital Organizations (PHOs) can coordinate a continuum of inpatient and outpatient services within their local communities and contract with health plans under both vendor and partner relationships. In its turn, this experimentation in physician organization spurs change in the strategies and structures of health insurance plans. Preferred provider organizations (PPOs) and network HMOs have displaced indemnity carriers and staff-model plans but will be displaced in their turn by new hybrids. The health insurance firms of the future will offer multiple provider networks, rather than remain wedded to a single design, in order to accommodate the heterogeneity among consumers in what they are willing to buy and among physicians in what they are willing to sell.

THE TRANSFORMATION OF INDEMNITY INSURANCE

Traditional health insurers forswear any attempt to influence the cost or quality of the health care services they finance. In their purest form, health insurers do not maintain any direct relationship with physicians but only with patients. The indemnity contract specifies a schedule of benefits to the enrollee in exchange for the premium, indicating the dollar amount that will be paid toward the cost of incurred services. The patient pays the physician's fees as charged and then submits a claim to the insurer for partial indemnification; the insurer makes no payment to the physician. Blue Cross and Blue Shield plans developed a service rather than indemnity contract, subsequently adopted by Medicare, according to which the physician bills the insurer rather than the patient for services rendered. The insurer adjusts the claim against its fee schedule, deducts the amount for which the patient is responsible under coinsurance provisions, and pays the remainder. In neither case does the insurer influence the patient's choice of physician, negotiate fees, second-guess the appropriateness of the therapy, or seek to improve the quality of the care provided.[1]

The three key components of the traditional insurance product, in terms of network design, physician payment method, and approach to medical necessity, simultaneously facilitate consumer choice and eviscerate provider efficiency. The indemnity or service contract covers clinical services provided by any licensed physician, without differentiation according to cost or quality. This any-willing-provider structure places no impediments on patient choice but rules out attempts by the insurer to negotiate volume discounts with particular physicians and hospitals. The patient obtains little economic reward from using the services of low price providers, which naturally undermines the incentives for providers to offer low prices and undermines their motivation to hold down costs. In effect, the consumer is offered free choice among an undifferentiated guild of high cost, high-priced providers. The open network design abjures any attempt to identify particularly high-quality providers or improve the average quality of the services covered. The indemnity contract assumes that all licensed physicians provide care of equal quality or, at a minimum, that high-quality providers should not be paid more than low-quality providers. The insurers lack any leverage to induce providers to disclose information on quality and traditionally have perceived no advantage to disseminating information developed by third parties.

The structure of indemnity contracts forces insurers to avoid risk sharing with providers and to rely on risk sharing with patients. Fee-for-service payment methods are doubly inflationary, since they reward physicians for increasing the number of procedures and for increasing the price charged per procedure. Fee-for-service does offer several desirable incentives, since it rewards physicians for working long hours, providing complex and unpleasant procedures, and treating very sick patients who need the greatest number of interventions. Historically its most obvious deficiencies lay in the distorted fee schedules, which reimbursed higher rates for invasive over noninvasive treatments of equal efficacy, paid specialists more than primary care physicians for similar services, and keyed payment rates to billed charges. These problems have been attenuated with the shift by Medicare and many private insurers to a fee schedule that tilts payments in favor of consultative services. But their open network structure prevents indemnity insurers from placing physicians even partially at risk for the cost of the procedures they provide, and thereby shifts the onus of cost control primarily onto the patient. The indemnity contract shares the risk of medical costs with the patient by requiring deductibles and coinsurance, by imposing annual limits on expenditures and hospital days, and by excluding some services from coverage altogether. Consumer cost sharing motivates the patient to evaluate the necessity of office visits and other minor forms of care, but is a very blunt instrument for controlling overall costs. The majority of health care costs are incurred by very sick patients who have crossed their deductible and coinsurance thresholds and, moreover, are incurred for complex services that patients cannot easily evaluate. Extensive cost sharing has been found to reduce hospital utilization, for example, but not to selectively reduce ineffective and inappropriate forms of care.[2]

The free-choice-of-procedure structure of traditional health insurance interferes with any attempt to influence the pattern of care being provided and reimbursed. The epidemiological evidence on geographic variations in medical utilization highlights the potential savings from more efficient patterns of delivery. Evidence of appropriateness and quality always lag behind the data on variability, but it is clear that many clinical services are overused and many are underused in the modern health care system. The ever more fierce resistance by taxpayers and employers to premium increases suggests that the primary source of funds to pay for underutilized services must derive from reduced payments for overutilized services. The arms-length nature of the provider relationship under indemnity insurance, however, prevents the insurer from discouraging or encouraging particular services. A procedure is judged necessary if it is recommended by a licensed physician and unnecessary if not so recommended, regardless of any clinical and epidemiological evidence to the contrary. Malpractice litigation and the professional licensure boards provide haphazard control on egregiously inappropriate interventions but do little to improve the average quality of the care provided.

PREFERRED PROVIDER INSURANCE

Traditional insurance fueled rather than dampened the inflation in health care costs during the 1970s and 1980s, and indemnity products rapidly lost market share to health maintenance organizations. As long as purchasers were willing to peg their health benefit contributions to indemnity rates, the HMOs set their premiums at similar levels and competed for enrollment by adding benefits and reducing consumer copayments. As purchasers pegged their contributions to the lowest market rates, HMOs held down their premiums and competed for enrollment by underpricing indemnity plans. Either way it seemed that traditional health insurance, with its broad network access, fee-for-service reimbursement, and aversion to utilization management, was doomed. But the predictions of its demise proved premature and, indeed, a re-engineered broad network product emerged as a successful competitor for the prepaid group practice.

Preferred provider insurance makes three key changes to the traditional indemnity product that significantly improve efficiency while only modestly restricting consumer choice. Most fundamental is the shift from an any-willing-provider structure to development of a contracted physician and hospital network, albeit one considerably more broad than the classic HMO network. Preferred provider insurance typically is a product developed by commercial or Blue Cross insurers, not a form of organization, but often is referred to as a Preferred Provider Organization (PPO). For present purposes, it will be referred to as PPO or preferred provider insurance. Preferred provider insurance identifies a subset of physicians and hospitals willing to accept reduced fee-for-service payment in exchange for more patient visits and admissions, and then creates economic incentives for patients to use these providers. The contract specifies one set of benefits and copayments for enrollees when they use services from contracted providers and a less generous set when they go outside the network. A typical benefit package, for example, pays 80 percent of the contracted rate for network providers and only 60 percent of the usual and customary fee for non-network providers, with the enrollee responsible for the difference. Some variants, often referred to as Exclusive Provider Organization (EPO) insurance, cover no benefits from non-network providers. In markets where indemnity insurance still prevails, it often is difficult for insurers to induce providers to accept discounted fees, but this reluctance evaporates as HMOs enter and contract with an even tighter network of medical groups and individual practices.

Once its provider network is in place, PPO insurance can introduce new payment incentives while retaining the basic fee-for-service structure. Most PPO products pay physicians according to a fixed or negotiated fee schedule, abandoning the usual, customary, and reasonable fee ceilings. Many adopt Medicare's relative-value scale as the basis for their fee schedules, converting Medicare's relative values into dollar prices for particular procedures according to local market conditions. Case rates or bundled episode-of-illness rates can be negotiated for elective surgery and other clearly defined procedures. Preferred provider insurers use their bargaining leverage to shift hospital payment methods from cost-based or menu pricing to negotiated rates per admission or per patient day. Significant cost savings can be achieved by pressing down prices for ancillary facilities and services such as skilled nursing and subacute care, rehabilitation and physical therapy, home health, pharmacy dispensing, durable medical equipment, ambulance, and outpatient surgery services. In each case PPO insurance uses the carrot of network inclusion and the stick of potential exclusion to obtain lower rates and more standardized forms of payment.

Preferred provider insurance introduces the rudiments of utilization management into its contracted network, abandoning the free-choice-of-procedure doctrine of indemnity products. The first changes target high cost hospitalizations, mandating second opinions for surgery and pre-authorization for admission.[3] Gradually these prior authorization requirements have been extended to high cost ambulatory tests and procedures, including magnetic resonance imaging and outpatient surgery. Admissions or procedures not obtaining authorization are subject to nonpayment by the insurer. Hospital lengths of stay are shortened through concurrent review of each day's necessity and with discharge planning focused on speedy transfer to subacute or home care. Very high cost procedures, such as organ transplantation, can be channeled to regional centers of excellence. Utilization review does not require a network structure, and has been adopted by most traditional plans, creating the "managed indemnity" insurance product. Enforcement of utilization review in the absence of selective contracting is difficult, however, and the PPO products have rapidly displaced all forms of indemnity insurance. In 1988, for example, 71 percent of Americans with private health insurance still were enrolled in indemnity plans, while 11 percent were enrolled in PPO products and 18 percent in HMOs. By 1993, however, only 49 percent remained in traditional plans, 20 percent had preferred provider insurance, and 31 percent were in HMOs.[4] Most of the enrollees in traditional plans were subject to utilization review through managed indemnity products.[5] By 1995, 25 percent were enrolled in PPO products and 48 percent in HMOs, with only 27 percent in a managed indemnity plan.[6]

Well-structured PPO products can obtain significant cost savings, allowing them to set premiums near HMO levels, while retaining consumer perception of broad access and unmanaged care. Health insurance plans with large market shares can bargain for prices dramatically lower than indemnity rates and pass these savings along to their enrollees. Their methods of utilization management steer a middle course between the wholly unmonitored structure of indemnity insurance and the more tightly structured programs developed by HMOs. PPO insurance allows patients to go directly to specialists for consultation or procedures, without requiring referral from a primary care physician, and does not second-guess office-based tests and procedures except in limited circumstances. It understands that the great bulk of savings are to be obtained by targeting the small number of very sick patients rather than by annoying the large number of generally healthy enrollees. With its broad network, fee-for-service payment, and nonintrusive medical management, preferred provider insurance often feels to the enrollee as indemnity insurance but at a lower cost. And of course this is its intent.

ECLIPSE OF THE SPOT CONTRACT

The evolution of indemnity into PPO products highlights the limitations of arms-length spot contracting in health insurance. Under the traditional indemnity arrangement, there is no written contract between the insurance company and the physician or between the patient and the physician. The patient can go to a different doctor for each new ailment or new manifestation of an old ailment, without committing to any provider. Free choice of provider for the patient is mirrored by free choice of patient for the provider. Physicians can refuse to treat any prospective patient and can terminate treatment for any continuing patient. In the larger economy, spot contracts typically are found in contexts where each interaction between buyers and sellers is discrete and hence where continuity and commitment over time offer no extra value.[7] For spot contracting to work well, the price and quality of the service need to be easily understandable, thereby ensuring that neither party to the transaction can take advantage of the other. Spot contracting prevails for bulk commodities such as wheat and coal and for consumer services such as restaurant meals and retail gasoline. Even in those instances, however, the value of continuity and difficulties of quality measurement often lead to more committed relationships. The potential for contractual disputes produce multiyear supply relationships for coal or the purchase of coal mines by electric utilities.[8] The potential for quality shading in restaurant meals is attenuated by the restaurant's need for repeat visits by satisfied customers. Where repeat visits are unlikely, as on interstate highways, the restaurant industry is dominated by chains whose outlets are linked through a single brand name to guarantee uniform quality.[9]

Spot contract relationships are problematic in health care because interactions between the patient and the provider, and hence between the insurer and the provider, are neither discrete nor easily monitored. Indemnity insurance does not reward continuity of care between particular physicians and particular patients, despite the obvious fact that patients benefit from the trust and clinical insight produced by long-term relationships. Indemnity insurance does not make any particular physician responsible for any particular patient. Rather, it pays any physician who provides a service and pays nothing if no service is provided. If the care received by the patient is comprehensive, it is despite rather than because of the reimbursement method. The disadvantages of spot contracting are aggravated by the patients' difficulties in measuring the quality of medical care services. The average patient is incapable of evaluating the technical competence of the services performed by the physician, and relies on anecdote and experience with peripheral indicators such as politeness and waiting times. Medical professionalism, including licensure and malpractice law, provides only limited protection. Outside health care, consumers often delegate responsibility for evaluating complex services to intermediate organizations. For example, consumers evaluate computers as a bundle of hardware and software, delegating to the manufacturers the responsibility for assembling the individual components. Users need not understand the performance attributes of each disk and drive. The health care equivalent of quality monitoring by intermediate organizations ranges from preferred provider insurance through more tightly structured HMO networks to fully integrated multispecialty medical groups. The most heavily monitored forms of medical care are found in environments such as the Mayo Clinic where individual physicians are screened prior to recruitment, are socialized into a culture of continual peer review, and are profiled against practice benchmarks for the group as a whole.

The indemnity insurance product is even more extreme than the typical spot contract in that it prevents volume discounting by purchasers. The individual patient accounts for only a small fraction of each provider's revenue stream and hence wields no leverage over rates. In most circumstances, of course, illness and deference rule out any thought of price negotiations. But the collectivity of patients enrolled in an insurance plan accounts for a large fraction of provider revenues. The centralization of purchasing through the preferred provider insurer allows individual patients to benefit from this latent economic leverage. Insurers have the technical expertise necessary to negotiate with physicians and are not compromised by illness or emotion from seeking the lowest possible price. Physicians and hospitals are willing to discount fees initially in anticipation of incremental revenue gains that offset fixed practice expenses. As discounted rates become the norm rather than the exception, providers are forced to accept the reality of thinner margins but also begin to contemplate organizational alternatives to traditional solo practice. Through its discounted fees and top-down utilization review, preferred provider insurance thus creates two quite distinct impacts on the structure of physician organization. By forcing physicians to practice in a more cost-effective manner, preferred provider insurance gives solo practice a new lease on life, permitting it to compete with more tightly structured medical groups. But by cutting fees and second-guessing utilization decisions, preferred provider insurance generates a provider backlash and stimulates the search for new forms of physician organization.

THE TRANSFORMATION OF THE STAFF-MODEL HMO

The first health maintenance organizations made no distinction between the insurance plan and the provider organization. Some HMOs were developed by visionary physicians who sought to stabilize practice revenues and patient coverage through prepayment.[10] Others were created by consumer cooperatives or industrial corporations intent on ensuring comprehensive benefits at an affordable cost. Prepaid group practices such as Ross-Loos, Group Health Cooperative of Puget Sound, and Kaiser emerged at a time when the spot contract principles of indemnity insurance were not yet firmly entrenched. To the first HMOs it seemed preferable, even natural, for physicians to be partners and employees in multispecialty medical groups that marketed their services to consumers on a prepaid basis, rather than to remain in solo practice with arms-length indemnity reimbursement. The original HMO contract guaranteed enrollee access to a defined set of services for a defined monthly premium, rather than specifying a partial indemnification schedule. Benefits were much more extensive than for commercial and Blue Cross plans, covering ambulatory, maternity, mental health, and preventive services long before these were covered by traditional health insurers. The HMOs eschewed deductibles and minimized reliance on coinsurance provisions as inimical to their belief in comprehensive coverage.

Prepaid group practice produced the alchemy of comprehensive benefits at affordable premiums by focusing its cost control attention on the supply rather than the demand side of the health care transaction. The central elements of this strategy were the adjustment of provider capacity to patient volume, salaried rather than fee-for-service compensation for physicians, and the fostering of a cost-conscious clinical practice style. In each of these instances the close coordination of clinical and insurance functions, the vertical integration between production and distribution, played an important supportive role. The HMOs hired physicians and built clinics in line with anticipated growth in patient volume. The insurance and marketing staff were responsible for attaining enrollment targets and the physician staff was responsible for providing services. HMOs were able to target clinic expansion in areas of anticipated growth while not exacerbating their physician surplus in areas already well served. They stringently limited physician referrals and patient self-referrals to outside providers in order to ensure the continual matching of patient volume with organizational capacity. This contrasted with the uncoordinated system of solo practice and indemnity insurance, which combined inadequate physician access in some areas with excess supply in others. The HMOs adopted the principles of group practice and salaried employment from Mayo and the other multispecialty clinics, but keyed salaries to training and tenure rather than to the number of tests and procedures each physician ordered. They worked hard to instill a culture of multispecialty cooperation within the budgeted structure of a prepaid practice, delegating to the physicians the responsibility for keeping clinical costs within their capitation revenues. The marketing staff and the physician leadership were jointly responsible for understanding the impact of increasing costs on patient enrollment. The cumulative impact of these organizational innovations were substantial. The vertically integrated HMOs provided significantly more preventive and ambulatory services than indemnity insurers, limited hospitalization by targeting less appropriate procedures, and incurred costs 30 percent below those of their indemnity competitors.[11] They passed these savings along to prospective enrollees in the form of lower premiums and better benefits, and rapidly grew their share of their local markets.

By far the most important of the prepaid group practices was the Kaiser Foundation Health Plan, which developed initially as an in-house medical care program for employees of Kaiser industries in the 1930s and opened to the public in 1945.[12] Kaiser proved successful in large part because it was not a vertically integrated firm but, rather, a partnership between one insurance plan and several medical groups tied together by exclusive contractual relationships. The physicians who provided clinical services to enrollees in the HMO were not Kaiser employees, but, rather, partners and employees in one of the regional Permanente Medical Groups. The distinction between the insurance plan and the medical groups allowed the physicians to retain control over both the administrative and the clinical dimensions of medicine while being assured of enrollment and revenues from the insurance plan. The Permanente groups, not the health plan, decided how many and which types of physicians to hire, how much they would be paid, and how they would be evaluated. There was no review of utilization patterns by the health plan, since all clinical decisions were delegated to the medical groups. The Permanente physicians had complete control over their affairs within the economic constraints of their prepaid budget, which derived from the premiums the insurance plan could charge in the outside market. This contrasted with the unimpeded control and open-ended payment of the professional guild under indemnity insurance and the impeded control and discounted payment of the guild under preferred provider insurance.

The contractual nature of the relationship between the Kaiser HMO and the Permanente Medical Groups fostered coordination between the distribution and the production sides of their enterprise without sacrificing the distinct cultures of each. In contrast to some prepaid group practices where physicians exerted unrestricted control, Kaiser retained an outward-looking, expansionistic strategy that fostered growth. Most physician-dominated health plans remained small and local, since they lacked the entrepreneurial will to expand. Kaiser expanded from its base on the West Coast to launch prepaid group practices in Hawaii, the Midwest, the South, and the northeast, often through the acquisition of struggling local plans. In contrast to prepaid group practices where the insurance plan exerted unrestricted control, however, the Permanente Medical Groups retained a strong physician culture and commitment. Staff-model HMOs, in which the individual doctor was an employee of the insurance company rather than of a medical group, were bedeviled by low morale and productivity. Lack of physician effort and entrepreneurship torpedoed efforts by indemnity insurers and Blue Cross plans to emulate Kaiser by building clinics and recruiting doctors. Aetna, CIGNA, Prudential, and other major plans lost millions of dollars on their HMO products before divesting their clinics and reverting to a contractual relationship with their erstwhile subsidiaries.

Despite its advantages over staff-model HMOs, Kaiser came to perceive even its contractual form of vertical integration as endangered by the changing health care marketplace. Attempts to expand into new geographic markets, often in response to requests by interested employers, incurred capital costs and time delays as the HMO and its Permanente partners struggled to build a delivery system. It obviously made no sense to build new hospitals in markets with high excess capacity, and Kaiser abandoned its early policy of owning inpatient as well as outpatient facilities. The time and money costs of constructing physician offices, even if restricted to primary care services, also proved to be limiting factors in areas with sufficient physician capacity. It was very expensive to maintain half-empty clinics and underutilized physicians while waiting for patient volume to grow. The regional Permanente groups began to contract with networks of independent physicians and hospitals, first in new communities but then in established markets where excess capacity made it cheaper to outsource than to provide particular services. The other leading staff- and group-model HMOs came to the same conclusion. The Harvard Community HMO merged with a network plan to form the Harvard-Pilgrim health plan and spun off its staff clinics into a semi-autonomous relationship. The Health Insurance Plan (HIP) developed a contractual network around its dedicated clinics in New York and divested its staff model altogether in New Jersey. A similar evolution from vertical integration to nonexclusive contracting occurred at the Group Health Cooperative of Puget Sound, HealthPartners in Minneapolis, and most of the other staff- and group-model HMOs.

THE NETWORK HMO

The success of Kaiser and the other HMOs posed a growing challenge to the professional guild of solo practice and the indemnity insurance industry that supported it. Preferred provider insurance offered some respite but could not match the economic savings and clinical coordination of the prepaid group practice. Most American communities lacked the multispecialty medical groups necessary to form conventional HMOs but would support prepaid HMO insurance if built on the available solo physician practices. The first HMO that combined prepayment with a network cobbled together from solo practices emerged in California's San Joaquin Valley under direct competitive threat from Kaiser. This form of insurer organization, eventually labeled the Independent Practice Association, or IPA-model HMO, contracted with individual physicians rather than medical groups, paid on a discounted fee schedule rather than through capitation or salaries, and monitored patterns of utilization directly rather than delegating this function to a physician organization. The IPA-model HMO was imitated and disseminated widely by medical societies, Blue Cross plans, indemnity insurers, and entrepreneurial start-ups, eventually outpacing the established plans.

The IPA-model HMO contrasts with the prepaid group practice in developing a contractual network of preexisting small practices that also provide services to non-HMO patients and often to the patients of competing HMOs. It pays physicians either on a discounted fee-for-service basis or through capitation for primary care services only, supplementing these reimbursement methods with a variety of withholds, bonuses, and other incentives for cost-conscious styles of practice. In most cases the enrollee is required to select a primary care physician as the coordinator of all care. Referrals to specialist consultations and procedures must be authorized by this physician. The IPA often imposes a supplementary level of oversight, requiring both primary care and specialty physicians to obtain prior authorization for high cost tests and procedures. In its network design, physician payment, and arms-length utilization management, the IPA stands between the staff-model HMO and the PPO insurance product. Its network typically is broader than the HMO's but tighter than the PPO's; its payment methods share less risk than the HMO's but more than the PPO's; and its methods of utilization management are weaker than the HMO's but more stringent than the PPO's.

The IPA is ideally structured for large metropolitan markets such as New York and Philadelphia that have excess provider capacity but lack large physician organizations. U.S. HealthCare and Oxford Health Plans came to dominate those markets by contracting with broad physician and hospital networks, obtaining significant fee discounts due to the excess market capacity, and retaining in-house rather than delegating the core functions of credentialing, claims processing, and utilization management. Over time, however, even the most sophisticated IPA plans find their ability to influence physician behavior without the benefit of intermediary physician organizations to be limited. After being acquired by the Aetna indemnity carrier and given a national agenda, U.S. HealthCare began to experiment with capitated and delegated relationships with physician organizations. Indeed, Aetna U.S. HealthCare signed the nation's first multimarket, multiproduct contract with a PPM firm after it divested its primary care clinics and IPAs to MedPartners in 1997. After its earnings debacle and stock price collapse in that same year, Oxford began shifting to tight networks and capitated contracts for its Medicare HMO enrollment, retaining broad networks and fee-for-service payment only for its relatively healthy commercially insured population.

The staff-model HMO is limited by its dependence on a single prepaid group practice for its delivery system, while the IPA-model HMO is limited by its dependence on a diffuse network of solo and small-group practices. The former cannot take advantage of the enhanced provider choice, price discounts, and physician productivity offered by the solo practitioners while the latter lacks the prepayment efficiencies and clinical coordination of the multispecialty medical group. One relies excessively on vertical integration through ownership or employment while the other relies on a spot contracting relationship little different from that of PPO insurance. The increasingly dominant form of HMO adopts a middle ground between these extremes, contracting with multispecialty medical groups where available but also with networks of physicians in solo practice. The key characteristic of this network-model HMO is that it owns neither staff clinics nor captive IPAs but contracts on a nonexclusive basis with both groups and freestanding IPAs. The medical groups and IPAs, in their turn, contract on a nonexclusive basis with multiple network HMOs, and continue to accept patients from indemnity and PPO insurers.

In one sense, the network HMO plan can be conceptualized as an intermediate form of organization that borrows elements from both the staff HMO and the PPO insurer. Like the staff HMO, it relies on capitated physician organizations rather than individual fee-for-service physicians. Like the PPO, it contracts with independent providers rather than owning a provider group. In another sense, however, the network HMO contrasts with both the staff HMO and the PPO, which bear an underlying similarity to one another. The staff HMO and the PPO deal with physicians as individuals, employing them in the first instance and contracting with them in the second. The network HMO, in contrast, fosters the growth of physician organizations. The network HMOs and the medical groups are independent but interdependent, with both mutual and conflicting interests. Their fates are intertwined but each maintains other partners. They are a single organization from the perspective of improving consumer service and hence revenue, but different organizations from the perspective of how revenues are to be divided.

In southern California the network HMOs, including Maxicare, PacifiCare, and HealthNet, initially offered exclusive franchises to medical groups in each local community. In the late 1970s and early 1980s, multispecialty medical groups maintained a gentleman's agreement to stay out of each other's backyards. As organizational islands in a sea of solo practitioners, medical groups had space to grow without competing directly with one another. A similar pattern was followed in the northern part of the state, where the TakeCare HMO was launched by Blue Cross in collaboration with a consortium of clinics. Very rapidly, however, the network plans found their contracting medical groups did not offer enough physicians and office sites to satisfy the market demand for choice. They encouraged the expansion of the multispecialty groups into underserved communities but recognized that the physician leadership and managerial talent needed to build medical groups were in short supply. It was necessary for the HMOs to incorporate solo practices directly into their networks. The health plans achieved this by contracting with IPAs as well as multispecialty groups. The IPAs were sponsored by local hospitals eager to retain HMO admissions and by medical societies whose physicians were eager to retain HMO patients. The most successful IPAs escaped dominance by hospitals and medical societies, evolving into entrepreneurial organizations committed to success through managed care rather than success against it. By 1990 many local communities exhibited multiple physician organizations, each contracting with multiple network HMOs.

The network HMOs shift both insurance risk and clinical responsibility to their medical group and IPA partners. The trend in contracting has been toward an ever greater number of services being covered through capitation rather than fee-for-service. Over time, capitation extended from primary care to all professional services and annual contracts evolved toward multiyear relationships where the providers received a percentage of the insurance premium. The largest physician organizations negotiated contracts covering multiple geographic markets and multiple insurance products, including HMO, PPO, and other options. The extension of capitation reflects an underlying trade-off between risk spreading and risk management. The health plans are larger and more diversified than the physician organizations, and thus better suited to bear the risk of unforeseen fluctuations in expenditures. The medical groups and IPAs, however, are better able to reduce expenditures by evaluating the clinical appropriateness of each test and procedure. As the physician organizations grow through mergers and acquisitions, they become better able to spread insurance risk while retaining their advantage in clinical performance. In this context it is in the interest of both sides to shift insurance risk from the plans to the providers through ever more comprehensive capitation.

An analogous shift occurs in clinical responsibility. Most physician organizations enjoy clear advantages over health plans in monitoring and managing referrals, high cost procedures, hospital admissions, and other elements of care. They are closer to the front line physicians, with better understanding of practice styles and ability to discuss difficult cases in a collegial manner. They are closer to the patients, with better understanding of the clinical idiosyncrasies as well as the preferences of each enrollee. Physician organizations are closer to local hospitals, nursing homes, and ancillary providers, with quicker access to information on changes in a patient's condition that require changes in the style or setting of treatment. Well-run IPA-model HMOs and PPO insurers can surpass poorly run medical groups, but the average insurer will always lag behind even the average physician organization in managing the process of care. Network HMOs need to perform utilization review for medical groups that are too small or poorly governed to conduct their own reviews effectively. But overall, the HMOs are able to step back from a primary into a supportive role. Their emphasis shifts to checking for potential undertreatment of patients by the medical groups, who now have the financial incentive to limit expenditures. This contrasts with the role of the PPO insurer, where the fee-for-service physician's financial incentive still is to overtreat and the health plan focuses on limiting unnecessary procedures.

ECLIPSE OF VERTICAL INTEGRATION

The accelerating shift from staff to network HMOs highlights the disadvantages of vertical integration, the exclusive linkage between a single health plan and provider organization, and the advantages of nonexclusive contractual linkages among multiple plans and providers. It contrasts with the principles of managed competition, which maintain that full integration of physician, hospital, and insurance functions produces the most efficient health care organization and will be the survivor in a competitive medical marketplace. The success of the network HMO stems from three interrelated factors: economies of scale, physician performance incentives, and rapid diffusion of innovations.

The separation of marketing and insurance functions from those of organizing and delivering care permits the health plans and the medical groups to achieve economies of scale in their respective sectors. While vertical integration increases the overall size of the firm by combining insurance with delivery functions, it typically leads to a narrower clinic network than that needed by the insurance unit and a smaller patient volume than that needed by the delivery unit. The optimal geographic scope of a health insurance plan is at least statewide, if not regional, while that for a medical group is local. Health plans need very broad scope in order to compete for contracts with multistate employers, to offer national delivery networks to the mobile American public, and to spread the costs of compliance with Medicare and Medicaid regulations. Once they have their core functions of marketing, purchaser relations, and regulatory compliance in place, they can add new enrollees at low cost while gaining significant new revenues. The capital costs required to build staff clinics to service these broadly dispersed consumers would be prohibitively high. Each HMO would need to build numerous clinics since competing plans rarely include each other's employed physicians in their networks. Competing HMOs are willing, however, to contract with the same medical groups so long as the groups are independently owned and give no preference to any particular plan. Independent medical groups do not require broad geographic coverage but need a high volume of patients at each site in order to keep their physicians fully occupied. Adding new patients in distant localities is of little benefit, while maintaining a constant flow of patients through their existing clinics is essential. Vertical integration limits their patient volume to the enrollees of a single health plan. Marketing difficulties at that health plan create disastrous drops in volume for the vertically integrated provider groups. Nonexclusive contracting with multiple health plans, on the other hand, shields the medical group from fluctuations in enrollments at any one plan. If one plan gains market share at the expense of the others, the physicians would see a different mix of membership cards but not a different mix of patients. Exclusive links to one health plan make the survival of the medical group depend on the prowess of one marketing team; nonexclusive contracts put multiple marketing teams to work for each medical group.

The advantages of the network HMO over its staff-model competitor would have been less substantial had either President Clinton's or the Jackson Hole version of managed competition been adopted. Large purchasing alliances can contract with many staff-model HMOs, allowing consumers to enroll in whichever plan offers their favorite physicians. HMOs that appeal to particular consumers can be successful without offering broad provider panels. In the absence of purchasing alliances, however, most employers contract with one or only a few health plans, giving preference to those with broad networks in order to accommodate their employees' desire for physician choice. The health plans are required to perform the role of ensuring consumer choice that the purchasing alliance would perform under managed competition. In this context, health plans vertically integrated with particular medical groups are at a severe disadvantage in marketing their services, compared to health plans that contract nonexclusively with many groups.

Vertical integration between production and distribution, as embodied in the staff-model HMO, can attenuate the incentives of each entity to work hard, take risks, and succeed in its individual market. Independent medical groups and health plans earn the full rewards of success and pay the full penalty of failure. When united in a staff model, however, each can coast on the efforts of the other. If medical groups develop a low productivity practice style in which each doctor sees only a few patients per day, for example, the health plan cannot terminate a contract but must engage in internal organizational politics. Similarly, if the health plan prices its product so high as to reduce membership or so low as to bring in inadequate revenues, the medical group must absorb the losses. In a system of nonexclusive contracting, plans and providers more easily exit an unsatisfactory relationship. In the normal course of events contract terminations do not occur, but the possibility of a rupture motivates each side to perform and not take the other for granted.

In its access to organizational innovations, the network HMO enjoys important advantages over the staff model. Vertical integration spurs investments in research and development by ensuring that the value of subsequent breakthroughs are appropriated by the firm, rather than being dispersed immediately to competitors.[13] Patent law ensures exclusive appropriation for a defined period, and hence offers an alternative to vertical integration, but is a notoriously weak method of protecting innovations that lack a clear blueprint or chemical formula. Unfortunately, the benefits of vertically integration in access to internally generated innovations often diminishes access to externally generated innovations. For example, computer companies that sought to directly manufacture all their component parts were outcompeted by networks of smaller firms that specialized in distinct but compatible components.[14] Virtual integration through nonexclusive contracts permits the rapid diffusion of innovations through the network by allowing all participants to benefit. While the length of time a firm can appropriate its own innovation is shorter than for vertically integrated organizations, the time necessary to identify and assimilate externally generated innovations is commensurably shorter.

Virtual integration between network HMOs and medical groups stimulates experimentation in new methods of payment and utilization management. Medical groups compete with each other but also copy each other's best ideas on how to pay primary care and specialist physicians, how to monitor patterns of referral and admission, and how to manage patients with chronic diseases. Network HMOs compete with each other but also copy ideas on how to structure risk sharing and incentives with providers, how to channel transplant patients to regional centers of excellence, and how to encourage use of preventive services. Innovative programs developed by one HMO with its contracting medical groups quickly diffuse to the other plans, since the physicians apply the new methods to all patients. Similarly, successful ideas developed by one medical group diffuse quickly to the others, since health plans apply the improvements to their entire provider networks. Staff-model HMOs with exclusive medical groups do not benefit from this rapid diffusion of innovation.

The loss of scale economies, performance incentives, and access to innovation experienced by the staff-model HMO parallel experiences elsewhere in the economy. Vertical integration between production and distribution should be viewed as the coordination mechanism of last resort, to be adopted only where contractual alternatives are not available.[15] In some industries, efficient production requires specialized methods of distribution or, conversely, efficient distribution requires specialized methods of production. The value of these specialized investments would be lost if the business relationships were terminated. In these contexts, vertical integration protects the party making the investment from the risk of termination and, by extension, the risk that the other party could extract more favorable payment under threat of termination. Unified ownership makes cooperation the best strategy for both sides. Specialized investments are found in manufacturing, railroad transportation, electric power generation, and other industrial sectors with extensive physical assets. They are not, however, an important feature of the relationship between health insurance plans and health care providers. Medical groups do not practice a different style of medicine for each health plan and health plans do not use different marketing methods for each medical group. Rather, the practice of medicine is imbued with the culture of standardization and disclosure. It would invite malpractice litigation for a medical group to withhold a quality-improving procedure from the enrollees of one health plan while supplying it to the enrollees in others. Conversely, as they evolve into organizations that structure consumer choice, HMOs develop standard methods of operation that should be applied to all providers rather than be specialized to any one.

In retrospect, the early prominence of staff-model HMOs was due not to any inherent efficiency of vertical integration but to the special features of the fledgling industry that changed as it matured. Pathbreaking firms in new industries frequently are forced to develop their own supply and distribution networks because independent firms are not present in the market.[16] As consumer demand grows, however, independent suppliers and distributors emerge and focus on particular segments of the industry, thereby reaping economies of scale. Formerly integrated firms find it profitable to divest their internal units and contract with independent suppliers and distributors. In some cases, suppliers, producers, and distributors develop joint ventures, partial ownership linkages, or franchise relationships. If consumer demand subsequently shifts away to other products, the industry may shrink to the point where independent suppliers and distributors no longer are viable, and a pattern of vertical integration will reemerge.

The early HMOs were staff models for analogous reasons. Most were spawned by industrial corporations or consumer cooperatives that built new physician group practices since none were to be found in their communities. During the 1980s, some Blue Cross and commercial insurers established staff-model HMOs as the only alternative to spot contracting with individual physicians, since no independent medical groups were available. Blue Cross developed clinics in Massachusetts and New Jersey, CIGNA purchased medical groups in Los Angeles and Albuquerque, and Prudential developed primary care centers throughout the southeast. In some cases, vertical integration occurred from the opposite direction, as medical groups or hospital systems established staff-model HMOs as an alternative to the local indemnity and PPO plans. Maxicare and FHP International began as group practices in Los Angeles while Humana was launched by an investor-owned hospital chain in the southeast. As the managed care industry matured, however, both medical groups and HMOs proliferated. Medical groups developed their capabilities for managing utilization under a capitation budget and it became less necessary for health plans to build their own delivery organizations. Conversely, HMOs developed skills in capitation contracting and delegation, and it became less necessary for provider organizations to build their own insurance plans.

THE MULTIPRODUCT HEALTH PLAN

Traditional indemnity carriers, having evolved into PPO insurers, and prepaid group practices, having evolved into network HMOs, each possess features attractive to the purchasers and consumers of health care. The PPO insurers build on their strengths in marketing and broker relationships, actuarial risk estimation, underwriting, pricing, claims processing, consumer service, and employer relations. They offer broad networks of physicians and hospitals with only modest constraints on referrals, procedures, and admissions. Preferred provider insurance can be sold as a fully insured product or be tailored to meet the needs of self-insured corporate purchasers. PPO networks can be developed quickly and marketed widely without the need for sophisticated provider organizations. The network HMOs, on the other hand, build on the strengths of prepaid group practice in capitation finance, utilization management, and organizational integration. The clinical and administrative efficiencies of their contracting providers have allowed the HMOs to charge low premiums, avoid deductibles, offer comprehensive benefits, and pioneer preventive medicine coverage. The network HMOs benefit from the innovations in incentives and practice styles occurring in the leading medical groups rather than avoid these organizations and contract with each individual physician directly.

PPO insurers and network HMOs now divide the private health insurance market between them, having squeezed out most traditional indemnity insurers and staff-model plans, and are making significant inroads into the public Medicare and Medicaid programs. Each has adopted some elements from the other yet they remain distinct products appealing to distinct customer segments. The PPO insurers excel in offering broad choice while the network HMOs excel at efficient delivery. The HMOs have broadened their networks but cannot achieve the almost universal inclusiveness of the insurers. Their point-of-service options and streamlined referral authorizations facilitate specialty referrals but cannot emulate the PPO insurer's claim to put the consumer in charge of all health care choices. Preferred provider insurance holds down premiums by cutting physician and hospital payments but imposes onerous deductible and coinsurance requirements to keep premiums near HMO levels. Insurers have tightened utilization management and extended it from inpatient to outpatient procedures, but cannot duplicate the continuous monitoring of care achieved by HMOs through their medical group relationships. An attempt by the HMOs to achieve the full breadth of choice offered by PPO insurance would undermine their provider relationships, while an attempt by the insurers fully to emulate the efficiencies of the HMO would alienate their choice-oriented customer base. In this context, individual health plans could remain specialized in a single provider network, offering either a PPO or an HMO design, and thereby reap the benefits of managerial focus and administrative simplicity. The alternative is to market both PPO and HMO products and then to add hybrid networks that balance in new ways the competing virtues of choice and efficiency.

Network diversification improves the health plan's leverage in contracting with physicians, medical groups, and other providers of care. Plans can combine enrollment across their various physician networks in negotiating volume discounts with hospitals, nursing homes, and drug manufacturers. Most of the rates negotiated with hospitals for inpatient days and outpatient surgeries can be applied to patients admitted under either the health plan's PPO or HMO network. In states where HMOs contract with individual physicians, rather than through independent medical groups, the plans can impose fee schedules covering procedures for both HMO and PPO patients. Beyond these advantages of scale, however, the maintenance of multiple networks helps the health plan understand the true costs of care and negotiate sustainable rates with providers. Capitation allows health plans to delegate utilization management to physician organizations. Over time, however, it undermines their ability to monitor the care being provided to enrollees and hence to evaluate the cost structure of the providers. Network HMOs often have difficulty demanding utilization data coded at the level of detail and accuracy comparable to the claims data generated by PPO products, which generate detailed claims and rely on individual physician contracting. While utilization and cost data are not fully comparable across PPO and HMO networks, information on one is invaluable as a benchmark of comparison for the other. Finally, the availability of non-capitated PPO networks limits the monopoly power of large physician and hospital organizations. Plans facing difficulties in obtaining competitive rates from their integrated HMO providers can fall back to more intensely marketing their PPO product.

Diversification offers important economies of scope through joint marketing and distribution. Whenever possible, firms seek to accommodate the diverse preferences of their employees by offering a choice of HMO and PPO networks. To the extent each health plan offers only a single network, purchasers must bear the administrative costs of contracting with multiple plans. To the extent individual plans offer multiple networks, however, the purchasers can sign one contract yet still offer choice to their employees. Diversification can be extended to triple-option structures, such as HMO, PPO, and point-of-service, as well as to multiple benefit designs. Network diversification is essential for health plans that market to small firms, for whom the administrative costs of contracting with multiple plans are prohibitive. It also is valuable for managing the self-insured accounts of large corporations, which seek to offer employee choice while retaining control over the risk pool. As Medicare and Medicaid extend their managed care programs to point-of-service and PPO designs, network diversification allows health plans to compete for beneficiaries who shun the traditional HMO structure. Most importantly, perhaps, diversification allows the health plans to retain the distinctive features of each network rather than dilute them down to the lowest common denominator. Some firms have sought to market a single product design to all market segments, typically combining a broad PPO network with a comprehensive HMO benefit package and out-of-network coverage to emulate indemnity insurance. These products force consumers interested in integrated delivery to pay the cost of the network breadth on which they place little value, preventing them from obtaining low price in exchange for limited choice. Yet these same products constrain consumers interested in indemnity-style coverage to obtain primary care referrals and specialty care authorization, preventing them from paying top dollar for unconstrained access.

Network HMO and PPO products embody different approaches to managing cost, access, and quality, which creates the potential for confusion if combined in a haphazard fashion but for cross-fertilization if coordinated correctly. HMOs are under much greater oversight than are PPO insurers from state insurance departments, the Health Care Financing Administration, and private accreditation entities such as the National Committee for Quality Assurance. They are obliged to develop internal structures for evaluating the processes and, to a more limited extent, the outcomes of care received by their enrollees. These structures and standards can be applied to PPO and indemnity products at less incremental cost by plans with HMO networks than would be incurred by plans not already subject to HMO oversight authorities. Conversely, health plans offering PPO products need to develop in-house capabilities for authorizing hospital admissions, surgical procedures, and the other elements of care that fall within their utilization management purview. The network HMOs have delegated most of these functions to their capitated physician organizations, since whichever party is responsible for the cost of care needs the authority for utilization management. Diversified health plans can use their in-house PPO capabilities to oversee their HMO networks, checking both for unnecessary care and for inadequate access to necessary care.

The most important scope economies derive from the ability of a diversified health plan to keep in touch with the rapidly evolving styles of care within the provider community. Through their capitated and delegated HMO networks, health plans maintain relationships with the most sophisticated physician organizations, those committed to rationalizing the mix of specialties and facilities and to reducing the variance in efficiency across clinics. The ideas and practices pioneered in these environments can be transferred to less sophisticated providers in the PPO networks. Conversely, health plans with strong PPO networks maintain day-to-day relationships with individual physicians and hospitals without the blending and aggregation engendered by medical groups and hospital systems. This keeps the health plans in touch with the small but cumulatively important changes that individual providers are implementing in their particular settings, innovations that respond to the changing preferences of consumers and patients. Many of these experiments can be applied to the larger provider organizations, which must struggle against the bureaucracy and nonresponsiveness that accompany large-scale organization. Virtual integration advantages the network HMOs over vertically integrated staff HMOs by linking them to a range of medical groups. By extension, multiple network relationships advantages diversified health plans over their single-product rivals by keeping them linked both with individual physicians through their PPO networks and with physician organizations through their HMO networks.

CONTRACTUAL INNOVATION

Preferred provider insurance and the network HMO preserve what is most important from indemnity insurance and the staff-model HMO while modifying them in ways essential for continued viability. PPO insurance retains the indemnity plan's broad physician network, fee-for-service payment, and patient self-referral to specialty care while exerting enough bargaining leverage and utilization review to hold down premiums. The network HMO retains a medical group, capitation, and delegation focus from its vertically integrated forerunner while broadening consumer access and rewarding physician productivity. The insurance industry continues to experiment with new network designs, benefit packages, and distribution strategies in response to changes in consumer demand, spinning out new products that will replace PPO insurance and the network HMO as they have replaced indemnity insurance and the staff HMO. Health plans now market multiple products that balance in different ways the competing virtues of access, coordination, coverage, and affordability.

Change within the health insurance industry responds to and stimulates change within the health care delivery system. PPO insurance sustains solo physician practice by holding down fees, limiting inappropriate care, and imposing the rudiments of quality oversight. For this support the insurers are excoriated by the medical profession, many of whose members believe that the unmanaged indemnity of yesteryear is still viable today. Physicians fail to realize that the PPO insurer is but a servant of the corporate purchaser, the rebellious taxpayer, and the individual consumer, all of whom are adamant about coverage costs. The network HMO sustains independent physician organizations, sharing financial risk through capitation and clinical responsibility through delegation. Multispecialty medical groups, IPAs, PPM firms, and PHOs derive their patients primarily from these health plans. Physician organizations are better able than individual physicians to recognize their debt to the network HMOs, without which they would never gain the revenues and responsibilities for managing care, and occasionally will join in partnership rhetoric. But day to day they are engaged in often bitter payment disputes and indulge themselves in the fantasy of squeezing out the insurance middleman.

Virtual integration in health care encompasses this ever-changing multiplicity of relationships between insurers and providers, including fee-for-service contracts with individual providers, capitated contracts with provider organizations, and every possible contractual hybrid. There exists no one best relationship between insurers and physicians, no ideal payment methodology, no final allocation of responsibility for utilization and quality. Purchasers and consumers differ in the networks and products they want to buy while physicians and physician organizations differ in the risks and responsibilities they want to assume. The multiplicity of contractual relationships under virtual integration characterizes both the health care industry as a whole and the individual firms within it. Health insurance plans contract in a nonexclusive fashion with competing providers and provider organizations. Conversely, physicians contract as individuals with PPO insurers and as members of IPAs and other organizations with HMOs. Exclusive contracts and franchise agreements are being displaced by organizational promiscuity as everyone contracts with everyone. Virtual integration supports cooperation between insurers and providers, given their common interest in improving network performance and market share, but also sustains conflict, as each struggles to obtain a greater portion of the joint revenue stream. The nonexclusive nature of the contractual relationships helps mediate these tensions by providing marketplace benchmarks on what is a competitive price for each particular service. This contrasts favorably with the regulatory price ceilings demanded by indemnity insurance and the internal transfer prices developed by vertically integrated HMOs, neither of which is based on meaningful standards of comparison.

Virtual integration creates confusion not only for insurers and providers but also for consumers, purchasers, regulators, and legislators. Critics demand a simpler insurer-provider structure, a one-size-fits-all solution to the effervescence of the marketplace, but cannot agree on what that ideal alternative might be. Some advocate a reversion to the spot contract of indemnity insurance, others praise vertical integration through the staff HMO, and still others promote new variants on the old themes. But the health care marketplace is too dynamic to coalesce around any one relationship. An element of chaos is the price that must be paid for experimentation in health care, for creative responses to the conflicting social demands for ever more costly medicine at an ever more controlled cost. The forms of health insurance prevalent today are no one's ideal, and no one will be dismayed to see them pass. They will be outmoded and outcompeted in their turn. Their most important impact will occur through the forms of innovative organization adopted by physicians and other providers of health care as they adapt to the risks, incentives, and opportunities of virtual integration.

The Multispecialty Medical Group

Solo practice and informal referral networks were well adapted to the rural demographics and modest clinical technology of the early twentieth century, but came under increasing stress with the urbanization of the population and specialization of the profession. The primary challenge came from the multispecialty medical group, pioneered by the Mayo brothers and popularized through the experience of cooperative medicine by army physicians during the First World War. The multispecialty clinic appeared to its proponents as the rational response to the complexity and fragmentation of medicine, which undermined the ability of the solo practitioner to comprehend and coordinate the full array of possible treatments. Yet medical groups spread only slowly in the face of ostracism by the professional guild, insurance mechanisms that subsidized inefficiency, and their members' only limited zeal for growth. Failures were frequent and the exceptions often owed their success more to the efforts of a few charismatic leaders than to any structural feature of the organization. Nevertheless, multispecialty groups did grow and diffuse throughout the nation, and today Mayo, Ochsner, Cleveland, Geisinger, Palo Alto, Scripps, Marshfield, and similar clinics enjoy the most prestigious names in medicine.

The growing pressure for cost containment and clinical coordination, embodied in the nation's transition to managed care, creates significant opportunities but also new challenges for multispecialty medical groups. Compared to their solo rivals, medical groups are well situated to bear the insurance risk of capitation and convert it into a long-awaited opportunity for population-based health care. Their physicians are paid on a salaried basis and face no direct incentives to provide unnecessary care or skimp on necessary care. Medical groups strive for a culture of peer review that contrasts with the clinical autarky of solo practice and accommodates the demand for systematic monitoring of quality. The leading groups are developing skills in managed care contracting, financial risk assessment, practice profiling, and quality reporting. They are rebalancing their membership by hiring primary care physicians to handle the patients' day-to-day needs and provide a referral base for the specialists. Each of these changes creates new stresses, however, for physician organizations. Capitation payment makes the medical groups responsible for the services provided by outside physicians and facilities, raising the very real specter of financial bankruptcy if they do not accurately anticipate and budget their costs. Salaried employment promotes cooperation but undermines incentives to work long hours and perform unpleasant procedures, threatening medical groups with low physician productivity. The fostering of cost-conscious practice styles is every day more difficult in a social context where outside specialists, hospitals, and drug manufacturers continually inform patients that more care is better care. Most challenging of all are the needed changes in structure and governance, as the medical groups embark on the difficult transition from what was often a professional fraternity toward a business firm capable of making disciplined decisions in a rapidly changing environment.

The growth and diffusion of the multispecialty medical group, paid prospectively and delegated authority for utilization management, is the single most important development in the contemporary organization of medicine. In some communities, the rise of the prepaid group practice has been led by historically dominant multispecialty clinics that have weaned themselves from exclusive reliance on fee-for-service payment. Elsewhere, however, multispecialty clinics were absent or had become too comfortable with a patrician style of practice to embrace the rigors of competition. New medical groups have arisen in these contexts, focused from the start on primary care, capitation, and utilization management. Either way, the multispecialty medical group is the natural clinical partner for the network HMO, which seeks to combine the advantages of broad physician access through nonexclusive physician contracting with the advantages of cost control through capitation. Medical groups certainly are not bound to any one form of reimbursement, receiving patients covered by indemnity and PPO insurance as well as by fee-for-service Medicaid and Medicare. They are not hermetically sealed off from the local medical community, referring some of their patients to outside specialists and receiving referrals from outside generalists. Nevertheless, the multispecialty medical group represents a qualitative disruption in the entropy of traditional physician organization, an island of formal structure and coordination in a sea of self-employed clinical entrepreneurs.

MEDICAL GROUPS AND MEDICAL MARKETS

Medical groups differ widely in their size and structure, reliance on capitation payment, and responsibility for utilization management. The idiosyncrasies of local history, leadership, and fortune account for much of the variety. But the key differences among medical groups stem from differences in the environments in which they arise, in the structure of insurance and clinical organization within their local communities. Two such features stand out. Most important is the penetration of managed care in the community and, in particular, the prevalence of network HMOs that embrace capitation and delegation with physician organizations. Medical groups have neither the incentive nor the opportunity to grow where indemnity or PPO insurance predominates or where HMOs pay physicians on a fee-for-service basis without delegation of credentialing, claims payment, and utilization management. The role of managed care in fostering medical group growth is accelerated in communities where a large fraction of Medicare beneficiaries have chosen HMO coverage, since senior citizens suffer from the chronic conditions that bring higher practice revenues but demand more sophisticated management skills than the younger, commercially insured, population. The second key determinant of medical group performance is the prevalence and proximity of other physician organizations similarly oriented toward success through managed care rather than success against it. Competition among sophisticated rivals forces improved performance, since payment rates fall to the levels acceptable to the most efficient groups and patients migrate to organizations that offer the best service. Competition is more than a threat, however, since it provides the opportunity for emulation and learning from like-minded organizations. As experienced so often in other industries, firms with monopoly power ultimately are disadvantaged by lack of benchmarks and best practices for which to strive. Medical groups compete but also cooperate with each other, formally through professional associations and informally through personal networks and the movement of physicians and managers across organizations.

Capitation payment, delegation of utilization management, statistical quality monitoring, and a strong primary care focus distinguish the multispecialty medical group from solo practice and the prepaid group practice from medical group practice under indemnity insurance. The importance of these factors can be highlighted by drawing on the experiences of multispecialty groups in environments that differ in the prevalence of network HMOs and in the proximity of competing groups. The HealthCare Partners Medical Group in California, Nalle Clinic in North Carolina, and Summit Medical Group in New Jersey are pioneers regionally but each has adjusted to the opportunities offered by its local community. As leaders they are atypical of the larger population of medical groups, most of which lag behind in scale and sophistication, but they illustrate the possibilities and pitfalls facing physician organizations under managed care.

HEALTHCARE PARTNERS MEDICAL GROUP

Los Angeles combines more than any other metropolitan area the features that nourish the multispecialty medical group. It has a long history of prepaid group practice, beginning with the Ross-Loos Clinic in 1929 and accelerating in the postwar period with the Kaiser Foundation Health Plan, the FHP staff-model HMO, and the multitude of medical groups that arose to compete with them. Kaiser exerted the greatest impact on the market, drawing ever more patients away from the solo physician practices and provoking a desperate market response. By the middle of the 1970s, a decade before managed care arrived in most American communities, provider organizations in Los Angeles were launching HMOs that linked together independent medical groups motivated by a combination of fear and admiration for their staff-model adversaries. The most successful network HMOs, including HealthNet, PacifiCare, and Maxicare, contracted on a nonexclusive basis with the same collection of small but growing medical groups. Mullikin, Harriman-Jones, Friendly Hills, Hawthorne Community, Beaver, Riverside, Pacific Physician Services, Rees-Stealy, Bristol Park, Facey, Santa Barbara, Buenaventura, and other medical groups grew from small clinics to become large organizations with dozens if not hundreds of physicians serving tens if not hundreds of thousands of patients.

The HealthCare Partners Medical Group traces its origin to a cluster of physicians covering emergency room services at California Hospital in downtown Los Angeles during the period when most paying patients and many physicians were fleeing to the suburbs.[1] The remaining patients were poor and elderly, often covered by Medicare but lacking in continuity of care and relying on the emergency room for routine medical services. In 1975 California Primary Physicians was formed with the intent of developing primary care services for this low income population. The group took its first capitation contract and suddenly found itself awash with patients. It grew rapidly but always maintained a strong financial balance sheet, paying the doctors a reasonable salary but retaining excess earnings for organizational growth rather than distributing it each year to avoid corporate income taxes. It was comprised mainly of primary care physicians, subcontracting with outside specialists for services to HMO patients under its capitation contracts. In 1992 California Primary Physicians merged with the Huntington Medical Group to form HealthCare Partners and subsequently affiliated with the Bayshores, Magan, and Memorial medical groups to span central Los Angeles from Long Beach east to the San Gabriel Valley. The rate of growth was exceptional even for the standards of the bursting southern California metropolis. In 1982 the various groups that eventually would comprise HealthCare Partners employed 52 physicians in four office sites and served 10,000 prepaid patients. Physician membership grew to 150 in 1990, 235 in 1994, and by 1998 exceeded 300 employed physicians in 30 clinic sites and 600 affiliated IPA physicians in a network of private offices. The group was governed as a professional partnership, with 190 partners drawn from the clinic and IPA physicians. Capitated patient enrollment had grown to 90,000 by 1990, topped 200,000 in 1994, and exceeded 250,000 early in 1998.

HealthCare Partners was in the middle of the medical marketplace most conducive to the growth of physician organization. HMO penetration of the commercial market exceeded 60 percent in much of southern California and all the health plans relied on capitation contracting and delegation of medical management to structure their provider networks. The HMOs contracted solely with physician organizations, not with individual physicians, and did not pay fee-for-service or seek to manage utilization patterns themselves. Of equal importance was the exceptional degree of HMO penetration among the elderly Medicare population. Over half of senior citizens were enrolled in HMOs which, with the exception of Kaiser, contracted with independent medical groups.

By 1998 HealthCare Partners served over 42,000 Medicare enrollees through HMO contracts in addition to those remaining with the Medicare fee-for-service program.

HealthCare Partners was surrounded on all sides by medical group competitors, which by 1997 had consolidated into very large physician systems. The Southern California Permanente Medical Group served 2.5 million patients through its Kaiser relationship; MedPartners had absorbed Mullikin, Friendly Hills, Pacific Physician Services, and numerous other groups with a capitated patient population exceeding 1.2 million; and UniMed Medical Management served over 600,000 patients in Los Angeles through the Facey, Harriman-Jones, Buenaventura, Beaver, and related organizations. Physician-hospital organizations and IPAs were crowding in from all directions. The stress from this competition was severe, leading as it did to a compression of capitation payment rates during a period when new drugs and heightened consumer expectations raised the underlying cost of providing care. But the proximity of medical group competitors was in part a result of the group's efforts. HealthCare Partners was an early and leading member of the Unified Medical Group Association (UMGA), an organization of prepaid group practices established in 1975 that by 1996 comprised 88 medical groups serving 4.5 million capitated patients, mostly in California.[2] The association drew on its member organizations to develop meetings and materials on best practices in capitation accounting, contractual language, medical management, pharmacy formulary compliance, data systems development, preventive services, and the numerous nuts and bolts of managed care. In 1997 the UMGA merged with the American Group Practice Association (AGPA), the long-standing association of fee-for-service clinics and prepaid practices such as Mayo and Permanente. The newly constituted American Medical Group Association, whose first president was the managing partner at HealthCare Partners, sought to combine the skills-building emphasis of the erstwhile UMGA with the policy focus of the erstwhile AGPA.

THE NALLE CLINIC

Charlotte, North Carolina differs strikingly from Los Angeles in demographics and culture but has developed a similar Sunbelt economy that continually attracts jobs, families, and managed care plans into a once conservative medical community. Kaiser came to North Carolina in the early 1980s at the behest of large employers in the Raleigh-Durham area and then expanded into Charlotte, followed by Prudential and other plans who emulated its principles of capitation and delegation. In seeking to develop their provider networks, however, these plans did not find ready at hand a multitude of independent medical groups but, rather, the more common American context of solo and small-group practices. They began to build medical groups almost from scratch to create vertically integrated staff- and group-model HMOs. They competed against indemnity insurers who gradually evolved into PPO insurers and launched IPA-model HMOs based on individual physician contracts. The hospital systems began to purchase primary care practices to ensure inclusion in the HMO networks and, in some cases, to lay the foundation for new provider-sponsored health plans. Payment rates under the Medicare program were too low to attract either national or indigenous health plans, and so physicians faced neither the threat nor the opportunity posed by prepaid senior services.

The Nalle Clinic was established in 1929 and soon became the center for specialty referrals from primary care physicians throughout the Charlotte area.[3] It prospered under fee-for-service reimbursement and added specialties as the population and referral base expanded. Over time, however, the medical profession in Charlotte underwent the same transition from predominantly primary care to predominantly specialty care composition as occurred throughout the United States. Rather than being the sole source of specialty care, Nalle found itself surrounded by single-specialty practices that competed aggressively for primary care referrals. The Clinic began to hire primary care physicians and subsidize their practices until they had sufficient patient volume, but then began to lose some of its revenue-generating specialists to more lucrative independent practice opportunities. In 1985 Nalle signed an exclusive contract for prepaid care with the Prudential HMO, confirming its course toward primary care and stimulating renewed internal debates over strategy and the distribution of physician earnings. Many specialists resisted the changes in physician composition and refused to continue subsidizing primary care practices through reduced specialty earnings. Clinic decision making was on the fraternity model, with every issue up for vote by the entire partnership, each specialty looking to its own economic interests rather than to the success of the enterprise. Nalle began to draw heavily on its bank credit line to finance expansion rather than tackle needed changes in structure and leadership. By the end of the decade the Nalle Clinic was comprised of 56 physicians, 34,000 HMO enrollees,

100,000 indemnity patients, an ineffective governance structure, and a looming financial crisis.

In 1990 the Nalle Clinic embarked on a strategic planning process that confirmed its commitment to primary care and capitation despite the foreseeable departure of key specialists and their fee-for-service revenues. It considered but rejected purchase offers from Prudential and the local hospital systems. The clinic affiliated with the PhyCor physician practice management firm, which contributed capital to continue primary care recruitment, the creation of satellite offices, and the paying down of the local credit line. The acquisition of smaller physician practices brought in contracts from other HMOs, which led in 1992 to the termination by Prudential of its Nalle relationship and the establishment of a rival HMO clinic in the community. Faced with the imminent loss of 34,000 Prudential enrollees, Nalle embarked on the fight for its life, signing with all Prudential's competitors and enjoining its patients to switch plans rather than switch doctors. This effort was largely successful, with the clinic retaining all but 4,000 of the Prudential patients and confirming its commitment to nonexclusive contracting with multiple health plans. Within five years the Nalle Clinic's managed care enrollment included 37,000 fully capitated and delegated patients from the Kaiser, CIGNA, Maxicare, Principal, and Aetna HMOs plus 25,000 patients under limited capitation from the Blue Cross Blue Shield HMO. Prudential's staff-model clinic steadily lost money and was divested to the FPA physician practice management firm, thereby becoming embroiled in the subsequent bankruptcy of that entity.

The Nalle Clinic exemplifies the medical group that embraces managed care and makes the difficult transition to a primary care and specialty physician balance, but which operates in an environment where capitation is limited and where competing medical groups are embryonic. By 1998 the Nalle Clinic had grown to 129 physicians practicing in a large central facility and nine primary care satellites. Only a quarter of its 700,000 annual patient visits derived from HMO patients, however, the remainder coming from publicly and privately insured fee-for-service patients. PPO products were the fastest growing form of insurance in Charlotte, attracting indemnity enrollees who wanted access to the Nalle Clinic but also to the physician-hospital organizations and the surrounding solo practitioners. The Clinic was interested in working with health plans to foster HMO options for Medicare beneficiaries, but was stymied by the low federal payment rates in North Carolina. Its growth strategy for managed care moved away from a clinic focus to the development with PhyCor of a statewide IPA structure that could link primary care physicians for capitation contracting in the surrounding rural environment.

THE SUMMIT MEDICAL GROUP

Summit, New Jersey is a high income suburban community many of whose residents commute to professional jobs on Wall Street and seek specialty care at the university hospitals in Manhattan. It is not an environment conducive to group practice, prepayment, and managed care. Primary care is subordinate to specialty services, with family practice unheard of and many internists and pediatricians maintaining part-time specialty practices. Solo practice predominates and even small groups are rare. Generous indemnity insurance is both a cause and a consequence of the patients' cultural proclivity to obtain care from across the metropolitan area rather than from a coordinated network of practitioners. HMOs entered the market during the 1980s but adapted themselves to the prevailing patterns of utilization. Oxford, Prudential, U.S. Health-Care, CIGNA, and the other leading plans developed broad networks of solo practitioners paid on a discounted fee-for-service or a limited primary care capitation basis. Capitation for all professional services, much less for hospital services, never was an option in an environment lacking independent medical groups. Frustrated with the limitations of unmanaged care, several health plans sought to develop staff-model HMOs by building clinics and employing primary care physicians. HIP extended its exclusive contracting model approach south from New York, the New Jersey Blue Cross Blue Shield plan began purchasing and consolidating primary care practices, and even Aetna threatened to bring in its staff model. Vertical integration failed here as elsewhere, with Aetna holding off, Blue Cross Blue Shield divesting its clinics, and HIP spinning off its physician network before sinking into financial disarray and state regulatory control.

The Summit Medical Group is an exception proving the rule that group practice cannot flourish in an environment dominated by university teaching hospitals, indemnity insurance, and a cultural antipathy to primary care.[4] Summit was founded in 1929 and grew to enjoy a reputation as the highest quality medical practice in the New Jersey suburbs, adding new physicians, patients, and specialties as the region prospered around it. By the late 1980s, however, it became aware that the hyperinflation of health care costs was not sustainable in the eyes of governmental and private purchasers and that severe countermeasures were in the offing. The adoption by Medicare of prospective payment for hospital services and a fixed fee schedule for physician services were straws in a stronger wind of change, which threatened to bring other forms of prepaid care to the New York region. The clinic was doing well financially but embarked on a planning process to evaluate its ownership structure, its recruitment of primary care physicians, and its involvement in managed care. The leadership visited medical groups in California and elsewhere in the northeast and became convinced that the comparative advantage of the multispecialty clinic lay in prepaid, primary-focused care rather than in its traditional fee-based specialty care. It joined the UMGA, recruited administrative staff from medical groups in California, built up its capabilities in utilization management, and affiliated with the Med-Partners physician practice management firm.

In 1998 the Summit Medical Group was the leading physician organization in its community, with 42 primary care and 35 specialist physicians practicing in a large central clinic and six satellites. Its 26,000 capitated enrollees accounted for a quarter of primary and specialty care visits, up from only 5 percent two years earlier. It received expressions of interest in affiliation from local primary care physicians but lacked the capital to expand, since the MedPartners organization had suffered severe financial losses and retracted its commitments of support. The group served as a point of reference and comparison for physician organization in the region as the cost control pressures stimulated growth in IPAs and physician-hospital organizations. But further growth would be slow unless or until the HMOs shifted from fee-for-service to capitation for their commercial enrollment and launched prepaid products for the Medicare market.

CAPITATION PAYMENT

There is no ideal mechanism for paying physicians. Fee-for-service reimbursement rewards individual physician productivity but also rewards heroic interventions at the late stage of disease rather than preventive interventions early on, encourages unnecessary treatment, and assumes that medicine is a series of discrete tasks rather than a cooperative process involving interdependent providers. Prospective payment through capitation rewards a focus on disease prevention but also the withholding of services, the cherry picking of healthy patients, and the avoidance of patients needing costly treatments. Salaried employment facilitates physician coordination but provides no reward for individual effort and can engender a dysfunctional mentality where every problem is someone else's responsibility. Each form of payment can be improved through judicious crafting. Fee schedules can be tilted to reward preventive and primary care services. Capitation payments can be adjusted for the patient's severity of illness. Salaries can be calibrated to performance. Hybrid payment mechanisms can blend elements of fee-for-service, capitation, and salary, such as capitation with extra payments for high cost procedures or fee-for-service with part-time salary for coordinating care. But not every form of payment can be used in every organizational setting. The size of the practice, its ownership structure, the mix of physician specialties, and the authority wielded by leaders exert a decisive influence over the methods that can be adopted to influence individual behavior. The limitations of payment mechanisms highlight the importance of the organizational setting in which the physician practices.

The key innovation of the network HMO in terms of physician payment incentives is to separate the reimbursement methods used for the medical group from the methods used for the individual physician. HMOs pay medical groups on a prospective, per-member-per-month basis for a defined set of clinical services. Payments do not increase if costs are allowed to rise but do not decrease if the medical group develops a more efficient style of care. Capitation payments shifts the risk of unexpected changes in health status, and hence need for health care services, onto the medical group. The group suffers financially if it attracts an especially sick mix of patients and enjoys above-average earnings if it attracts an especially healthy patient mix. The health plans attenuate the insurance risk borne by the groups by adjusting capitation rates according to the age and gender of each enrollee, by creating special reimbursements for patients with selected illnesses, by sharing upside and downside risk for hospital and pharmacy costs, and by offering stop-loss reinsurance that covers medical group costs exceeding a defined threshold. The HMOs and medical groups agree on the principle that the insurer should be responsible for the underlying epidemiological determinants of health costs and that the physicians should be responsible for those cost components that are subject to clinical analysis and control. Capitation is not designed as a means of shifting insurance risk but, rather, of creating financial incentives for medical groups to improve the efficiency of their services. It contrasts directly with fee-for-service payment, which retains all insurance risk in the health plan but rewards inefficient physician practice styles with higher payments and cuts practice revenues dollar for dollar if the doctors develop lower cost methods of care.

The network HMO does not apply capitation payment to the individual practicing physician within the multispecialty medical group. Employed physicians are paid their salaries by the group, not a capitation rate, according to their training, tenure, and performance. Capitation of primary care physicians for all professional services received by their patients would make individual physicians responsible both for the unpredictable fluctuations in health status and for the practice efficiency of downstream specialists. Doctors would be making daily trade-offs between their own family's college tuition payments and their patients' surgical referrals. With salaried employment, however, the medical group physicians' personal income is not directly influenced by their practice decisions. Over time, of course, earnings and employment of the medical group physicians are very dependent on their collective practice efficiency. But at the decision making moment, individual physicians face only weak and diffused economic incentives. They know that less costly treatment will benefit the group, whose revenues are fixed prospectively, but also that more costly treatment may generate higher patient satisfaction and loyalty, both of which are essential for sustained enrollment and group profitability.

The structure of financial incentives facing the salaried medical group doctor contrast with those in solo practice, where no distinction can be made between the payment method for the group and the method for the individual physician. If solo practitioners are paid fee-for-service, they earn direct financial rewards from performing more tests and procedures, including for those that create little benefit to the patient but merely fuel the fires of health care cost inflation. If, on the other hand, solo practitioners are paid individual capitation, they earn direct financial rewards from withholding tests and procedures, even ones that are clinically beneficial, so long as neither the patient nor any third party notices. The organizational fragmentation and absence of collective clinical accountability in the physician guild virtually insures that the solo practitioner can respond to the financial incentives of fee-for-service and individual capitation without stepping outside the bounds of acceptable medical practice.

Medical groups can be capitated for a narrow or broad set of services. A small group might be capitated only for primary care services, with specialty referrals and hospital admissions being paid by the HMO on a fee-for-service basis. A larger group might be capitated for all professional services, including primary and specialty care, while allowing the insurer to share the risk for hospital costs. A very large group could be capitated globally for all clinical services, including primary, specialty, hospital, nursing home, home health, and pharmacy services. Breadth of capitation increases the insurance risk, since the medical group is responsible for an increasing share of the costs incurred by its patients. Primary care services account for approximately 10 percent of the health insurance premium, specialty referrals for 30 percent, and hospital and ancillary services for 40 percent. Hence moving from primary care to professional services capitation triples the insurance risk assumed by the medical group and moving to global capitation doubles it again. But broader capitation also increases the incentives for efficient practice, since the physicians are now responsible for coordinating a broader set of clinical services. Medical groups limited to primary care capitation have no incentive to examine the necessity of the services provided by referral specialists. Indeed, physicians capitated only for primary care services have the financial incentive to limit the range of services they provide personally and to refer everything out to the specialists. In contrast, professional services capitation gives the medical group the incentive to rethink the interactions among all physicians working on a particular patient's illness. For a patient with mild or moderate disease, the best approach often is to encourage the primary care physician to manage the care and refer out only in acute circumstances. For a patient with a severe illness, however, the best approach often is to delegate case management to the specialist with most experience in the particular condition. For a patient requiring coordination among disparate specialists, the best approach often is to rely on an internist to manage the case, albeit with frequent specialty referrals and feedback.

A hallmark of the multispecialty medical group is broad professional services rather than narrow primary care capitation. HealthCare Partners, Nalle, and Summit all favored capitation that covers specialty referrals, tests, and procedures since this rewards rather than punishes efficiency-enhancing changes in clinical practice. But the potentially most significant benefits to physician organization come when the medical group accepts full or partial capitation for hospital, pharmacy, and ancillary services. Decades of public subsidies for hospital construction and technological diffusion have produced a vast institutional infrastructure in search of doctors and patients. In the context of fee-for-service insurance, this supply is able to create its own demand. Epidemiological studies routinely report unnecessary hospital admissions, medical interventions, and surgical procedures but have little impact as long as the financial incentives reward more costs with more revenues.[5] Here lie the greatest potential gains from new payment mechanisms. Medicare's system of prospective payment limits the profitability of adding ever more tests and procedures to a patient's hospital visit, but leaves untouched the physician's ability to gain extra revenue from extra expenditures if procedures are shifted to the outpatient, subacute, or home settings.

Capitation that does not cover hospital services gives physicians the incentive to substitute inpatient for outpatient services, while global capitation creates the incentive to find the lowest cost setting for each patient's treatment. Outpatient office visits, freestanding laboratory and radiology centers, and ambulatory surgery facilities provide an economical alternative to hospital admission. Patients who need inpatient procedures often can be discharged a few days earlier if a subacute facility, nursing home, rehabilitation unit, or home health service is available. In some cases, however, reliance on the acute care hospital is the cheapest alternative. It hardly makes sense to discharge a patient early from a hospital with many unused beds if so doing requires numerous follow-up visits by a home health nurse. Furthermore, medical groups must evaluate the influence of treatment setting on the patient's perception of quality. Globally capitated medical groups led the effort to decrease hospital lengths of stay for uncomplicated delivery, for example, since the clinical benefits of longer stay are counterbalanced by heightened risk of hospital-acquired infection. This policy created a backlash among mothers who wanted inpatient recovery and respite before taking their babies home. Now the physicians must pay for these extra hospital days or offer home nursing support sufficiently attractive that their patients will opt for speedy discharge.

Global capitation opens vast possibilities for well-run medical groups but is ruthless in exposing the weaknesses of groups that do not grasp the necessity of putting aside reserves for incurred but not reported claims. In the 1970s and 1980s many physicians focused on the risks and underappreciated the potential rewards from capitation, clinging to fee-for-service payment. A few made the opposite mistake, rushing into global capitation before they had built the administrative infrastructure and changed the physician culture to accommodate it. The most successful medical groups went into capitation one step at a time, taking on progressively broader financial responsibilities as they built the group's competencies in evaluating and managing risk.

HealthCare Partners recognized quite early the advantages offered by capitation payment but also the risks that attend it. Its first contracts were for professional services capitation, which quickly came to cover ancillary services such as laboratory tests and radiology. Learning to practice medicine under a capitation budget was like learning to walk, and the medical groups needed the health plans to hold their hands as they wobbled the first steps. The HMOs limited the medical group's risk in many ways, inserting stop-loss provisions, rolling deficits from one period over to the next, and reimbursing some charges that nominally lay within the capitation budgets. Over time the group learned to walk without help, putting aside reserves, negotiating low prices with subcontractors, reviewing hospital admissions and specialty referrals, and nurturing a clinical culture that accepted the reality of limited resources. Capitation accounted for the lion's share of operating revenues to the medical groups and provided the financing for growth. Between 1990 and 1997, for example, HealthCare Partners' total revenues grew from $87 million to $300 million, with professional services capitation accounting for three-fourths of the total.

Until the 1990s, physician organizations in California could not be capitated for hospital services unless they owned an inpatient facility. Several medical groups bought or built community hospitals to enable them to contract for global capitation and erase the budgetary barriers between inpatient and outpatient care. Mullikin, Friendly Hills, Pacific Physician Services, and Bristol Park created their own form of physician-hospital organization, but one that differed from the standard PHO in being dominated by physicians and focused on maximizing ambulatory care rather than being dominated by administrators focused on maximizing inpatient admissions. HealthCare Partners considered purchasing a community hospital but recognized the difficulty of convincing patients to travel from across its wide geographic range to any one facility. Managing an institution was not something HealthCare Partners thought it could do well, being a primary care physician group not structured to manage capital-intensive institutions. Without ownership of a hospital, the medical group could not accept global capitation, but obtained virtually the same revenues by contracting creatively with the HMOs. Nursing home, home health, outpatient surgery, and ambulance services that traditionally were part of hospital capitation budgets were reassigned to the physician capitation budget, which was augmented commensurably. HealthCare Partners negotiated with each HMO an inpatient services budget and with each local hospital the rate at which the budget could be charged for inpatient services. It could bargain for better hospital rates than could the HMOs since it had a larger patient population in its geographic region than did any one plan. The medical group then negotiated with the health plan for the lion's share of all savings in the hospital risk pool at the end of the year, seeing no logic in an even split between health plan and medical group when the physicians bore the cost of higher outpatient visits that resulted from reduced inpatient admissions. Of its $206 million in 1994 revenues, for example, Health-Care Partners obtained 77 percent from enhanced professional services capitation, 15 percent from the savings in hospital risk pools, 3 percent from noncapitated HMO payments, and 4 percent from fee-for-service patients.[6]

Capitation has diffused rapidly as other medical groups followed the example set by the medical group pioneers. The prevalence of each payment method on the West Coast was indicated in a 1997 survey of medical groups providing services under 640 HMO contracts in California, Oregon, and Washington. Of the 4 million patients served by these groups, 90 percent were capitated for all professional services. Even more striking were the contractual incentives for hospital services, where 57 percent of patients were covered by global capitation and an additional 37 percent were covered by shared risk capitation. Capitation was slower to penetrate mental health services, where 50 percent of patients were covered by full risk and 19 percent by shared risk contracts, and especially to outpatient pharmacy benefits, where only 5 percent were covered by full capitation and 31 percent by shared risk contracts.[7] Capitation plays a much less significant role for medical groups in eastern markets less heavily penetrated by network HMOs. In 1997, only 23 percent of the Nalle Clinic's $80 million revenues derived from capitation, with 16 percent stemming from Medicare, 54 percent from PPO and indemnity insurance, and the remainder from Medicaid and patient self-pay. The distribution of revenue shares was similar in the Summit Medical Group, which received approximately equal income from capitation, indemnity insurance, Medicare, and discounted fee-for-service.

DELEGATION OF UTILIZATION MANAGEMENT

The imperative to control health care costs cannot be met merely by reducing the price paid for each medical procedure. Sustainable reductions in inflation require control over the quantity and mix of services as well as over the unit prices. Indemnity and PPO insurers that started by demanding discounts off "usual and customary" physician fees soon added administrative controls on the quantity of services provided. Early efforts at utilization review were bolstered by studies documenting unjustifiable geographic variations in patterns of care and large numbers of unnecessary procedures. But the gains achieved by arms-length utilization review systems are limited, offering a one-time 10 percent cost reduction, since insurers have only meager resources at their disposal to influence the physicians' style of practice.[8] It is not economical to monitor the large number of relatively low cost clinical decisions made in private offices, and so most indemnity and preferred provider insurers focus on big-ticket procedures done in the hospital. These utilization review mechanisms, typically involving nurses armed with clinical protocols, can deny authorization for a procedure but do not offer a substitute that achieves the same or better outcome at a lower cost. Practicing physicians loathe what they consider a top-down system of controlling care that is not sensitive to their patients' particular conditions. They quickly learn to circumvent the controls.

The traditional structure of health care organization discourages the physician from paying attention to the economic implications of the process that begins with the initial referral to specialty consultation. Primary care physicians may grumble that their specialist colleagues are living a Mercedes-Benz lifestyle by performing unnecessary procedures, but there is no motivation to intervene. After receiving the initial referral, the specialist takes control of the case, often recommending repeat visits and procedures without consulting further with the referring generalist. As medical students recognized the financial attractiveness of careers in specialty care, swelling the excess supply of cardiologists, dermatologists, and orthopedists, many Americans patients have become habituated to go directly to specialty treatment without a primary care referral. Direct patient access to specialty care contrasts with the more regulated systems in Canada and Great Britain, where primary care physicians coordinate specialty referrals.

The core philosophical belief of the multispecialty medical group is that coordinated care is better than fragmented interventions. The individual patient often is unable to understand the nature of his or her illness and to choose the most effective form of care. The role of the primary care physician is to provide guidance to the patient throughout the whole course of treatment, including those phases where the hands-on services are provided by others. Medical groups such as HealthCare Partners, Nalle, and Summit require each HMO patient to choose a primary care physician who takes responsibility for the overall pattern of care. Patients can change their personal physician whenever they want, but need to be linked to a physician at all times. These family practitioners, internists, and pediatricians provide most services to their patients and refer to specialists when they believe the patients' conditions require it. If the patient seeks an appointment with a specialist member of the medical group, he or she often is instructed to get a referral from the personal physician. If the patient goes to a specialist outside the group without first obtaining a referral, the medical group may refuse to pay the specialist's fee.

Medicine is as much an art as a science, and individual physicians often treat patients with similar conditions in quite dissimilar ways. Some primary care physicians are very conservative, relying largely on tests and procedures that they perform directly, while others refer patients frequently to specialty consultations. Frequent referrals may reflect the belief that more treatment is better treatment or may be simply a way of making the primary care physician's life easier by sending challenging patients to someone else. In the fee-for-service context, this ping-pong pattern of referrals is economically lucrative, since every new visit generates a new fee. Under capitation, however, extra visits generate no extra income and the diversity in referral patterns demands attention.

Some medical groups seek to reduce the variability in referral patterns by requiring primary care physicians to obtain authorization from the group prior to referring patients to specialty care. Typically this prior authorization is required only for specialties and procedures where costs and clinical variation are of particular concern. A 1993 survey of 94 medical groups in California found that 23 percent permitted patients to self-refer to gynecologists, 47 percent required a referral from the primary care physician, and 30 percent required prior authorization from the medical group in addition to the primary care referral.[9] None of the groups permitted patient self-referral to a surgical subspecialist, with 66 percent requiring prior authorization from the group in addition to a primary physician's referral. A similar pattern was observed for uncommon and high cost procedures. While only 9 percent of the medical groups required prior authorization for a chest x-ray, 54 percent required authorization for a pulmonary function test and 95 percent required authorization for magnetic resonance imaging. Additional requirements for authorization were imposed on high cost specialty procedures even after the initial referral had been authorized. Cardiologists were required to obtain authorization for exercise stress tests by 55 percent of the med-

ical groups, for echocardiograms by 64 percent, and for coronary angioplasty by 96 percent. This survey overstated the prevalence of prior
authorization requirements in multispecialty medical groups, since it included IPAs that have weaker physician commitment and hence stronger
reliance on formal administrative controls.

The scope of utilization management developed by physicians in their
own medical groups often exceeds that imposed by insurance plans. The
medical groups are able to rely on their physician members to staff the
utilization management committees and to fulfill the key role of medical
director. Nurses are trained to perform the first level of review, approv-
ing referral requests that are clearly justified and passing the more questionable cases to the physicians. These nurses make daily visits to hospitalized patients and develop plans for postdischarge care. Utilization
management can be performed on a more intensive basis by medical
groups than by health plans for several interrelated reasons. The medical groups often have more patients going to the local hospital than does
any one health plan, and so enjoy economies of scale in reviewing patterns of care. More importantly, the medical groups have a better appreciation of the strengths and limitations of the physicians in their
groups and know where the problems are likely to occur. Individual physicians easily can be contacted for further information if a referral seems
unjustified. This documentation can include clinical specifics such as co-
morbid conditions but also social dimensions of care such as the patient's
preferences and the availability of family support. Extra days in the hospital and follow-up home visits that might look unnecessary to a distant
health plan might look quite necessary to a medical director who knows
that the patient has no family members at home. Conversely, a diagnostic procedure that might pass review by the health plan's oversight system might be questioned by a medical director who knows that the referring physician routinely recommends expensive tests prior to any
clinical exam. Utilization management serves its most important function in keeping the individual physicians thinking about cost as well as
quality, rather than in actually denying authorization for referrals. The
1993 survey found that the groups denied less than 10 percent of referrals to high cost procedures and permitted the referring physician and
patient to appeal. Approximately 17 percent of denials were appealed,
and 35 percent of the appeals were upheld by the medical directors reviewing the cases.[10]

The clinical infrastructure and administrative systems of utilization
management produce dramatic changes in patterns of care at prepaid

medical groups, reducing specialty referrals, hospital admissions, and hospital lengths of stay. Impacts on total physician visits are mixed, since reductions in specialty referrals and hospital use lead to extra primary care appointments. The trend over time can be illustrated using the experiences of Mullikin Medical Centers, a large multispecialty clinic that competed with HealthCare Partners in Los Angeles. Mullikin was a pioneer in utilization management, owning a hospital and obtaining some of the first globally capitated contracts in California, and took pains to document its early experiences. In 1983, Mullikin physicians used 525 hospital days of care for every 1,000 patients, a level not far from the national average. This implied that approximately 10 percent of Mullikin's patients were admitted to the hospital each year and that each hospital stay lasted approximately five days. Over the next four years, Mullikin reduced hospital utilization to 359 days per 1,000 patients.[11] By 1990 hospital days were down to 166 per 1,000 patients and by 1994 to 139. This compared to the 1993 national average of 433 days.[12] The reductions in inpatient days were achieved largely by reduced admissions rather than by shorter length of stay. Admissions per 1,000 patients declined from 64 in 1990 to 44 in 1994, while average length of stay for those patients who were admitted rose from 2.6 to 3.2 days. Outpatient visits increased slightly during these years, from 3.4 to 3.5 visits per patient. Similar trends occurred in other medical groups. HealthCare Partners experienced 218 hospital days per 1,000 patients in 1990 but by 1994 had brought utilization down to 149 days per 1,000 patients. Annual outpatient visits declined from 4.2 to 3.1 visits per patient during these years.[13] During this period inpatient days rose from 850 to 936 and outpatient visits declined from 7.5 to 6.8 for Medicare patients. In 1994 the national average of hospital days was 1,578 for Medicare HMO patients and 2,422 for Medicare fee-for-service patients.[14]

The spread of utilization management exerts a huge impact on the hospital industry, as experienced in California subsequent to the growth of large medical groups. Between 1983 and 1995, despite 25 percent growth in state population, the number of hospital admissions in California declined from 3.11 million to 3.03 million. Average length of stay declined from 6.4 days to 5.4 days even though the reduction in admissions left a sicker average mix of patients in the hospital. The combination of fewer admissions and reduced length of stay produced an 18 percent decline in total inpatient days, from 20 million in 1983 to 16.4 million ten years later. Hospital capacity declined from 82,966 beds in 487 facilities to 75,016 beds in 424 facilities.[15] The changes were most dramatic in those areas which experienced the greatest growth in capitation contracting. Total expenditures on hospital services grew during this period, in large part due to movement by hospital organizations into the provision of outpatient and nursing home care, but the rate of growth was 44 percent lower in areas with high HMO penetration than in markets with low penetration.[16]

The ability of medical groups to manage care leads to a withdrawal by HMOs from day-to-day review of individual physician decisions and a delegation of responsibility for utilization management. On the West Coast, the major HMOs have delegated to medical groups and IPAs the responsibility for utilization management, rather than seek to authorize referrals and procedures centrally. The 1997 survey found that 98 percent of the medical groups' patients were covered by contracts that delegated full responsibility for review of specialty referrals, 93 percent were covered by contracts delegating hospital admissions, and 59 percent were covered by contracts delegating hospital length of stay. In contexts where the medical groups were not fully delegated for utilization management, they shared this responsibility with the HMOs. The delegation of responsibility for case management of especially ill patients was less complete, with 40 percent of patients covered by contracts entailing full delegation and 54 percent covered by contracts specifying joint responsibility.[17] Delegation of utilization management is much less widespread in regions such as New York where multispecialty groups are embryonic and lack the internal information and administrative mechanisms to monitor patterns of care.

The system of utilization management in multispecialty medical groups now is undergoing extensive reanalysis and revision. Prior authorization requirements create uncertainty and frustration for primary care physicians and patients who must wait for a medical director or committee to review their request for an elective procedure or nonemergency admission. Reliance on primary care referrals for specialty consultations converts the personal physician from a coordinator to a gatekeeper, antagonizing specialists and adding to the patients' antipathy toward managed care. Many state legislatures and regulatory agencies are placing limits on utilization management mechanisms. HMOs are shifting to open-access products that allow patients to self-refer to specialty consultation and allow specialists to perform procedures without medical group authorization. Medical groups have responded to the weakening of administrative controls by extending capitation payment incentives to outside specialty physicians, which balances the accentuation in consumer-induced demand by an attenuation of provider-induced demand.

In some regions, strong utilization management programs never got going. HMOs in New Jersey, for example, did not permit the Summit Medical Group to channel all referrals to the group's employed specialists, thereby guaranteeing to enrollees access to the health plans' much broader contracted network. Some delegated responsibility for big-ticket procedures such as magnetic resonance imaging while others required that the group obtain prior authorization from the health plan. The most popular managed care products in the New York region have point-of-service features that allow patients to self-refer out of network, even though the capitated medical group is partially responsible for the cost of outside claims. The culture of physician cooperation partially buffers the multispecialty medical group from the inflationary impact of open-access insurance products, since the generalists and specialists share a similar clinical outlook and aligned financial incentives. The Nalle Clinic, for example, annually utilized 155 hospital days per 1,000 HMO patients, only 60 percent of the rate prevalent in the Charlotte area, without imposing significant utilization management on its physicians. The Summit Medical Group moved away from micromanagement of care, focusing on overall patterns rather than on individual referrals and authorizations. No review of medical necessity was performed for referrals to specialists within the group, though the organization tracked all such referrals as the basis of its statistical analyses. Prior authorization was required for outside referrals but the group moved to streamline this process and replace it with an educational campaign to convince patients that within-group referrals result in better care since the information feedback is more thorough. Between 1994 and 1997, the group was able to reduce outside specialty referrals from 30 percent to 18 percent of the total. It worked to reduce out-of-group and out-of-network referrals even for patients covered under insurance that did not capitate outside claims, recognizing that the payment rate it is able to negotiate for covered services ultimately depends on the total cost of the care received by its patients.

QUALITY MONITORING AND IMPROVEMENT

The fragmented medical system offers prepaid groups many simple but effective opportunities for improving quality by enhancing coordination. Many patients traditionally have used hospital emergency rooms for primary care because their doctors' offices are closed on evenings and weekends. Asthmatic children are admitted to hospitals for conditions that should be treated earlier, cheaper, and better in an outpatient setting. Senior citizens easily confuse the medications prescribed by multiple providers who act in ignorance of each other's interventions. Capitation payment provides the financial incentive and medical group organization provides the administrative infrastructure to change the process of care. Large medical groups extend their office hours and operate urgent care centers on weekends and holidays. They develop patient education materials, encourage additional doctor checkups, and distribute inhalers to children with asthma. Their nurses visit frail Medicare patients at home to check the medicine cabinet for incompatible drugs, install handrails in bathrooms to reduce falls, and arrange transportation for physician office visits.

It is easy for multispecialty medical groups to pick the low-hanging fruit from the vast orchard of potential quality improvements. But continued progress requires more radical changes in the process of medical care, especially for chronically ill patients who are frequent users of hospital services. A large fraction of all medical care expenditures are incurred by a small fraction of the total enrollees; these are precisely the patients most likely to suffer adverse outcomes from the fragmentation of services. For example, in 1987 the sickest 1 percent of Americans accounted for 30 percent of total health care expenditures, while the healthiest 50 percent accounted for only 3 percent of expenditures.[18] While primary care physicians can be expected to oversee specialty referrals, it is unreasonable to assume that they have the time to intervene each time the patient undergoes tests at a clinical laboratory, is admitted and discharged from a nursing home, interviews competing vendors for durable medical equipment, and requests extra visits from a home health nurse. Medical groups establish case management programs for patients with these special needs. Administrative staff and licensed vocational nurses handle the clinically simple but administratively complex processes of arranging for medical equipment and office appointments. Registered nurses consult the physicians concerned with a particular patient to ensure that each is apprised of the other's actions, that the medical record is carefully documented, and that the patient and patient's family understand what is happening. Nurse practitioners with special training in geriatrics and physical therapy conduct rounds in subacute and rehabilitation facilities, overseeing the quality of care and thereby permitting greater use of these institutions by patients who otherwise would need admission to a hospital.

The accelerating shift of medical care from hospital to nonhospital facilities has a dramatic impact on the type of care still being provided in hospital settings. As the less severely ill patients are treated elsewhere, hospitals are left with patients suffering from very serious conditions. Primary care physicians, who used to have many patients in the hospital and who would make daily rounds to oversee their care, now find they rarely have more than a few patients hospitalized on any one day. The traditional daily rounds, which once permitted the efficient treatment of multiple patients, now require the same amount of travel time for the physician to cover only a two or three patients. Physicians in large metropolitan areas often admit to multiple hospitals, depending on the patients' preferences, and so have even fewer patients in any one facility than do physicians whose patients are willing to go to the same institution. As medical science advances, it is increasingly difficult for the primary care physician to keep abreast of the most recent innovations in clinical treatment for severely ill patients. Hospital patients are being treated by various specialists, each of whom performs a particular procedure and then leaves, making it difficult for the primary care physician to get direct feedback on what has been done.

As the process of hospital care becomes more complex, the need for coordination grows but the role of the primary care physician in the hospital declines. Medical groups are developing special teams of physicians to take responsibility for the care of all hospitalized patients, permitting primary care physicians to focus their activities on the outpatient setting.[19] These new "hospitalists" have training in internal medicine, often with emphasis in pulmonology, and take principal responsibility for the patient's course of treatment while hospitalized. The hospitalist brings in medical and surgical specialists for particular procedures, but retains ultimate authority as the attending physician on the case until the patient can be discharged back to the primary care physician. The full-time presence of the hospitalist on the wards permits a much more efficient coordination of testing and treatment than the traditional framework in which the floor nurses do what they can to interpret test results and coordinate specialist interventions while waiting for the primary care physician to make rounds after the long day in the office. The patient's primary care physician now is encouraged to make social rounds in the hospital to reassure the patient and explain the course of treatment but does not as a matter of course write orders to the hospital staff. The hospitalist model was pioneered in capitated medical groups such as HealthCare Partners but since has diffused widely, as health plans, hospitals, and specialized firms have recognized the potential economic savings and as primary care physicians have recognized the potential clinical benefits.

Insight into the prevalence of various quality assurance initiatives is available from a 1994 survey conducted in California of 94 capitated medical groups.[20] Over 90 percent of the groups monitored rates of cesarean section, a dangerous and costly surgical intervention that is commonly overused. Patterns of use for outpatient drugs were monitored by 70 percent of the medical groups; emergency department visits were monitored by 78 percent. Approximately half the medical groups monitored preventive services for underuse, including childhood immunizations, screening mammograms, follow-up visits for abnormal Papanicolaou test results, prenatal care for prospective mothers, and flu vaccines for the elderly. Approximately one-fourth of the medical groups monitored hospital admissions and readmissions for asthma, follow-up treatment for heart attacks, and annual retinal exams for diabetic patients. Medical groups with the most active quality assurance programs were those that had been established longer and those with a higher proportion of capitated patients.

Some medical group initiatives lower costs while improving quality of care, but many others require higher expenditures in order to achieve higher quality. Not surprisingly, medical groups are more eager to invest in the former programs than in the latter. The capitation payments they receive are adjusted partially for the expected costs of their enrollees, using demographic data on age and sex, but not for the quality of care that is subsequently delivered. In this respect, capitation is no different from fee-for-service, which rewards the quantity but not the quality of the services provided. The new frontier for clinical improvements depends on payment systems that reward higher quality with higher payments. As a crucial first step, data systems are being developed to measure improvements in the process of care and to report these findings in a format permitting comparison across different organizations.

The professional guild relied on a bad-apple approach to monitoring and improving the quality of care. Physicians who provided egregiously poor care could be deprived of their medical license or sued for malpractice. This approach removed the worst actors but did little to improve the quality provided by the average practitioner. Improvements in average performance require an epidemiological approach to quality, one that compares the outcomes of different patterns of care after accounting for the special characteristics of individual patients. The shift from a bad-apple to a statistical approach to quality, often denoted "continuous quality improvement," has produced dramatic improvements in manufacturing industries but is coming only slowly to medical care.[21] The epidemiological approach to quality improvement builds on the quality programs developed by HMOs at the behest of large purchasers. The National Committee for Quality Assurance pioneered a system for monitoring and measuring the process of care that permits quantitative comparisons of performance across health plans.[22] The initial focus of its HealthCare Employer Data Information Set (HEDIS) was on the rate of utilization for preventive services such as immunizations and mammograms, since these cost-effective interventions commonly are neglected by plans and providers. The NCQA process requires independent audits of patient medical charts rather than accepting unverified data from the health plans. NCQA steadily has expanded the scope of the audits to encompass process and outcome measures for patients with chronic illnesses, for elderly patients, and for patients enrolled through state Medicaid programs.[23]

Medical chart audits measure the provision of services and outcomes as evaluated by physicians, but not the quality of care as evaluated by the patients themselves. Patients cannot understand many of the technical dimensions of medicine, but can provide important information on the cumulative impact of medical interventions on their functional ability. Epidemiological studies report a strong correlation between the patients' evaluations of their health status after treatment and the evaluations produced by laboratory tests and clinician judgments.[24] Patients also provide valid assessments of the service dimensions of care, including the accessibility to regular, urgent, and emergency appointments, courtesy and caring by the professional and support staff, and the extent to which diagnoses and treatments are explained in a comprehensible fashion. To obtain insight into these dimensions of quality, purchasers have developed surveys to query HMO enrollees concerning their satisfaction with their health plan, with their personal physician and specialty referrals, and with the hospital care they receive. These surveys elicit information on the patient's use of preventive services, as a check on the physician's records, and on the patient's self-assessed health status. Repeated surveys of large groups measure changes in health status as evaluated by the patient. The survey data can be disaggregated to examine satisfaction, use of services, and changes in health status for children, patients with chronic conditions, and other groups of special concern. Together, chart audits and consumer surveys facilitate comparisons across health plans, thereby assisting purchasers to make better use of their financial leverage, consumers to make more informed choices, and health plans to improve their performance against industry benchmarks. To date these efforts largely have been limited to physicians and patients linked through HMOs. The quality of care received by patients enrolled in indemnity and PPO plans and in fee-for-service Medicare has not been subject to systematic monitoring and comparison.

The new quality measurement initiatives began with the health plans since HMOs are the principal source of network coordination in many regions. Staff-model and IPA-model HMOs can be held responsible for the quality of the services they cover since they directly manage the individual physicians in their networks. This HMO unit of analysis makes less sense, however, in a world where independent medical groups assume responsibility for utilization and quality management. Groups chafe under the demands of multiple HMO quality initiatives that raise administrative costs by duplicative auditing and surveying, preferring to participate in a single quality program applicable to all health plans. The audits are taxing on staff and disruptive of practice, since patient charts are removed from physician accessibility during the audit process. Audits by multiple HMOs require repeated sampling but generate the same results, since the physicians do not apply different styles of care to enrollees in different plans. The same problems afflict patient satisfaction data, with medical group patients being surveyed by multiple health plans using noncomparable survey instruments. The medical chart and satisfaction data are collected at the level of the individual doctor and patient but aggregated to the level of the health plan, rarely permitting the medical group to evaluate its own performance against the previous year's results or against a benchmark of other medical groups.

As medical groups grow in scale and sophistication, the focusing of quality initiatives exclusively on health plans becomes anachronistic. The logic of the emerging organizational structure in regions with high managed care penetration suggests dual focus on the medical group and on the health plan. The medical group is larger than the individual physician, who does not serve enough patients to be monitored by epidemiological methods, but is smaller than the health plan, which contracts with a heterogeneous physician network. The medical group can be subjected to statistical oversight and be responsible for monitoring the quality of care provided by each of its clinicians. The obvious starting point has been to reduce duplicative monitoring and to disaggregate chart audit and patient satisfaction data to the medical group level. The California Cooperative Healthcare Reporting Initiative combined the expertise of large corporate purchasers, health plans, and medical groups to field a single set of chart audits for each medical group each year.[25] A similar logic was applied to patient-focused measures of quality. The Physician Value Check Survey was developed as a cooperative venture by purchasers and medical groups to query patients from participating medical groups on access to services and quality of care. Results were published in a manner facilitating comparisons among medical groups.[26] This quality monitoring developed farthest and fastest in California due to the vigorous competition among multiple network HMOs and multispecialty medical groups, with comparative quality data quickly being posted on various Internet Web sites.[27]

Medical care encompasses diverse services in diverse settings and quality measurement necessarily produces multiple indices. There is a great value in accreditation initiatives that synthesize measures of performance into a few overall indicators. The NCQA developed an HMO accreditation program that plays a central role in corporate purchasing decisions and subsequently has been extended into the Medicare and Medicaid programs. As medical groups took the lead in quality improvement efforts in California, accreditation programs began to refocus to that level. The Medical Quality Commission was established in 1991 by the Unified Medical Group Association to evaluate and accredit medical group quality. The Joint Commission on Accreditation of Healthcare Organizations moved beyond its historical focus on hospital oversight to include medical groups. The Foundation for Accountability was sponsored by large corporations and governmental programs with a focus on outcomes measurement in the managed care setting. NCQA, the industry leader, extended its certification program to encompass medical groups. Quality oversight mechanisms continue to devote their greatest effort at the health plan level, however, since many regions of the nation have only incipient physician organizations. Indeed, the Medical Quality Commission ceased its activities in 1997 due to insufficient interest among health plans and purchasers to reward medical groups with the best documented performance, which undermined the groups' willingness to finance the accreditation process.

PRIMARY CARE AND SPECIALTY MIX

The multispecialty medical group arose in response to the increasing complexity of medical knowledge, which challenged the ability of the individual physician to coordinate the full course of treatment. In the fee-for-service era medical groups were composed almost entirely of specialists, who viewed the group as a locus of coordination that substituted for the physician generalist. This tilt toward specialty care was not only ideologically congenial but financially remunerative, since the indemnity insurance carriers paid higher fees for specialty procedures than for primary care office visits. Many medical groups relied on specialists to treat conditions that normally would fall within the definition of primary care. Dermatologists removed warts, obstetricians provided prenatal care, and cardiologists managed hypertension. Medical groups typically began with common specialties such as gastroenterology, gynecology, and general surgery, adding subspecialties as the patient base grew. The biggest groups proudly offered a full range of medical and surgical subspecialists able to treat the rarest conditions with the most advanced techniques.

Capitation payment radically changes the economics of medical group membership. Now revenues do not increase with the increased number and complexity of procedures but are capitated prospectively based on the costs that a conservative style of medicine is expected to incur. It no longer makes sense to substitute high paid specialists for moderately paid generalists to perform primary care. Neither prestige nor profit flows to groups of specialists that conceptualize medicine as the search for rare conditions, treating every headache as a possible brain tumor and testing every fussy baby for meningitis. Specialists have become cost centers rather than revenue generators. For the first time medical groups composed predominantly of primary care physicians have become viable. Specialty services can be obtained from independent practitioners on a contracted basis rather than merely from salaried group members. Medical groups always outsourced services for which they lacked sufficient patient volume to justify an employed specialist. In the fee-for-service environment, groups that referred a patient outside the group were not responsible for the subsequent costs of treatment, which were paid directly by the insurance company. Under capitation, however, the medical group usually is required to pay the trail of claims that the referred patient generates.

The new financial context increases the importance of close coordination between primary and specialty care and hence would appear to reward medical groups that bring the full range of physician skills inside the organization. Physical proximity facilitates the informal peer review that controls unnecessary procedures without heavy-handed utilization review. Salaried specialists are more likely to identify their personal goals with those of the group than are outside contractors and to cooperate actively with cost containment rather than gaming the system to squeeze out more referrals and more fees. This commonality of goals and values is very important for the economic success of the organization, since specialists greatly influence the patients' perceptions and choice of primary care providers. Most importantly, a group that fosters enthusiasm among all its physicians has the best chance to develop the innovations in practice style that improve quality as well as reduce cost. Medicine is becoming ever more complex; those organizations that successfully combine specialization with coordination will prosper.

Coordination among primary and specialty care is essential, but group employment is not the only means to achieve the goal. When well done, contracting can induce a cost-conscious style of practice among outside specialists that equals or even exceeds that of employed specialists. Medical groups do not refer to outside specialists at random but build formal relationships with a subset of independent physicians in each specialty. These specialists may receive a significant fraction of their total referrals from the group, and thus come to view their economic fates as commingled. Outside referrals for specialty care often help rather than hurt the patients' views of the medical group, since it opens up more choices. The medical group achieves a wider geographic coverage and greater diversity of physician gender, ethnicity, and personal style if it accounts for a fraction of the practices of many contracting specialists than if it fills the entire practices of a small number of employed specialists.

Multispecialty medical groups now apply economic logic to their physician mix : should they "make" each specialty service by hiring new members or "buy" that service on the open market through referral contracts? Outside contracting is especially advantageous in a period when the excess supply of specialists and inadequate supply of primary care physicians is changing relative incomes in the larger medical marketplace. The fee-for-service era permitted specialists to raise their incomes relative to primary care, but now the pendulum is swinging the other way. The specialist salary scales in most medical groups have been benchmarked to the old market and the differentials have proven resistant to change despite the decline in relative earnings of outside specialists. Medical groups find it easier to reduce rates for outside contractors than salaries for inside employees.

Until the advent of managed care in North Carolina, specialists almost exclusively composed the Nalle Clinic, since the indemnity insurance plans paid poorly for primary care services and nothing for the service of coordinating care. The route to clinic profitability lay through the recruitment of procedure-oriented specialists and the acquisition of revenue-generating clinical technology. With the signing of the Prudential HMO contract and even more dramatically after the switch to nonexclusive HMO contracting, however, the Clinic reoriented itself toward a balanced primary and specialty care membership. Recruitment of generalists accelerated while recruitment of specialists slowed. In 1990 the Nalle Clinic was composed of 50 specialists and 6 generalists, but by 1998 had grown to 62 specialists and 67 primary care physicians. Health-Care Partners represented the novel phenomenon of medical groups that were focused on primary care at the start. HealthCare Partners began as a primary care group and gradually added specialists as it expanded its geographic scope and especially when it began attracting large numbers of elderly Medicare patients through capitated HMO contracts. It picked up additional specialists through the mergers with the Huntington and Bayshores medical groups. In 1994, however, 81 percent of its employed physicians were still in primary care, with most specialty services being contracted out to a large referral panel.

CHALLENGES TO THE MULTISPECIALTY MEDICAL GROUP

The changing physician mix and reliance on outside contracting symbolizes a fundamental restructuring of the multispecialty medical group. In the fee-for-service era most medical groups were small in size, owned in equal partnership shares, governed by a democratically elected board, and staffed by physicians who viewed the group as a fraternity of quasi-independent practitioners rather than as a business worth more than the sum of its parts. Managed care creates new opportunities but also new challenges for these organizations, forcing them to change ownership, governance, compensation, clinical practice, and, ultimately, the very concept of what it means to be a medical group.

The increasingly competitive environment rewards large physician organizations that spread the insurance risk of capitation payment, achieve economies of scale in managing utilization, and increase bargaining leverage with upstream health plans and downstream hospitals. But large scale undermines the mechanisms by which multispecialty groups have been governed. As long as a group has only one clinic setting and a small number of physicians, it can rely on informal methods for evaluating prospective partners, adjusting compensation, purchasing equipment, and operating the day-to-day business. The partners share a common vision of the organization and of their roles within it. As the group brings in new physicians and places them in satellite sites throughout the community, however, this informal governance comes under strain. The heterogeneity in status, income, and perspective across the various specialties is compounded by the influx of primary care physicians, who resent their subordinate role and demand control commensurate with their rising importance under managed care. The evolution of organizational revenues from fee-for-service claims attributable to individual physicians toward capitation contracts linked to the entire group forces a painful change in internal compensation methods. No longer can physicians be paid merely a percentage of the claims they each bill. More complex payment methods need to be devised that reward collective as well as individual initiatives. The growing size of the organization complicates compensation even further since ownership shares now have great value. Distinctions between senior partners, junior partners, and nonpartner physicians become more important, creating ever stronger stresses on one-doctor-one-vote governance mechanisms.

Multispecialty medical groups face the problems that confront all large organizations, especially the attenuation of individual incentives and the strengthening of internal factions. As long as they are small and closely knit, medical groups can rely on social pressures and a tight link between individual effort and reward to sustain the productivity of each physician. As the groups grow larger and more diverse, however, collegial sanctions weaken and the doctors are less able to perceive the impact of their individual contributions on the success of the organization. Some use the opportunity to work fewer hours, see fewer patients, and perform fewer unpleasant procedures, taking longer vacations and filling out their work schedules with more meetings. The attenuation of individual incentives is aggravated by an accentuation of internal politics.

The democratic procedures and large board of directors make for unwieldy and inefficient governance, with long and rancorous assemblies whose decisions often are overturned in the face of subsequent opposition. Factions develop between primary and specialty care, among the various specialties, by age and gender, and between partners and physician employees. Leaders who make necessary but unpopular decisions often lose their jobs, to be replaced by weak administrators afraid to question the status quo. Weak governance undermines the medical group's efforts to retain organizational profits to hire new primary care physicians, build clinic satellites, acquire computer systems, and buffer operating revenues from the trail of incurred but not reported claims.

Medical groups unable to overcome the challenges of growth disappear. Successful groups recognize the imperative to develop smaller and more committed governing boards, to recalibrate relative earnings and redistribute ownership shares in favor of primary care, and to retain and reinvest in a strong bottom line. Sustained success against free-riding and political faction ultimately require, however, a restructuring of the membership and boundaries of the physician organization. Partnership units no longer are distributed equally but, rather, on the basis of individual contribution. The infrastructure often is spun off as a legally distinct though contractually linked management services organization, whose ownership is concentrated among the most committed physicians and administrators. Medical groups reduce the proportion of physicians who are partners and increase the role of physician employees, then reduce the proportion of employees and increase the role of outside physician contractors. With each passing year the multispecialty medical group comes to function less like a professional fraternity and more like a nexus of contracts. Integrated multispecialty clinics historically have played an important role in American medicine and their salience is increasing in the era of constrained revenues. But for the foreseeable future the majority of doctors will remain in solo or small-group practice. For them, an alternative, network form of organization is emerging, one that balances clinical coordination and ownership autonomy within the independent practice association.

CHAPTER 6

The Independent Practice Association

Physicians are socialized to value autonomy and individual responsibility in their clinical decision making. Many also prize autonomy and independence in the business aspects of medicine. The multispecialty medical group, with unified practice ownership and salaried physician employment, runs counter to this widely diffused and deeply felt sentiment. The vast majority of American physicians, generalists as well as specialists, remain in solo practice or in small groups with less than 15 members.[1] The imperative for enhanced coordination across diagnoses and enhanced cooperation among specialties grows ever more insistent, however, as the economic pressures intensify. The combination of physician preference for independent practice and market pressure for cost control thus have stimulated the growth of a network form of medical group, one that mimics the multispecialty clinic in fostering physician interdependence but is based on solo practice to retain physician independence.

The Independent Practice Association (IPA) brings physicians together for purposes of performing the functions of managed care but leaves them separate for purposes of operating the day-to-day aspects of their practices. It negotiates capitated contracts with HMOs and point-of-service plans, develops payment incentives for its primary care and specialty physicians, monitors and manages patterns of health care utilization, and strives to improve the quality of care through greater attention to prevention, patient satisfaction, and the measurable aspects of clinical outcomes. But the IPA leaves its physician members as the owners and managers of their individual practices, in charge of their work hours, their support staff, their office facilities, and the other aspects of running a small business. The organization typically does not get involved with the care for patients from indemnity plans and has only limited involvement with preferred provider insurance plans.[2] The physicians compete among themselves for these patients while cooperating with each other for the care of the HMO patients.

The functions and significance of the independent practice association have been difficult to grasp for many observers of health care organization. The term IPA sometimes is used to describe a form of insurance plan, rather than a form of medical group. In markets without physician organizations, HMOs contract with individual physicians and are referred to as IPAs. The term also is confused by the historical development of many IPAs as a defensive strategy to stop managed care rather than as a proactive strategy to succeed at managed care. The early IPAs sought to make as few changes as possible in the traditional organization and financing of medicine, and some of their successors are focused more on anticompetitive efforts to fix prices rather than on pro-competitive efforts to coordinate care.[3] For purposes of understanding innovation under managed care, the indiscriminate use of the same term is unfortunate, since it commingles some of the most innovative with some of the most conservative tendencies in health care organization. It would be better to adopt an alternative nomenclature, such as "network medical group," that could distinguish the physician-run from the insurer-run IPAs and the new from the old form of physician organization. Using the term "network medical group" would highlight the similarities between the IPA and its integrated multispecialty rival and point to the similarities between IPAs and network forms of organization in the broader, nonhealth economy. With advances in computer and communication technologies, firms in many industries are evolving away from traditional hierarchies toward looser structures that rely on contract rather than ownership, on incentives rather than authority, and on information systems rather than physical proximity to coordinate their activities. These new technologies also stimulate the coming together of small firms into chains, joint ventures, franchises, and other partially integrated but partially autonomous organizational structures.

The analysis of the evolving IPA requires several steps. The first will be to sketch briefly its historical evolution and to distinguish the new network organization from the traditional IPA. It then will be important to identify the key differences between the network and the multispecialty medical groups and to highlight the challenges that confront the IPA. While benefiting from the many virtues of decentralization, the network organization is forced to pay greater attention than its multispecialty rival to the manner in which it pays individual physicians, since financial incentives are the link between the member and the group to a much greater extent than in contexts where the physicians are partners who share a single physical facility, a common clinical culture, and a joint economic destiny. The IPA also must strive to develop internal organizational structures, including specialty departments and quality committees, that replicate those of the multispecialty group yet are consonant with the preferences and priorities of the dispersed physician membership.

THE TRADITIONAL IPA

The independent practice association emerged originally to mediate the quite different needs of HMOs and practicing physicians.[4] The health plans needed physicians willing to accept some limits on fees and some oversight over practice patterns so that the plans could fulfill their commitments to purchasers and enrollees for comprehensive benefits at a fixed premium. The HMOs sought to hold down the costs of identifying, credentialing, contracting, and monitoring thousands of individual physicians dispersed in small practices across broad geographic areas. The physicians, for their part, wanted to retain ownership of their practices but needed to continue generating revenues adequate to cover expenses in an environment where many patients were switching from indemnity to HMO coverage. They sought to minimize the frustrations of dealing with distant insurance entities and were more willing to participate in locally focused and physician-controlled networks.

The impetus for IPA formation varied across regions depending on the presence or absence of multispecialty medical groups. On the West Coast, the early network HMOs built their provider networks around multispecialty groups that were willing to accept capitation payment and delegation of utilization management. The health plans grew much faster than the medical groups, however, as the rising cost of indemnity insurance induced ever greater numbers of patients to switch to HMO coverage. The plans turned to IPAs to fill the gaps in their provider networks and to expand into completely new communities.[5] They happily discovered that competition between IPAs and multispecialty groups held down the capitation rates they were required to pay, further contributing to HMO growth through lower costs and premiums. In the east, there were very few multispecialty medical groups, and the HMOs needed to build their networks from individual physician practices. Here the insurer often owned and managed the IPA. Some indemnity carriers jump-started their HMO products by purchasing IPAs from physician or hospital sponsors, canceling contracts with competing plans, and incorporating the now captive IPA as a corporate subsidiary. Over time, however, the complexity of managing dispersed physician networks led to efforts by the health plans to outsource the IPA functions. By the end of the 1990s even many of the most obdurate plans were contracting with freestanding IPAs to coordinate their physician networks.

Independent practice associations were sponsored by a wide variety of organizations and individuals. The pioneering groups were created by local medical societies in response to competitive threats from both staff and network HMOs. Hospitals funded many start-ups in hopes of retaining patient admissions and leveraging higher payment rates from HMOs. Some IPAs were established by entrepreneurial individuals, usually physicians, who recognized the market opportunity, invested their own money, and subsequently controlled the organization themselves. By the 1990s large corporate entities, including physician practice management firms and multihospital systems, were building IPAs to deepen their market penetration.

Freestanding IPAs have grown very rapidly since they meet the needs of both insurers and physicians. For the insurers, the IPAs present a ready-made network of physician practices that are well established in their communities and whose core practice expenses already are covered by payments from indemnity insurers. There is no need for the HMO to build or lease new clinics, hire physicians and support staff, and then cover operating losses until patient volume is sufficient to sustain the practices. The IPA is willing to negotiate a capitation rate that, when translated down to the individual physician, covers the incremental costs incurred by the HMO patients and makes a contribution toward overhead but does not need to cover all the fixed costs of the practice. Reliance on IPAs reduces in a dramatic fashion both the time and the capital costs of developing an HMO network. The IPA is advantaged in this respect over both the staff-model HMO, which directly owns clinics and employs physicians, and the network HMO, which contracts with independent multispecialty clinics. Multispecialty medical groups can grow more easily than staff-model clinics since they attract enrollees from multiple HMOs as well as from indemnity insurers, but nevertheless face the same basic need to invest first and then wait for practice volume to grow. The evolution of many HMOs from owning physician clinics to contracting with multispecialty groups and then to contracting with IPAs exemplifies one of the most important advantages of market relationships and the disadvantages of vertical integration between insurance and delivery. Through their IPA contracts the health plans are able to achieve large economies of scale, compared to what it would cost them to establish similarly broad networks composed of wholly owned clinics.

The IPA offers even greater potential advantages to HMOs as a marketing mechanism. The foremost obstacle to growth in a staff or network HMO is that prospective enrollees must switch primary care physicians when they switch health plans. HMOs that contract with IPAs, however, obviate this often distasteful requirement. The IPA physician practices are full of indemnity and PPO patients who now can switch to HMO coverage without changing their physician. HMO enrollment feels similar to indemnity coverage and is particularly attractive to patients for whom the inconveniences of utilization review are outweighed by the enhanced benefits and reduced coinsurance. IPA networks can accelerate HMO growth even more rapidly to the extent the physicians come to view the IPA as more congenial financially and culturally than the traditional insurance companies. Physicians have numerous opportunities to encourage their indemnity patients to switch coverage if they so desire. Many are hostile to HMOs and would rather encourage their HMO patients to switch back to indemnity coverage than the opposite. As market competition forces indemnity insurers to cut fees and impose draconian utilization controls, however, a physician-run and locally focused IPA can become increasingly attractive to its members. Moreover, the IPA as an organization has its incentives aligned with those of the HMOs. The success of the medical group depends on growth in order to achieve economies of scale in administration, utilization management, and capitation risk bearing. This organizational growth depends on recruiting new primary care physicians and on the conversion of patients to HMO coverage. The IPA leadership gradually comes to view the HMOs as their business partners and the indemnity and PPO insurance plans as their competitors.

Many private practice physicians find the network medical group better able to meet their needs than the alternative of joining a multispecialty clinic or staying aloof from managed care. The independent physician practice is a small business with a high ratio of fixed to variable costs. The support staff payroll is due weekly, the office lease and electricity bill must be paid monthly, and the interest payments on bank loans must be met quarterly regardless of how many patients visit and procedures are performed. Even a modest erosion of the patient volume toward competing HMO providers can spell financial disaster, especially when conventional insurers become resistant to visit-churning, procedure upcoding, and other desperation tactics. Participation in an IPA can allow individual physicians to hold onto their existing patients and even gain new ones, as the health plan actively markets its coverage and channels enrollees to network providers. Incremental business through IPA contracts can contribute significantly to practice profitability even if the fees or capitation rates are lower than what physicians obtain on their indemnity patients.

The IPA structure has proven useful to hospital sponsors as they struggle to adapt their amorphous medical staff organizations to the needs of managed care. Hospitals are directly at risk of losing inpatient admissions if their medical staff loses HMO patients to physicians linked to other institutions. Hospitals suffer from a cost structure as inflexible as that of their physicians, since the core expenses of the physical facility, the administrative staff, and even much of the clinical support staff cannot be adjusted quickly to accommodate fluctuations in patient volume. Over time, many hospitals have proven themselves adept at converting fixed to variable costs by imposing flexible work schedules, by outsourcing laundry and food service, and by contracting with employment agencies for temporary nursing staff. Nevertheless, the progressive loss of admissions to competing facilities sets the hospital onto a downward spiral of excess capacity, organizational downsizing, acrimonious employee relations, poor public relations, and further hemorrhaging of referrals and revenues. A successful IPA can help the hospital in its rate negotiations with the HMOs. Most obviously, the HMO is less able to threaten contract termination and thereby demand lower rates for inpatient care and ancillary services such as ambulatory surgery and subacute care. In some instances, the IPA affiliation permits the hospital and the physicians to negotiate with the HMO for a global capitation payment, through which the providers obtain a single payment for all clinical services and divide it among themselves without subsequent interference from the insurer. A few hospital systems have used their IPA relationships as a stepping stone toward full economic and clinical integration with their physicians, negotiating percent-of-premium contracts with HMOs or bypassing insurers altogether and contracting with the ultimate purchasers of care.

The IPA enjoys the advantages but also suffers the disadvantages of maintaining its base in solo practice, compared to the alternative of integrating the physicians into a multispecialty clinic. The advantages lie most clearly in the enhanced productivity of the physicians who retain ownership of their individual practices and gain the full reward of additional effort. The solo physician practice is the ultimate for-profit enterprise, with ownership and control combined in one person. The physician is not paid a predetermined salary but keeps as personal income all revenues that remain after paying the practice costs. The combination of fee-for-service payment with for-profit ownership creates extremely high-powered financial incentives for the physician, for whom each additional patient visit or procedure contributes directly to personal income and lifestyle. Especially in the IPAs' early years, they pay member physicians on a fee-for-service basis, and so each additional patient visit brings additional revenue. Investments in the practice that attract patients, such as longer hours and more attentive support staff, create financial benefits that accrue directly to the individual physician rather than being diffused across a much larger medical group. Even when IPAs shift from fee-for-service to subcapitation payments for physicians, their members remain motivated to streamline operations and enlarge their patient panels. Despite all the changes in technology and organization, the practice of medicine remains a one-on-one interaction where the energy and ingenuity of the individual physician is the prime determinant of profitability. Multispecialty medical groups with salaried physicians face a continual struggle to sustain individual productivity, since there is an ever present tendency for the doctors to see fewer patients, to accept less responsibility for evening and weekend backup, and to coast on the efforts of their partners. This free-riding tends to worsen as medical groups get larger and especially when they come to be owned by impersonal entities such as staff-model HMOs, hospital systems, practice management firms, and governmental agencies.

Despite some incontrovertible advantages, the IPA suffers from serious disabilities that accompany its fragmented organizational setting. The commitment of the physicians to the success of the organization often is very low, since the profitability of the physician's practice is determined by many factors unrelated to the IPA. This is especially true in markets weakly penetrated by HMO coverage, since indemnity and PPO patients are obtained without reliance on the IPA. Moreover, in markets heavily penetrated by HMOs, IPAs compete with one another for HMO contracts and then for primary care physician affiliations. Individual physicians often belong to multiple IPAs and feel no special sense of commitment to any one. They frequently view the IPA's payment and utilization management mechanisms as obstacles to be circumvented rather than as necessary features of an organization that must live within a budget. Although individual physicians receive the full reward for initiatives that benefit their individual practices, they receive little direct reward for initiatives that benefit the IPA as an organization, and they adjust their actions accordingly. Many IPAs face difficulties in convincing member physicians to participate in governance and management activities.

The liabilities of the network structure are accentuated by the cultural context in which the network medical groups evolve. IPAs sponsored by medical societies are dominated by specialists and subspecialists, who naturally resist the transition to a primary care focus. They frustrate attempts to strengthen the role of primary care physicians in governance and to tilt the compensation schedule in their favor, both of which are essential to control costs and facilitate growth of the organization. Many IPAs are governed using the principles of representative democracy, whereby each specialty has one member on the board of directors and interprets the role of that physician as promoting the interests of the specialty rather than of the organization. Hospital-sponsored IPAs naturally favor the specialists on their medical staffs. Even hospital administrators who understand the central role of primary care are hamstrung by the organizational imperative not to antagonize the specialists, who account for most fee-for-service admissions. Hospital sponsorship can cripple an IPA with kindness by allowing it to continue operating at a loss, with the deficit made good by the hospital. Hospital subsidies permit the physicians to retain their traditional indifference to the costs of the care they provide and their willful neglect of financial controls. And, needless to say, hospital subsidies come with a price. The dominant institution often impedes efforts to reduce unnecessary admissions or to grow the IPA by adding physicians who admit patients to competing hospitals.

THE NETWORK MEDICAL GROUP

Economic behavior within the traditional IPA resembles the tragedy of the commons, in which physicians each pursue their own individual good at the expense of the group. Most traditional IPAs survive, therefore, only so long as they face no serious competition. Few are able to achieve the efficiencies in reduced hospital admissions, length of stay, and overall costs earned by prepaid group practices.[6] Many observers have believed that the IPA is merely a transitional organizational form, useful only to introduce physicians to prepayment and utilization management, and destined to be outcompeted by fully integrated groups. And indeed many IPAs did dissolve after the physicians sucked the last dollar out of the capitation budget and the hospital finally refused to continue its subsidies. Others sold out to insurance companies, who used the ready-made physician networks while instilling financial discipline and utilization controls from the top down. A minority of IPAs, however, recognized their early weaknesses and took the steps necessary to control costs and ensure survival. The new generation of network medical groups has benefited from the innovations by multispecialty clinics in methods of capitation contracting, utilization management, and quality monitoring. But they do not pattern themselves on integrated groups to the extent of acquiring practices and transforming their physicians from owners to employees. They demonstrate the advantages of being second, following the trail blazed by the first movers while avoiding the wrong turns and the blind alleys.

The single most important determinant of success in the network medical group, compared to the traditional IPA, is the shift from an anti–managed care orientation with a specialty focus toward a pro–managed care orientation with a focus on primary care. Most IPAs were formed around medical societies or hospital medical staffs where the numerically and politically dominant specialty physicians were dedicated to maintaining traditional income and status distinctions within the profession. Success within managed care requires, however, that a medical group be able to attract the participation and commitment of the primary care physicians, who are the magnets for patient affiliation. It certainly is not desirable for the network medical group to gain a reputation as hostile to specialty interests, but it must find means to make the primary care physicians feel it is their organization. The IPA must aggressively recruit primary care physicians to join the organization and, once they have joined, foster an allegiance relative to competing network and multispecialty medical groups. The IPA must rebalance the distribution of the capitation income it receives from the HMOs in favor of the primary care physicians and to the detriment of the specialists. If primary care physicians are paid on a fee-for-service basis, the

IPA can raise the rates paid for office visits and other primary care interventions and lower the rates paid for surgical and other invasive procedures. If the generalists are paid on a subcapitation basis for primary care services, the rates can be raised and the budget for specialty payment commensurably reduced. These changes in compensation and culture are important for convincing the primary care physicians to favor rather than resist the conversion of their patients from indemnity insurance to HMO coverage. These conversions are the most important short-term means to growth for the network medical group, and constitute an important competitive advantage over multispecialty medical groups. A growing multispecialty group must hire new physicians and then wait for patients to leave their accustomed doctor and switch to the group, whereas new physician members in a network group come with established patient loyalties.

Long-term growth of the IPA requires the addition of new HMO contracts and new hospital relationships for its physician members. In some markets HMOs contract with different IPAs, but over time the most successful network groups become desirable partners for all the health plans. The more contracts held by a particular IPA, the less is the need for individual physicians to belong to more than one organization. Indeed, access to HMO patients is one of the most immediate and tangible benefits of IPA membership for the physicians. IPA growth through addition of primary care physicians is furthered to the extent the physician organization is not linked in an exclusive fashion to one hospital. Doctors and patients oriented to distant or competing facilities will not wish to participate if doing so requires changes in admission patterns. The separation from a particular hospital or hospital system forces the IPA to become a financially self-sustaining medical group rather than a loose confederation subsidized and therefore dominated by a hospital institution. Non-exclusive relationships with multiple HMOs and multiple hospitals are a mark of the mature network medical group, and clearly distinguish it from IPAs that were established by particular health plans or hospitals to serve their purposes rather than those of the physicians.

The network medical group must develop an infrastructure of departments, committees, and activities that mimic those of the multispecialty medical group if it is to compete successfully against those groups for capitated contracts. Indeed, formal departments and committees are often more important in a network medical group than in its multispecialty counterpart. The IPA's physicians are dispersed geographically and compete with one another for non-IPA patients, and are little inclined to see their personal interests as aligned with those of the group. Some IPAs designate clusters or pods of primary care physicians in each community as suborganizations within the organization, capable of sharing primary care capitation and bonus payments, developing protocols for referrals, and ideally to view each other as partners rather than rivals. Many IPAs create departments for each particular specialty, either across the whole network or by geographic region, to perform risk-bearing and utilization management functions. The infrastructure components based on specialty and geography are then supplemented by committees based on particular functions, such as utilization management, quality improvement, membership, finance, and health education. The chairs of these clusters, departments, and committees constitute the grassroots leadership of the organization. They are the lieutenants who communicate the vision and directives of the senior partners to the rank and file physicians and, conversely, articulate the concerns of the membership to the leadership.

The development of a solid departmental and functional infrastructure requires compatible changes in the overall governance of the network medical group. As long as IPAs are democratic organizations rent by factions seeking personal advantage, management cannot impose the fiscal discipline essential for independence from hospital control. Many traditional IPAs have large and unwieldy governance boards that serve as debating societies more than as business directors. Meetings are lengthy, acrimonious, and inefficient, with decisions made one month subject to renewed debate the next month when a different mix of members happens to attend. Successful IPAs reduce the number of seats on their boards and ensure that primary care physicians play a dominant role. The boards become self-perpetuating and elections are an unexciting event. There are few spoils for physician factions to contest. Board members come to interpret their role as promoting the interests of the organization rather than of their specialty. In governance respects IPAs begin to resemble the models established by leading multispecialty clinics, where power is concentrated in the hands of senior partners rather than diffused on a one-physician-one-vote basis to all participants. The limitation of direct democracy is particularly important in the network medical group since many of its physicians belong to competing IPAs and some would like to use the IPA to stop HMO penetration rather than to accommodate it. These changes in governance and culture are the most difficult but the most important over the long term, and clearly distinguish the network medical group from a conventional medical society.

The administrative component of many network medical groups is structured as a separate organization that provides management services to the physicians' professional partnership on a long-term and exclusive basis. The formal separation between the Management Services Organization (MSO) and the professional corporation is important since the individual physicians manifest quite different degrees of commitment to the success of the IPA. The MSO is owned by the most entrepreneurial physicians and managers, often in part by the partners in the professional corporation, and sometimes with an investment by a hospital system or practice management firm. This allows senior management to obtain an ownership stake in their enterprise, which confers important incentives, without violating the corporate practice of medicine statutes that prevail in many states. It also allows the network medical group to gain access to the outside capital necessary for growth. The MSO performs key administrative functions for the network group such as contracting with insurance plans, subcontracting for hospital and ancillary services, establishing financial targets, processing claims, and keeping track of patient enrollment and disenrollment. The clinical functions of monitoring utilization and quality typically remain within the physicians' professional corporation. In these contexts the network medical group manifests a dual structure of MSO and professional corporation, the former focusing on administrative concerns and the latter on clinical concerns. The MSO is a business firm with a culture of strong financial controls that can counterbalance the diffusely governed professional corporation. The split between management services organization and professional corporation is not essential to the IPA, however, and many continue to operate with a single organizational structure.

The primary care focus, organizational infrastructure, and nonexclusive relationships with health plans and hospitals combine to position the network medical group for rapid growth in physician membership and patient enrollment. Growth invariably poses challenges to the IPA but also can stimulate a virtuous cycle of enhanced efficiency, lower costs, higher profits to be divided among the physician members, stronger physician commitment, and further growth in patient enrollment. Most obviously, higher patient volume allows the IPA to spread its fixed costs over a broader base and thereby reduce the burden on the individual physicians. Overhead costs are lower than in multispecialty medical groups but are substantial nevertheless. The IPAs contract with vendors for outsourced services, employ medical directors and nurses to monitor utilization and quality, install computer systems to track financial revenues and expenditures, review the credentials of individual physicians, and respond to demands from public regulatory agencies and private accreditation entities. Higher enrollment permits the IPA to contract with HMOs for a broader range of capitated services, including hospital care and pharmacy benefits, since it better can spread insurance risk. Greater patient volume increases the dependency of physician members on the organization as a source of practice revenue, and thereby strengthens their willingness to participate in risk pools, utilization management committees, and other medical group activities. Some IPAs seek exclusive commitment from their primary care physicians, who are paid higher rates and offered practice supports if they resign from competing groups. Other IPAs seek to ensure physician commitment by accounting for a large share of patient volume but avoid exclusivity as inviting scrutiny from governmental antitrust agencies.

THE ADVANTAGE OF BEING SECOND

The experiences of the network medical groups can be illustrated using examples from the San Francisco region. The Hill Physicians Medical Group and the Brown and Toland Medical Group contrast with each other in terms of geographic scope, specialist mix, and historical relations with hospitals. But they resemble each other in their pursuit of growth through capitation contracting, strong MSO and physician group governance, tight financial and administrative controls, and broad panels of primary care and specialty members. Whereas multispecialty medical groups came to dominate much of the managed care system in southern California, the northern part of the state historically proved more congenial to network physician organizations. Most of the early IPAs failed for the conventional reasons, including specialist dominance, loose governance, and weak management, but they created a context in which the survivors could adopt new strategies and tactics while adhering to the network structure. Ironically, perhaps, the salience of IPAs in northern California derived in part from the extremely important role played by the nation's largest multispecialty clinic, the Permanente Medical Group. Permanente contracted on an exclusive basis with the Kaiser HMO, and grew at a phenomenal rate in the 1970s and 1980s when there were few effective managed care competitors. Many physicians and patients who were attracted to multispecialty clinics joined Permanente, depriving the independent multispecialty groups of their natural constituents. When the network HMOs entered the market seriously in the late

1980s, they immediately perceived the imperative to support the IPAs since there were so few independent clinics. The growth of multispecialty groups also was stunted by the prominence in northern California of large and prestigious hospitals, which gradually merged into systems that sought to incorporate physicians as well as nursing homes, ambulatory surgical centers, and home health agencies. If southern California is composed of large medical groups and small hospitals, northern California is composed of large hospitals and small physician practices.[7]

Hill Physicians Medical Group, founded in 1982 by doctors affiliated with the hospitals on Oakland's "Pill Hill," initially had all the characteristics of an IPA destined to fail.[8] It was initiated and subsidized by hospitals, defensive and anti-HMO in orientation, and lacking any meaningful administrative infrastructure. Financial difficulties led the physicians to recognize the need for independence, financial stability, and strong administration. In 1984 the IPA linked its destiny with the PriMed MSO and decided to extend its reach beyond the geographic market of its original hospitals. The IPA grew rapidly throughout the eastern suburbs of San Francisco by offering administrative efficiencies and prompt payment to small physician practices that otherwise were unable to participate effectively in HMO networks. Hill Physicians contracted with all the major network HMOs and allowed enrollees access to the large panel of physician members. It erased the distinctions among the HMOs for its primary care physicians by developing a single specialty network, single hospital network, single network of ambulatory surgery centers, nursing homes, and ancillary facilities, and a single pharmacy formulary. Most importantly, Hill Physicians established a consistent method of paying physicians and a consistent method of managing utilization, thereby freeing its members from the variability among methods used by the HMOs.

In 1993 Hill Physicians formed a partnership with the Catholic Healthcare West (CHW) hospital system as a means of entering the Sacramento market. CHW owned the Mercy IPA, composed of the medical staffs at its five Sacramento hospitals, plus an integrated multispecialty group.[9] The hospital-owned IPA was dominated by specialists and almost bereft of primary care physicians, was having no success at attracting new patients, and was requiring ever greater subsidies. CHW had come to recognize that it lacked the political willpower to impose discipline on the physicians, who controlled the flow of its hospital admissions. The sale of the Mercy IPA to Hill Physicians solved those immediate problems and laid the groundwork for joint initiatives in other areas where CHW owned hospitals but lacked physician commitment. Within a year Hill Physicians had increased substantially its patient enrollment in Sacramento while attracting new primary care physicians and earning a profit on the enterprise. The subsequent three-year record was quite revealing of the physician rebalancing that was both a cause and a consequence of successful growth. By the end of 1997 Hill's Sacramento division had 114 primary care and 476 specialist physicians to service 96,000 HMO enrollees, compared to 21 primary care physicians and 650 specialists for 20,000 enrollees in 1993. The IPA as a whole had 700 primary care and 1,800 specialty physicians to care for 325,000 HMO enrollees.[10]

These gains were not made without pain. Physician payments were reduced and referrals were more tightly managed. The true test of willpower came when Hill Physicians dropped 180 specialists from its membership in order to channel more referrals to the remaining physicians. Multispecialty medical groups always limit their physician membership to the number they can support off their patient base, but IPAs often include any willing provider in the community. Nonselective physician membership is advantageous from the standpoint of marketing to patients, for whom more choice is always better, but impedes the development of physician commitment to the organization. After slimming down its physician membership and expanding patient enrollment, Hill Physicians accounted for 35 percent of the practice volumes for its primary care physicians and 10 percent of referral volumes for its specialists.

The Brown and Toland Medical Group was formed in 1996 through an affiliation between the IPA at California Pacific Medical Center and the faculty group practice at the University of California's medical center in San Francisco, UCSF.[11] The California Pacific IPA, which constituted the larger part of the new organization, had been established four years earlier on the urging of the hospital trying to survive in a market with great excess capacity and ever-growing HMO penetration. The hospital and the IPA jointly owned an MSO that handled contracting, provided administrative services to physician practices, and performed inpatient and outpatient utilization management. The IPA included most members of the hospital's medical staff and accounted for 83 percent of all hospital admissions, counting the physicians' fee-for-service as well as HMO patients. HMO patients accounted for 35 percent of admissions. The administrative infrastructure and relation with the prestigious California Pacific Medical Center attracted primary care physicians previously affiliated with other hospitals, with the concomitant growth in patient enrollment. The IPA benefited from the urban geography of San Francisco to combine a primary care presence in every neighborhood with a concentration of specialist practices in two office buildings near the hospital. This geographic proximity facilitated the development of the cohesive specialist culture that often eludes IPAs in geographically dispersed markets. By 1996 the California Pacific IPA was composed of 40 percent of all HMO patients in San Francisco and 70 percent of HMO patients outside the Kaiser plan.

The California Pacific IPA benefited from its affiliation with its hospital partner but also chafed under the limitations this partnership imposed. As a dominant provider in the San Francisco market, the IPA negotiated high capitation rates with the HMOs but then paid above-market rates to the hospital for outpatient surgery, magnetic resonance imaging, and laboratory tests that could have been obtained more cheaply from freestanding providers. Moreover, its commitment to exclusive use of the California Pacific facility limited its appeal to new patients and prevented it from exploiting the excess capacity in neighboring institutions. The IPA solved the problem of limited hospital access by merging with the faculty practice group at UCSF, whose member physicians would continue using the University of California's teaching hospitals. The contracting limits imposed by the California Pacific partnership were loosened by dissolving the joint ownership of the MSO, which subsequently was owned exclusively by the medical group and its physician shareholders. The IPA obtained a license from the state of California permitting it to contract on a globally capitated basis with HMOs for hospital as well as physician services, thereby obviating the need to make prior agreements with the hospital over the division of capitation revenues between professional and institutional components. By the end of 1997 Brown and Toland included 1,350 physicians serving 189,000 patients from a dozen HMOs. The following year the IPA expanded as far south as Palo Alto, incorporating the HMO business of the faculty at Stanford University's medical school and recruiting primary care physicians in the communities along the San Francisco peninsula. The transformation from a hospital-centered to a physician-centered organization was symbolized by its new name. Prior to the merger the California Pacific Medical Group and the UCSF Medical Group had been clearly identifiable in terms of their hospital affiliations, but the new Brown and Toland Medical Group linked the names of two historically prominent local physicians and was no longer identifiable by its institutional relationships.

THE EVOLUTION OF PHYSICIAN COMPENSATION

The methods by which individual physicians are paid is more important in the network than in the multispecialty medical group. All physician organizations need their physicians to be dedicated to patient satisfaction, to maintain a broad scope of practice yet recognize the limits of their competency, to refer patients with specialized needs to colleagues with specialized training, to work hard as individuals, and to participate cooperatively as members of a larger team. The multispecialty group screens potential members more closely than the IPA, commands attention by paying the physician's entire salary, owns or leases a clinic building that facilitates peer monitoring, and wields the threat of termination in cases of egregious malfeasance. The network medical group, in contrast, takes in large numbers of physicians who often are screened only for their clinical credentials, retain many sources of practice revenues, and remain in geographically dispersed offices where performance is difficult to monitor. The strongest link among the physician members, the one thing they invariably recognize as binding them to the IPA, is the manner in which they get paid.[12]

Despite their dependency on financial incentives for motivating physician performance, many IPAs begin with a compensation system singularly maladjusted to the needs of an organization whose revenues derive from capitation contracts. IPAs do not employ their members and so cannot pay them on a salaried basis. Most initially adopt fee-for-service reimbursement methods since these are familiar to the physicians and congenial to the diffuse organizational setting. Claims are reimbursed using a fee schedule or discounts off the physicians' usual and customary prices. In either case, payments are subject to a "percentage withhold." If total physician claims fall within total capitation revenue, the surplus in the withhold account is distributed among the members, often in proportion to their individual billings. If there is no surplus in the withhold account, the physicians receive no bonus. Budgetary deficits are rolled over to the next accounting period when the percentage to be withheld from each claim can be increased.

The fee-for-service payment system used for individual physicians works at cross purposes from the capitation payment system used for the medical group. Collectively the physicians have the incentive to practice conservatively in order to regain the percentage withheld from their claims, but individually they have the incentive to increase the number and complexity of the procedures they perform. Individual physicians obtain personally the fee for their extra procedures while the loss imposed by those claims on the withhold pool is spread across the entire membership. Not surprisingly, withhold pools rarely exhibit a surplus. Many network groups find themselves caught in an ever-tightening financial bind, as individual physicians respond to the cuts in claims payments by churning additional procedures. The system penalizes the committed member, who refrains from opportunistic increases in billings, while rewarding those who would milk the organization dry. Discounted fee-for-service payment invariably works to the advantage of the specialists, who find it easier to order additional tests and upcode procedures than do the primary care physicians. Many IPAs find themselves nurturing a culture of cynicism, with both resentful generalists and defensive specialists looking to their own personal advantage and none concerned with the advantage of the others.

The payment reform most commonly instituted by the IPA moves the primary care physicians to capitation payment for the services they provide while continuing to pay specialists fee-for-service. Patients are linked to individual primary care physicians, who can be paid in a manner somewhat analogous to the salaried generalists in multispecialty groups. Under individual capitation, individual physicians' income from the IPA is proportional to the size of their patient panel. Physicians with half their practice consisting of IPA patients would receive half their income from the organization, the equivalent of working half-time on salary. Patients cannot be linked easily to individual specialists, however, since most do not use specialty services in any one year and cannot be expected to identify a personal physician in each specialty. But despite its understandable organizational logic, the combination of primary care capitation and specialist fee-for-service creates severe difficulties. Once paid on a capitated basis, primary care physicians receive no additional income for providing additional services and can only increase incomes by adding new patients to their panels. In order to free up time to manage new patients, they may reduce the services they provide to each patient and refer more services to the specialists. The specialists are happy to cooperate with this, since they earn a new fee for each referral. The solution is to move to payment methods that blend elements of both capitation and fee-for-service.

The Brown and Toland Medical Group paid its primary care physicians on a capitated basis, adjusted for the age and sex of each patient and with special case rates for newborns and AIDS patients. Physicians with fewer than 50 IPA patients were paid completely by fee-for-service in order to protect them from the variability in costs associated with small numbers. All primary care physicians were protected by stop-loss limits for particularly sick patients. Brown and Toland supplemented the capitation base with fee-for-service payments for a long list of procedures, allowing the individual physician to either perform these services or refer them out. The list included immunizations and other preventive services for which the medical group and its contracting HMOs were being held responsible by the National Committee for Quality Assurance. The majority, however, concerned diagnostic and therapeutic procedures that lay on the boundary of primary and specialty care. They were carved out of the capitation in order to allow primary care physicians to refer them to specialist colleagues but were made reimbursable on a fee-for-service basis to encourage primary care physicians to extend the scope of their own practice. The same fee was paid regardless of whether the procedure was performed by a generalist or a specialist. The primary care physicians also were paid on a fee-for-service basis for visits occurring in a hospital emergency room, nursing facility, or the patient's home. Partial fee-for-service protected the physician against the economic risk of having a particularly sick patient population, supplementing the age and sex capitation adjustments, the case rates for newborns and AIDS patients, the fee-for-service payment for physicians with small panels, and the stop-loss provisions for high cost cases.

Specialty procedures account for three-fourths of total physician costs and hence specialist compensation incentives are of particular importance. In some communities specialists have coalesced into large groups willing to be paid on a per-member-per-month basis for all tests and procedures within their specialty. Individual specialists within the groups are paid a salary. This replicates the alchemy performed by the multispecialty medical group, resolving the high-powered incentives of collective capitation into the low-powered incentives of individual salary. The specialty structures of most American cities, however, remain a diaspora of small practices, each competing vigorously with the others and each averse to bearing the insurance risk that prepayment entails. The excess supply of specialists is holding down professional incomes, which generates difficult political pressures on administrative mechanisms. Finally, maintaining a broad mix of specialist choices is an important marketing advantage for IPAs competing with multispecialty groups, and they do not want to unduly limit specialty participation.

Brown and Toland blended fee-for-service and capitation payments for panels of specialists who shared risk while continuing to own their individual practices. The medical group defined a per-member-per-month budget for the services falling within the purview of each specialty, and allowed each panel to allocate this budget among its member specialists as it saw fit. Most panels paid individual specialists on a fee-for-service basis, retaining a percentage withhold to ensure that the sum of claims payments did not exceed the departmental budget. Departmental capitation replicated the structure of the IPA at the level of the individual specialty. Churning or upcoding by one physician would come at the expense of other specialists, who were better positioned than primary care physicians to distinguish necessary from unnecessary procedures and culturally more willing to cooperate with fellow specialists than with the entire IPA.

Departmental capitation limits but does not eliminate the depletion of the specialty budget by individual physicians. It is particularly problematic in specialties where the individual physician can recommend repeat visits that generate new claims while requiring little of the physician's personal time. The monitoring of this high volume, low intensity churning is difficult for IPAs extended over broad geographic areas. In these contexts the logic of capitation can be extended down to the individual physician. Rather than dividing the departmental capitation budget among member specialists based on the number of the procedures each performs, it can be allocated based on the number of distinct patients that are referred by primary care physicians. The initial referral triggers a lump sum payment to the specialist, who then is responsible for the specialty services required by that patient for a prescribed period of time.[13] This referral-based capitation resembles the case rates sometimes adopted by surgeons, according to which a single fee is charged for the preoperative workup, the major procedure, and the postoperative care. But referral-based capitation can be applied to cardiology, dermatology, and other specialties where treatment typically is not structured around a single procedure. For these specialties, the capitated episode is defined as a period of time, often two, six, or twelve months, following the initial referral.

The blending of capitation and fee-for-service within specialty departments suggests analogous hybrids for primary care physicians. The need to protect the individual physician against insurance risk is less pressing in primary care, since generalists can refer the most expensive tests and treatments to specialists. Rather, the liability of individual capitation is that it discourages primary care physicians from providing the full scope of services for which they have been trained. The ideal payment mechanism would provide extra compensation to those primary care physicians who provide a procedure they otherwise could refer to a specialist, while including in the capitation budget funds to cover services that lie unequivocally within the domain of primary care. The extra compensation would equal the cost that an efficient primary care physician would incur to provide the procedure to the patient with an average severity of illness, thereby motivating primary care treatment of the less severely ill patients and referral of the more severely ill.

Hill Physicians long retained fee-for-service payment for primary care in order to encourage its physicians to maintain a broad scope of practice. The group recognized, however, that fee-for-service rewarded physicians who were particularly aggressive in their treatment styles and penalized those with conservative clinical management. Moreover, fee-for-service rewarded individual procedures but not improvements in overall practice efficiency. The IPA developed a blended payment method of fee-for-service supplemented with partial capitation, in contrast to the Brown and Toland method of capitation supplemented with partial fee-for-service. Under the new system, primary care physicians would continue to submit claims for all visits and procedures, but would be paid at 60 percent rather than 100 percent of the Medicare fee schedule. This was the IPA's estimate of the marginal cost to the physician of providing a particular procedure, with the remaining 40 percent being needed to cover practice overhead. Setting the fee equal to marginal cost would neutralize the economic incentives for the physician, who could provide the procedure personally or refer it to a specialist based on clinical considerations. Individual primary care physicians would receive an additional 40 percent of revenue from the IPA in a capitated payment, based on the number of patients in their panel and adjusted for age and gender mix. This capitation payment would favor physicians with conservative practice styles, since they would gain an average capitation rate while losing a below-average amount of fee-for-service revenue. Conversely, physicians with an aggressive treatment style would give up 40 percent of an above-average amount of fee-for-service revenue while receiving an average capitation payment. The capitation incentives could be fine-tuned to further reward physicians maintaining conservative referral patterns, receiving high scores on patient satisfaction surveys, and participating actively in IPA governance.

Despite continual experimentation and innovation, payment incentives remain blunt instruments for rewarding the range of behaviors desired from physicians. The basic split between generalist and specialist reappears within each individual specialty, where the general surgeon jostles with surgical subspecialists and the internist disputes turf with the medical subspecialists. Capitation payments designed to discourage unnecessary services can encourage excessive referrals and the avoidance of costly patients. Fee-for-service payments designed to encourage service provision can encourage the churning of unnecessary visits. Hybrid payment methods can lead to ping-pong referrals from generalists to specialists and back again. Despite their indispensable role in every medical organization, payment mechanisms need to be supplemented by administrative mechanisms and a clinical infrastructure to motivate appropriate physician performance.

A CLINICAL INFRASTRUCTURE

The process of utilization management in the network medical group has climbed a steep learning curve in tandem with the experiments in physician compensation. The amorphous IPA entity has been forced to institute more formal mechanisms for monitoring utilization than the integrated medical group since it relies less on informal peer review and socialization. Given their origins in physician communities hostile to managed care, many IPAs seek to limit disruption in the accustomed standards of practice. The inevitable failure of these minimalist efforts threatens the IPAs with insolvency and may create panic reactions in the direction of maximal control. Physicians sometimes find their IPAs interfering with day-to-day clinical decisions to a much greater extent than the oft-maligned insurance companies. Resentment undermines physician commitment to the organization and legitimizes further churning and upcoding of procedures. The path away from mutually assured destruction is to be found partly through the specialty departments that are formed to support capitation payment but subsequently provide an organizational infrastructure for managing care.

The foundation of utilization management within the network medical group is the requirement that every patient select a primary care physician responsible for coordinating all aspects of care. This doctor performs preventive and primary care services personally and refers more complicated cases for specialty consultation. In principle, the primary care physician plays the role of the symphony conductor, coordinating the full range of clinical services for each patient. In practice, however, primary care physicians often find themselves playing the role of gatekeeper, forced to deny patient requests that the physician thinks unnecessary but that the patient desires. Patients in nations such as Great Britain and Canada are accustomed to receiving most services from general practitioners and seeing specialists only upon referral. In the United States, however, aggressive consumer demand and excess specialist supply generates strong pressure for patient self-referral. Primary care physicians are anything but enthusiastic about their newfound gatekeeper role. While appreciating the philosophy that they should coordinate care, primary care physicians find themselves caught between patients who believe they can see any specialist for a ten-dollar copayment and specialists who interpret referral denials by primary care physicians as incompetence or greed. Moreover, the primary care gatekeeper can only limit a specialty referral. The greatest expenses are incurred not in these initial visits but in the tests and procedures performed at follow-up appointments. Individual primary care physicians are in a weak position to monitor these, since they often do not see the patient between specialty visits and are not trained to evaluate highly specialized treatments.

A multispecialty medical group impresses upon its member specialists the importance of a conservative practice style in a capitated environment and wields the threat of discipline in case of flagrant noncompliance. The network groups, however, are forced to construct an organizational infrastructure that brings together members of each specialty to develop methods of utilization management. The specialty risk pools established for departmental capitation offer just this infrastructure. Once each specialty is subject to its own capitation budget, it has the incentive to develop specialty-specific protocols for appropriate use of tests and treatments. It can elect its own department director with responsibility to monitor protocol adherence by panel members. The department leader, the assistant medical directors, and the IPA's support staff review requests for interventions with more knowledge of the technical issues than that available to the primary care gatekeeper. In contexts where the individual specialist is paid on a referral-based capitation method, the departmental emphasis switches from monitoring for unnecessary treatment to monitoring for insufficient treatment.

The Hill Physicians Medical Group experimented with various physician payment incentives, methods of utilization management, and organizational structures to coordinate care across its broad physician network. The group began with a fee-for-service payment system and spent its first decade preparing to adopt primary care capitation. Each time it got close to the transition, however, it forced itself to reflect on the il-logic of rewarding a shift in services from primary care to specialist physicians. By the early 1990s it was willing to be proud of a payment system that encouraged primary care physicians to practice to the full extent of their competency and rewarded the active promotion of preventive services. Patients were required to obtain primary care referrals for specialty visits, but the IPA did not impose any oversight or prior authorization requirements on the primary care physicians themselves. It permitted specialists to schedule follow-up visits at will but required prior authorization for any procedure costing more than $500.

Hill Physicians's oversight structures worked tolerably well because of the tight review of high cost procedures and encouragement of primary care. They reached their limits in 1994, however, when the HMOs responded to demands for premium reductions by large corporate purchasers by demanding commensurate reductions in the capitation rates they paid to the medical groups. Hill Physicians had been developing specialty departments as a means to bring its diffuse physician membership together in clinically cohesive units. In early 1995 it established capitation budgets for each department, based on two years of claims history in each department and discounting the totals by the percentage required to stay within the overall IPA budget. Each department chose its own mechanism for paying physician members. In most instances individual specialists continued to file claims on a fee-for-service basis, the solvency of the departmental accounts being ensured by the continual adjustment of the fee schedule. Departments that had a dominant single-specialty group could assign the full departmental budget to that group and allow it to pay claims from independent specialists. Each department also was responsible for developing its own clinical protocols and methods of monitoring utilization.

The cardiology department in the Oakland region, to cite one example, included 50 cardiologists, pediatric cardiologists, and cardiovascular surgeons who were responsible for the cardiology services of 120,000 Hill Physicians patients in their area. One group with four office sites accounted for a large fraction of cardiology services provided by Hill Physicians though it also provided services to fee-for-service patients and to competing IPAs. The departmental chair and his four assistant medical directors continued to practice medicine and surgery full time while assuming responsibility for protocol development and for review-of-procedure requests. One set of protocols focused on referral criteria for primary care physicians and the other on treatment criteria for cardiologists and surgeons. Departmental capitation stimulated specialists to train the primary care physicians on management of mild and moderate cardiac conditions in order to reduce unnecessary referrals. The capitated department was more strict in the oversight of its cardiologists than was utilization management in the absence of the departmental structure. Ten cardiologists were dropped from the Oakland region as part of the general streamlining of the IPA in 1994; these included several individuals that the group felt were churning procedures and several who had received few referrals and were only tangentially involved with the IPA. The cardiology department met quarterly, with approximately one-third of its members participating in any given meeting. Practice profiles on each cardiologist were presented at these meetings, which also discussed protocols and prevailing patterns of care. Executive leaders from the medical group attended these meetings to help with boundary issues, such as the division of responsibility between primary care physicians, cardiologists, and cardiac surgeons for postoperative patient care. The leaders of the various specialty departments met regularly to discuss common concerns and learn from each other's experiences.

The development of specialty departments, capitation pools, and specialty-specific protocols exerted a dramatic impact on patterns of utilization and expenditure in the Hill Physicians Medical Group. Cardiology in the Oakland region experienced a 30 percent drop in hospital utilization and a 20 percent drop in claims costs in the first year. The decline in hospital admissions and length of stay was observed throughout the organization. Total inpatient days per 1,000 enrollees declined from 196 in 1993 to 158 in 1995 and 148 in 1997. These figures were comparable with the shifts from inpatient to outpatient care achieved by integrated multispecialty clinics. The decline in hospital utilization produced surpluses in the hospital risk pools, but thereby renewed discussion concerning distribution of those surpluses among members of the IPA. In order to attract and reward primary care physicians, Hill Physicians had divided hospital savings just among physicians in family practice, internal medicine, and pediatrics. Sustained reductions in hospital use, especially once clearly unnecessary admissions had been eliminated, required extra outpatient visits and procedures from specialists more than from generalists. Discussions over the appropriate participation by specialists in hospital risk pool savings were accompanied by discussions over how to mitigate the churning of primary care visits that derived from fee-for-service payment. The principle of blending capitation and fee-for-service, well established for specialists, reinforced the blending of capitation and fee-for-service for primary care physicians.

CHALLENGES FACING THE NETWORK MEDICAL GROUP

The network medical group brings marketplace incentives for effort and entrepreneurship inside the physician organization. As owners of their individual practices, the physicians are motivated to work long hours, be attentive to patient preferences, hold down expenses, and constantly think of new ways to grow their business. As members of a medical group, however, the physicians are motivated to cooperate with one another to an extent never achieved in the era of guild professionalism. The network medical group contracts with HMOs in a manner similar to its multi-specialty counterparts and hence faces the same imperatives. It must build a clinical infrastructure of medical directors, specialty departments, quality committees, and case managers for chronically ill patients. It contracts with hospitals, nursing homes, rehabilitation facilities, ambulatory surgery centers, medical equipment vendors, and home health agencies for ancillary services. By combining the capabilities of the multi-specialty group with the incentives of independent practice, the network group has silenced the skeptics who once considered it as nothing more than a transitional organizational form.

The multispecialty medical groups have responded to the IPA challenge by imitating its key innovations. They are reviewing compensation mechanisms, replacing salary schedules based on job tenure with performance-based pay linked to physician productivity, patient satisfaction, and the measurable aspects of quality. They are disaggregating large clinic staffs into compact practice teams and distributing them in satellite offices throughout the community. Many continue to benefit, moreover, from a greater organizational commitment by their physicians and stronger recognition by their patients. The physicians in HealthCare Partners understood that their personal destinies were inextricably linked to that of their organization, while many members of Hill Physicians participated in competing IPAs to diversify their allegiances. Consumers in Charlotte easily recognized the Nalle Clinic but Brown and Toland needed extensive advertising to achieve a brand name in San Francisco.

In the end there is no single best way to organize the delivery of physician services. The network IPAs and the multispecialty groups remain distinct alternatives even as they borrow features from one another. Some physicians and patients prefer the stability and coordination of the multispecialty clinic while others prefer the intimacy of small practices brought together by the IPA. The most entrepreneurial physician organizations have responded by coordinating both multispecialty groups and IPAs. Some multispecialty groups have developed wraparound IPAs that benefit from the clinical infrastructure of the integrated group while allowing physicians to retain ownership of their practices. Some IPAs have brought multispecialty groups as well as solo practices under their contractual umbrellas, paying each the same blend of capitation and fee-for-service and not favoring either over the other. Diversified physician organizations are built around MSOs that combine network and multispecialty groups and negotiate on their behalf with hospitals and other vendors. The dynamic of experimentation is moving from the consolidation of physician practices to the consolidation of medical groups into larger health care systems.

CHAPTER 7

Physician Practice Management

Multispecialty medical groups and independent practice associations enjoy substantial advantages over the unaffiliated solo practice but even these entities often perceive themselves to be too small to survive in the ever more competitive economic environment. They begin to evaluate opportunities for affiliation with other medical groups, with a local hospital, or with a larger corporate system. Physician Practice Management (PPM) firms use capital from institutional investors, banking consortia, and the public equity markets to acquire medical groups, expand them through recruitment of new physicians and patients, and merge them with similar organizations within their local communities. This consolidation may offer advantages to medical groups. Large and well-capitalized organizations can develop the infrastructure necessary to manage financial risk and clinical practice patterns. Large physician systems may negotiate higher rates from health plans and lower rates from hospitals, outside referral specialists, and ancillary vendors. Systems linked to leading medical groups can identify and disseminate best practices throughout their networks. But the consolidation of physician organizations into corporate entities also incurs great risks. The amalgamation of small practices into large groups and of large groups into larger systems invariably engenders diseconomies of scale and scope. As experienced by the staff-model HMOs, the employment of once independent physicians attenuates incentives and entrepreneurship. Key local leaders may use the PPM buyout as their opportunity to retire, taking their expertise with them and weakening the cultural continuity of the organization. PPM firms inject the volatility of the capital markets into once stable medical practices. Driven by investor growth expectations they may bid too high for medical group affiliates and too low for HMO contracts.

The PPM industry experienced a meteoric rise and spectacular fall in its first decade. The industry spawned innumerable firms and business models, enjoyed phenomenal growth in service volume and revenues, and was lionized by investors and analysts. Then it overreached its operations, overextended its finances, and was subjected to the frontier justice of the corporate economy. Firms large and small were threatened by litigation, write-offs, divestment, and dismemberment. The PPM survivors and their hospital competitors emerged strengthened from the chaos, with new opportunities to acquire physician organizations at bargain-basement prices but also with new appreciation of the risks of conglomerate consolidation.

FINANCIAL CAPITAL

Physician organizations need capital for several purposes. Many medical groups have unfunded liabilities to senior partners and most require improvements in information systems, clinic facilities, and administrative infrastructure. Physician organizations seeking a regional presence require funds to acquire individual practices and merge with existing medical groups. Finally, all large physician organizations require seed money to develop new revenue sources and to reduce costs through clinical and administrative efficiencies. These capital needs can be conceptualized as bridge loans, growth funds, and operational investments. The bridge loans have the most immediate urgency, given the perilous financial state of many medical groups, and the growth funds have their greatest value during the consolidation phase of physician organization. Operational investments are the most important over the longer term, however, since they alone stimulate improvements in medical group performance and yield to capital partners the requisite gains in revenues and earnings.

The immediate financial needs of medical groups stem from the weak governance of the traditional physician organization. Most multispecialty clinics and IPAs have been structured as partnerships that pay out surplus funds to physician shareholders at the end of each year to avoid corporate taxation. In the era of unmanaged care, physician organizations had little administrative infrastructure and no need for reserves to cover the trail of incurred but not reported claims that become important determinants of financial performance under capitation. In the managed care era, they need professional administration, cash reserves, information systems to monitor utilization patterns, and claims processing capabilities. The traditional sources of capital are insufficient for the task at hand. Banks once were willing to make short-term loans to individual physicians, often on no more security than a medical license, but have become cautious. Local hospitals once were willing to make unsecured loans to medical groups to obtain patient admissions but now want tighter control. Medical groups often were owned in unequal amounts by individual physicians, with senior members having large but illiquid shares. In some cases these physicians can be bought out through group conversion to a nonprofit medical foundation, but in most cases they expect to get paid through buy-ins levied on new physician members. Many medical groups thus have entered the era of managed care with no retained earnings and with significant unfunded liabilities.

Managed care offers new economies of scale and scope, but growth requires capital. Funds are needed to purchase individual physician practices and, more importantly, to merge with other multispecialty clinics and IPAs. The consolidation of medical groups guarantees access to payer contracts, since it is impossible for the plans to market insurance without the larger provider system. Individual physicians find it attractive to join established groups to gain access to these contracts. As managed care penetration deepens and competition intensifies, however, access to HMO contracts becomes less important. Employers and consumers force health plans to include most primary care physicians and medical groups in their networks. In these contexts, the consolidation of physician practices enhances revenues not through more health plan contracts but, rather, through better contracts. This involves broadening the range of capitated services from primary to specialty and hospital care. Further revenue growth is to be found in less traditional services. In some cases these market niches already are being pursued by single-specialty physician organizations, which come into direct competition with the multispecialty groups. One major new area of medical group activity is the contractual provision of physician services to hospitals, such as staffing emergency rooms, neonatology units, and radiology services. Other institutions in need of services, including universities, military bases, and prison medical units, also beckon to entrepreneurial physician enterprises.

The most important use of capital is to improve the efficiency of the services provided by physician organizations. Medical groups require computerized information systems capable of producing administrative and clinical reports by health plan, region, physician, patient, and diagnosis. Information systems, however, are only the visible tip of an iceberg of investments needed to re-engineer physician practice. The invisible bulk of investments is devoted to building competencies in financial risk assessment, network contracting, utilization monitoring, and quality accreditation. The prepaid group practices pioneered a style of health care that emphasizes outpatient, subacute, and home health services and de-emphasizes the acute care hospital.[1] Efficiencies in practice styles require an organizational infrastructure consisting of medical directors, utilization management committees, utilization review nurses, and case managers for chronically ill patients. These individuals and committees are needed to implement the principles of continuous quality improvement: the measurement of processes, identification of outliers, reduction of variance, and benchmarking of best practices.[2]

One historical source of capital for physicians was the local hospital, which often made subsidized loans or offered free clinic space in the expectation of patient admissions. In the managed care era, some hospital systems offer to be the financial and strategic partners for medical groups, buying up the practices and incorporating the physicians as employees in integrated systems. In the ideal scenario, Physician-Hospital Organizations (PHOs) contribute not only cash but brand-name recognition, enhanced clinical coordination, and stronger bargaining leverage with health plans. The primary force driving medical groups toward consolidation, however, is not lack of patient loyalty, practice efficiency, or bargaining power but lack of strong management and governance. One-doctor-one-vote democracy impedes the ability of medical groups to make rapid and at times difficult decisions, to rebalance primary care and specialist incomes, to retain excess earnings as capital rather than distributing it to the partners, to standardize practice patterns, and to document the process of care for health plans, purchasers, and regulators. Sale to a hospital system may compound rather than resolve these failures of governance. Most PHOs are dominated by nonprofit hospital boards beholden to multiple constituencies with multiple objectives. Few of these constituencies are focused on achieving success under managed care.

The alternative to seeking investment funds from hospitals is to tap the public debt and equity markets. Institutional investors, individual stockholders, corporate bond underwriters, and venture capital firms are eager to participate in what they interpret as a major growth industry, the social transformation of American medicine.[3] The conversion of many health plans and some hospitals to publicly traded corporations has fueled growth in market share and revenues, though it has led to great volatility in profits and organizational fates. Many problems encountered by insurance and hospital corporations stem from lack of physician commitment, which has sparked investor interest in organizations focused directly on physician services. Investor meetings and stock prospectuses trumpet the fact that physicians account for 80 percent of the health care dollar through their own professional services and through the tests, treatments, and hospital admissions they prescribe. Whoever invests in medical groups could displace insurance plans and hospital chains as the center of the health care system. The stock market may be well structured to finance the high risk but potentially high reward enterprise embodied in the multispecialty medical group. In contrast to institutional lenders such as banks and bond underwriters, equity investors are able to finance firms that have few existing assets but great expectations. Start-up firms, whether in software, biotechnology, or physician services, need not pay current dividends if they can sustain rapid growth. Short-term earnings can be plowed back into the firms to enhance services, invest in new products, and grow through mergers and acquisitions. However, the public capital markets are inherently anxious, unsure of the sustainability of past trends, and prone to overreact to rumors, tidbits of information, and short-term profits and losses. The volatility of the public investor creates volatility in the publicly traded physician organization, impeding focus and long-term investment in administrative and clinical capabilities.

In principle, medical groups interested in access to the capital markets could go public by building on a record of profitability and then issuing stock in their own name. Typically this would be preceded by private investments from venture capital firms with the financial resources and management expertise to navigate the turbulent waters of an initial public offering. A few groups did follow this route. Medical groups quickly discovered, however, that the skills they possess in organizing doctors, managing practice patterns, and contracting with health plans do not ensure success in the equity markets. Outside investors are unsure as to the boundaries of the physician services industry, to say nothing of the viability of any particular medical group. They are betting on rapid revenue growth and are quick to exit at the first sign that a group might miss its targets. The prices commanded by particular stocks are based on earnings expectations and fall precipitously if those expectations are disappointed. Alternatively, the medical group could exchange its private equity for the publicly traded equity of an established physician practice management firm. The PPM firm provides financial capital, owns the clinics, employs the nonclinical personnel, and administers the business side of the operations, but usually does not employ the physicians or control the clinical aspects of the practice. The physicians remain owners and employees of professional corporations that hold the health plan contracts, establish physician salaries and work expectations, manage utilization patterns, and accept responsibility for quality of care. Some firms focus on IPA management, avoiding the need to purchase clinic assets and thereby limiting their capital outlay. The infant PPM industry exhibits many different ownership, governance, financial, and compensation models, and it is not important to dwell on the details of each. Rather, the term "physician practice management" can be used in a more generic sense to denote corporate organizations that seek to consolidate physician practices, single-specialty networks, multispecialty clinics, and IPAs while remaining independent of HMO and hospital ownership.

ECONOMIES OF SCALE

PPM firms potentially enjoy three economies of scale, compared to small physician organizations. The most obvious is in the cost of capital, where scale and risk diversification lower bank interest rates and create access to more flexible equity and debt financing. Centralized purchasing can reduce costs for supplies and equipment obtained from national vendors. Large physician corporations potentially gain bargaining leverage with insurer organizations, although contracting dynamics vary widely from market to market.

A fundamental business principle for the PPM firm is that the return on each medical group investment must exceed the cost of the capital used in the transaction. This produces a dual focus on increasing return on investments through improved performance and on lowering the cost of capital through a portfolio of financial instruments. National physician corporations develop credit lines through consortia of financial institutions at lower interest rates than those available to any individual clinic. The most important source of long-term capital, however, is through the public equity markets. Not all physician corporations sell ownership shares to the investing public. Some are owned solely by their managers and physicians, while others have taken in private investors such as venture capital firms. Turbulence in the stock market can drive formerly public firms to buy back all their stock and go private, using funds from bond offerings or institutional investors. Physician organizations with a national growth strategy ultimately will enter the stock market, however, since it provides the most flexible capital in the long run. Most PPM companies do not issue standard corporate debt since leverage imposes fixed repayment schedules that impair flexibility in the face of expansion opportunities. Some issue debt that converts to equity at trigger dates and prices. The capital markets prefer convertible over standard bonds for growth companies and are willing to support that debt at a low interest rate. The availability of bank credit and debt offerings permit publicly traded firms to time secondary stock offerings for periods when their share price is high. The cost of capital is important not only to the corporate entity but to individual clinics that need investment funds for replacement and expansion of facilities, clinical equiment, and local market penetration. The PPM firm serves as an internal capital market for its clinics, reviewing and negotiating requests with each site and charging affiliates at the interest rates achieved in the larger outside market.

Each medical group and IPA operates in its own geographic market and pays local rates for labor and supplies. Affiliation with a corporate entity does not reduce the cost of these inputs. National affiliation brings volume discounts, however, for administrative and clinical inputs purchased through national contracts. Large PPM firms achieve discounts on mundane and exotic supplies, from bandages to brain scanners. The potentially most significant savings, as capitation contracting spread, lie in drugs and devices if PPM firms can develop preferred vendor relationships with pharmacy benefits management firms and direct contracting relationships with manufacturers.

Large physician organizations enjoy potentially strong bargaining positions since HMOs cannot market their insurance products without having the medical groups and IPAs in their networks. However, most of the advantage in bargaining leverage stems from consolidation within markets rather than expansion across markets. Nationally diversified PPM firms are disadvantaged rather than advantaged in this respect, compared to locally concentrated PHOs. Some PPMs aggressively pursue multimarket contracts with national plans. But a large presence in one geographic market does not increase the PPM firms' bargaining power in a distinct market where it has only a small presence. Bargaining power cannot be leveraged across geographic markets, and a rate increase achieved in weakly penetrated markets will be offset by a commensurate decrease in highly penetrated markets. Indeed, in their headlong pursuit of growth, some PPM firms negotiated low rather than high rates with HMOs, thereby gaining high patient enrollment but creating subsequent budgetary difficulties.

ECONOMIES OF SCOPE

The geographic dispersion of medical clinics and IPAs limits economies of national scale but increases the potential advantages for economies of scope. The heterogeneity of physician practice styles, clinical cultures, managed care penetration, and population demographics across states and localities hamper efforts at standardization but offer possibilities for comparison, benchmarking, and organizational learning. PPM companies may be able to combine the advantages of diversity, which stem from operating in multiple local markets, with the advantages of consistency, which stem from integration into an organization with one mission, one information system, and one bottom line. Indeed, this is the only long-term advantage to multimarket organization in a locally focused industry that places no significant value on national brand names for the intimate services delivered by physicians.

The scarcest resource in American health care is management and physician leadership that understands how to balance competing needs: the needs of the patient for the best care regardless of cost and the needs of society for the best care at an affordable cost. Traditional hospital and insurance management was insensitive to the professional goals and clinical culture of the physician community and did a poor job at what it continually referred to as herding cats. Conversely, traditional physician leadership was insensitive to the budgetary concerns of purchasers and did a poor job of building solvent organizations with strong administrative structures. Regional and national physician organizations have the opportunity to scour their clinics for local leaders, promote them to larger spans of authority, and apply their ideas and methods across the organization as a whole.

The practice of medicine no longer approximates the nostalgic imagery of the individual practitioner whose clinical armamentarium fits within a black bag. Medical groups are labor- and capital-intensive organizations that require large numbers of physicians, nurses, technicians, computers, laboratories, examining offices, and on-site pharmacies. The efficient management of these complex organizations requires continual evaluation of performance against benchmarks. The PPM administrative databases ideally draw on their medical groups to establish average and best achievable standards for staffing, space, supplies, and expenditures by specialty department and clinic size. The corporate staffs can provide internal consulting services to their local clinics on operations, finance, marketing, and other administrative functions.

Medicine exhibits huge geographic differences in rates of surgery, diagnostic procedures, hospital admissions, pharmaceutical regimens, and overall standards of care.[4] These geographic variations are a source of frustration but offer the potential for improvements in both quality and efficiency once data-based methods of analysis are in place. Governmental and professional entities are pursuing protocols and guidelines on a condition-specific and procedure-specific basis yet often encounter difficulty in translating their recommendations into practice at the grassroots level. National organizations have the potential to contribute to this larger effort by drawing on their physician constituencies to develop internal committees and collaborate with external organizations. The greatest potential benefit from regional and national expansion, though the hardest to achieve in practice, is the transfer of best administrative and clinical practices from leading to lagging medical groups. The most important form of competition over the long run will not be reductions in price for the existing set of clinical services but, rather, fundamental changes in the manner in which health care is delivered. Innovation and technology transfer have been the engines of productivity improvement and cost reduction in the larger nonhealth economy.[5] They will play only a modest cost-reducing role in medicine, however, as long as physicians are fragmented into small practices unconnected with each other except through informal referrals and medical society memberships. Academic medical centers and clinical journals provide only a one-way transfer of information, helping practicing physicians keep abreast of their research-oriented colleagues but not encouraging innovations in real-world practice to diffuse throughout the profession. Innovations trickle down but cannot easily percolate up. This unidirectional learning is particularly limiting once managed care creates incentives for innovations at the grassroots level while allowing the traditional centers of professional prestige to cling to fee-for-service reimbursement.

CONSOLIDATION

By 1995 the PPM industry had captured the imagination of Wall Street. The logic of the business plan seemed compelling. The physician, not the hospital or the insurer, was the central figure in health care. Medical groups and IPA networks were essential to achieve the scale and scope necessary for success in the competitive health care economy. Consolidation of medical groups required capital. Whichever firms could bring the financial capital of Wall Street together with the intellectual capital of the multispecialty groups would be poised to dominate a trillion-dollar industry. Venture capitalists and investment bankers filled a pipeline with promising start-ups ready to make their initial public offering and then expand into new markets on an upward spiral of investment, earnings, and continued investment.

The rush of new capital and companies into the PPM industry created a whirlwind of creative destruction as new firms were launched into a turbulent environment where success could reap huge rewards but where any slip brought disaster. It proved easier to articulate a successful strategy than to implement one. Many once promising entities stumbled briefly, lost the backing of their investors, and were forced into consolidation with an erstwhile competitor. Pacific Physician Services held an almost impregnable competitive position in the Inland Empire of California, linking medical groups that served 300,000 capitated patients from all the network HMOs. Its stock price surged from $8 at the initial offering in 1991 to a high of $29 one year later but then plummeted on the news that the company's expansion efforts into other states had proven more costly than anticipated. Pacific Physician struggled on for several years with a sluggish stock price and a tarnished image until it sold out in 1996 for the equivalent of $20 per share. AHI sought to avoid the capital costs that burdened multispecialty medical groups by organizing primary care IPAs and leaving the physicians in ownership of their practices. The IPA model could be established rapidly in markets where the health plans were happy to outsource the difficult task of developing and managing physician networks. AHI began in California and moved into Texas and Georgia with a strategy for expanding nationwide. It quickly discovered that the infrastructure costs of expansion could cripple growth during the initial phase when revenues were thin. AHI also sought to manage referrals in multiple states from a central office in California, re-creating precisely the arms-length utilization review that physicians had come to detest in health plans. After an initial public offering at $14 per share, AHI traded down to $12 and then collapsed to $6 on the day it announced its earnings shortfalls. By the end of 1996 AHI recognized its options as an independent company were finished and sold out for the equivalent of $8 per share. Coastal Physician Group completed an ini-tial public offering in 1991 as a company managing hospital emergency rooms and then refocused itself on acquiring primary care physician practices. It made the salient mistake of believing the rhetoric of vertical integration, acquiring a small HMO and thereby competing with the health plans that contracted with its clinics in Florida. When Humana, the HMO market leader, severed its contracts, Coastal found its clinics empty of patients but full of red ink. By 1998 the Coastal stock price, which had reached a high of $40, had plummeted below $1 per share and the company was shedding divisions and directors at a rapid rate.

These early years produced three PPM firms that grew to a truly na-tional scale, enjoyed exceptional reputations among investors, and then suffered spectacular difficulties when costs caught up with revenues. PhyCor, FPA Medical Management, and MedPartners had different or-ganizational cultures and pursued different business strategies but shared the same fundamental agenda. They bought multispecialty medical groups, built IPAs, coordinated primary care, specialist, and hospital-based physicians, and struggled to earn profits within an increasingly constricted financial environment. They eschewed ownership of or by health plans, favoring contracts that linked their fates without making either fully responsible for the other. In analogous fashion they avoided ownership of and by hospitals, maintaining a flexible range of contracts that accommodated the idiosyncrasies of local medical markets and the power of hospital-based systems within them. The happenstance of merger and acquisition sometimes left them owning a small HMO or hospital, since some medical groups had embraced vertical integration, but these entities were retained only so long as they generated profits on a stand-alone basis. PhyCor, FPA, and MedPartners pursued full service diversification, providing physician services in clinic, IPA, and hospital settings in multiple communities across multiple states. Corporate fi-nance and strategy were centralized; the practice of medicine was de-centralized.

PHYCOR

PhyCor acquired its first medical group in 1988, soon followed by other acquisitions and a public stock offering in 1992.[6] In its first decade the company pursued a strategy of affiliation with multispecialty clinics in midsized markets, same-store growth through recruitment of new physicians and patients, and the formation of wraparound IPAs that linked clinics and independent physicians for capitation contracting and utilization management. The pace of growth accelerated over time, with prominent affiliations including the Straub Clinic and Hospital in Hawaii with 190 physicians, the Toledo Clinic in Ohio with 80 physicians, and the Lewis-Gale Clinic in Virginia with 130 physicians. As of 1998 PhyCor was affiliated with 57 multispecialty medical groups that employed 3,890 physicians in 515 office sites and contracted with 26,000 physicians through IPAs in 36 markets. It held managed care contracts for 1.5 million capitated patients and an equal number of noncapitated patients, and offered services on a noncontracted basis for large numbers of Medicare and commercially insured fee-for-service patients. The company operated in 28 states with widely diverse demographics and managed care penetration, with the largest numbers of clinics located in Florida, Virginia, and Texas.[7]

PhyCor's core strategy was to purchase the tangible assets of multispecialty clinics, including facilities and equipment, and then establish local subsidiaries to manage these in cooperation with the affiliated medical groups. Each medical group was owned by member physicians and retained its own board of directors and executive leadership. Each clinic was governed by a joint policy board composed of three PhyCor management staff and three physicians chosen by the medical group. PhyCor was responsible for establishing capital budgets, managing daily clinic operations, employing the nonphysician staff, purchasing supplies and information systems, and the other business aspects of the enterprise. The medical group was responsible for physician employment, performance, and payment, for quality and utilization management, and for the other clinical aspects of the enterprise. The joint policy board was responsible for establishing growth objectives in patient services and revenues, prioritizing capital expenditures, contracting with health plans, and the other strategic aspects of the enterprise.

The key financial dimensions of the relation between the PPM firm and its affiliated physicians was the initial clinic acquisition and the subsequent management services agreement. Each clinic was valued based on five-year projections of revenues and expenses, adjusted for growth opportunities, and net of outstanding liabilities. Physician shareholders were paid a combination of cash, PhyCor stock, and notes that had a face value in cash but could be converted to stock at specified dates and trigger prices. The physicians' choice of payment mix depended in large part on considerations of personal tax minimization. PhyCor and the medical group signed an exclusive long-term management services agreement that specified the allocation of revenues after payment of clinic expenses. This distribution pool was defined as revenues minus expenditures for clinic operations, excluding physician compensation, and typically was allocated 85 percent for the medical group and 15 percent for PhyCor. The higher the initial purchase price demanded by the medical group, the lower was the subsequent split of the distribution pool it received. The tradeoff between initial purchase price and subsequent revenue split was determined by the internal politics of the medical group. Senior physicians with large ownership shares and a short time horizon before retirement favored a higher price and lower revenue share. Conversely, junior physicians favored a lower price and higher revenue split. After acquisition, PhyCor continued to invest in the upgrade of facilities, addition of satellite sites, physician recruitment, subsidies for new physicians until they filled their practices, and clinic expansion through IPA formation and acquisition of nearby practices.

Recognizing that the number of multispecialty clinics was limited, PhyCor expanded its strategy to encompass the development and management of IPAs, beginning with the acquisition of the PPM firm North American Medical Management in 1995. By 1998, over half of the capitated patients served by PhyCor came through its IPAs and there was potential for significant growth. In areas where PhyCor maintained both a clinic and an IPA, the clinic was brought under the IPA umbrella for managed care functions such as contracting and utilization management. The IPAs focused exclusively on capitation contracting, in contrast to the dominant role of fee-for-service in the clinics. Only 15 percent of PhyCor clinic revenues but 100 percent of its IPA revenues came from capitation. By 1998, 38 percent of the PPM firm's total revenues were capitated. Another potential area for growth lay in relationships with hospitals that were losing money on their PHO operations. PhyCor explored joint venture possibilities under which the PPM firm and each hospital system would co-own a local subsidiary to manage physician practices, establish IPAs, and coordinate contracting and utilization management. Alternatively, the hospital could own the practices and PhyCor could limit itself to IPA and management activities. The prototype was to be Phy-Cor's joint venture with the New York and Presbyterian Hospitals Care Network, which would establish IPAs at community institutions affiliated with the Cornell and Columbia University hospitals in New York City, northern New Jersey, and southern Connecticut. All this was favorably evaluated by the financial community, which rewarded PhyCor with share prices consistently above $30 and the highest price to earnings ratio in the industry.

FPA MEDICAL MANAGEMENT

FPA Medical Management grew out of a primary care medical group in California, made its initial public offering in 1994, and then moved to buy IPAs in Arizona, Texas, and New Jersey.[8] It contrasted with PhyCor in avoiding multispecialty clinics and the purchase of physician practices. FPA believed that doctors would work longer hours and be more sensitive to patient preferences if they continued to own their practices than if they were brought together as employees in larger clinics. FPA could help the physicians retain their independence by negotiating and managing HMO contracts on their behalf. Access to contracts was a strong concern for physicians in markets newly exposed to managed care, since HMOs initially developed tightly structured networks that excluded many physicians and included others only after extracting substantial fee discounts. FPA's focus was on utilization management and tight control over specialty referrals, believing strongly in the role of the primary care physician as gatekeeper to the health care system as a whole. It acquired Sterling Healthcare, a PPM firm focused on hospital staffing, in recognition of the parallel role of emergency room physicians as gatekeepers to hospital admission in many circumstances.

FPA required broad geographic breadth and significant market depth in order to control specialty costs and retain primary care physician allegiance to its IPAs. Local market penetration was important to achieve volume discounts from specialists, hospitals, nursing homes, and ancillary vendors. The commitment of primary care physicians, many of whom belonged to multiple, competing IPAs, would be strengthened to the extent FPA attracted more health plans and patients. Geographic breadth was important to make FPA a desirable partner for the geographically diversified health plans. Many HMOs were interested in reducing the time and money required to develop networks of individual

physicians in each community and were willing to outsource those functions to PPM firms large enough to handle broad regions under a single
contract. FPA purchased captive IPAs from several health plans as a
means of establishing national contracts and of growing into new markets. Diverging from its historical preference for IPA structures, FPA
purchased the primary care clinics serving 70,000 members of the
PCA health plan in Florida, leading to a relationship with the Humana
health plan that subsequently acquired PCA. It acquired the IPAs and
staff clinics serving 200,000 patients of Foundation Health in California, Arizona, and Florida, which led to a national contract with the
health plan that formed when Foundation Health merged with Health
Systems International. FPA soon signed national capitation contracts
with other major health plans, including Aetna U.S. HealthCare and
PacifiCare.

Entry by a PPM firm into a new market clearly was easiest when it
could purchase an established medical group as the anchor for further
practice consolidation. But many parts of the nation, and especially the
northeast, lacked indigenous physician organizations, forcing the PPM
firms to build off small foundations or launch completely new groups.
The experiences of FPA in New Jersey, a state with large hospital systems
and small physician practices, highlighted the challenges posed to corporate physician entities as they moved into these uncharted waters.
Through the 1980s and into the 1990s New Jersey had lagged behind
most urban states in managed care penetration. Capitation payment and
utilization management were embryonic, health insurers contracted with
individual physicians rather than with physician groups, and hospitals
were purchasing physician practices in order to keep their beds full. FPA
decided to enter the mid-Atlantic marketplace in order to demonstrate
to Wall Street analysts that its model of IPA capitation and delegation was
replicable outside the California context. It developed two IPAs in New
Jersey, which by 1997 had 600 primary care physicians and 28,000 enrollees from the Oxford, United, NYLCare, and Blue Cross HMOs. Each
IPA had a board of directors and medical management committee composed of practicing primary care physicians and FPA staff. Specialty physicians contracted as individuals with the PPM firm rather than belong
to the IPA, and did not play a major role in governance.

Some HMOs in New Jersey were reluctant to delegate to the IPAs responsibility for utilization management, physician credentialing, and
claims payment. They were willing to capitate medical groups for professional and hospital services, albeit with mental health and pharmacy

carve-outs, but were unsure whether physician organizations were the proper candidates to manage the process of care. Medical groups in New Jersey lacked a tradition of responsibility for utilization management, which had been imposed from outside by health plans. This contrasted with managed care in California, where financial capitation and clinical delegation went hand in hand. FPA was unwilling to contract with health plans that would not work toward delegation of these functions. It conducted a more stringent review process than most health plans, requiring authorization for nonemergency specialty referrals as well as for hospitalizations. It developed its own hospitalist teams to coordinate medicine, surgery, and specialty procedures at major facilities. In 1997 FPA acquired the HealthPartners PPM firm, which served 100,000 HMO patients in New York and Connecticut and had previously been owned by the Oxford and WellPoint health plans. After consolidating its New Jersey, New York, and Connecticut IPAs, FPA had the largest prepaid physician organization in the tristate New York area and appeared poised to expand rapidly into the most populous region of the nation. Wall Street was enthusiastic, and in October 1997 FPA's stock price peaked at $40.

MEDPARTNERS

MedPartners had been founded by executives from HealthSouth, the nation's largest chain of rehabilitation hospitals and ambulatory surgery centers, with an initial focus on single-specialty practices. What it lacked by way of expertise in capitated care, MedPartners offset by expertise in capital finance. In this way it was the complementary opposite of Mullikin Medical Centers, which led the California market in capitation contracting but had struggled to achieve profitability and grow beyond its home state.[9] Mullikin had engaged an investment banking firm to assess the possibilities of a public stock offering but then mitigated the risks of launching into the financial markets by merging with MedPartners. At the time Mullikin had 360,000 patients in medical groups and IPAs in Los Angeles, San Francisco, and Portland, Oregon. Now armed with publicly traded MedPartners stock, Mullikin could move rapidly to consolidate its home market. In 1996 MedPartners acquired Pacific Physician Services, extending the Mullikin strength in central Los Angeles into inland areas and doubling the number of patients served. Six months later MedPartners acquired Caremark International, a diversified health services firm whose PPM division owned multispecialty medical groups in several metropolitan areas. Caremark owned the Friendly Hills Health-

Care Network, one of the pioneering physician organizations in Orange County, and had recently added the staff clinics from CIGNA Health-Care, for a total of 400,000 patients in southern California. MedPartners went on to assimilate Talbert Medical Management, the former staff-model component of FHP International, which had 270,000 patients in California and nearby states, plus a variety of smaller IPAs and medical groups. By the end of 1997 MedPartners served 1.2 million HMO patients in Los Angeles, employing or contracting with 15 percent of the physicians in one of the largest health care markets in the nation.

MedPartners was much more than a regional powerhouse in southern California. It had taken advantage of a window of opportunity to consolidate that market but understood Wall Street's preference for geographic and product diversification. Through the Caremark merger MedPartners came to acquire Kelsey-Seybold, Oklahoma City, North Suburban, and other multispecialty clinics in major cities such as Houston and Chicago. MedPartners absorbed 47 primary care clinics and 6 IPAs formerly owned by Aetna U.S. HealthCare, laying the foundation for the nation's first multiyear, multimarket contract between a health plan and a physician organization. Similar expansions were achieved by purchasing staff clinics from Prudential HealthCare in Houston and Memphis and from Massachusetts Blue Cross in Boston and Springfield. Through Pacific Physician Services, MedPartners had acquired Team-Health, a subsidiary focused on contracted physician services for hospital emergency rooms and surgical services. Acquisition of the InPhyNet physician practice management firm in 1997 greatly expanded Med-Partner's hospital physician contracting as well as bringing in 116,000 capitated patients in Florida. MedPartners inherited the nation's largest independent pharmacy benefit management company and several disease management programs, legacies of Caremark's origins in the pharmaceutical and medical supply industries. By the end of 1997 MedPartners was affiliated with 3,385 clinic physicians and 7,482 IPA physicians in 40 states, serving 2.1 million HMO patients plus numerous fee-for-service patients. The stock price for the nation's largest publicly held physician organization peaked at $32.

THE CHALLENGE

The meteoric rise of PhyCor, FPA, and MedPartners masked serious structural problems within the PPM industry. These firms were bedeviled by the same incentive and governance problems as smaller physician organizations, now compounded by aggregation. The amalgamation of multiple groups and IPAs within one market created potentially serious conflicts over leadership, employment security, referral patterns, and brand names. Expansion into distant geographic markets embroiled the PPM firms in new clinical practice styles, novel regulatory and economic contexts, skeptical consumer and provider attitudes toward managed care, and ambivalent health plan attitudes toward physician organization. Pressure to sustain their rapid rates of growth drove the firms to pay high prices for money-losing medical groups and to accept low capitation rates in exchange for higher HMO patient volume. As they grew larger and more diversified, physician organizations found themselves experiencing the diseconomies of scale and scope.

The Achilles' heel of vertical integration between health care insurers and providers had been the attenuation of incentives for medical groups and individual physicians. PPM firms focused exclusively on physician services in the hope of retaining physician culture and commitment, but often found themselves perceived as merely one more large corporate entity. The firms struggled against the decline of effort and entrepreneurship that occurred when physicians switched from being owners to employees, but with only limited success. Joint governance, profit sharing, stock options, and performance-based compensation swam upstream against a current of apathy and alienation that threatened to grow stronger with each new merger and acquisition. Many local clinic and IPA leaders used the PPM affiliation as the moment to exit the organization, cashing out their shares for early retirement or the pursuit of other business opportunities.

Rapid geographic expansion brought ever greater differences in practice styles and attitudes toward managed care inside the PPM organization. Some physicians were excited about the possibilities for a re-engineering of medicine in favor of preventive and primary care, chronic disease management, and clinical coordination. But others wanted the system to change as little as possible, and felt betrayed if the PPM firm did not embrace stasis as a guiding principle. Partners in multispecialty clinics quickly forgot the money they were paid for their ownership shares and focused on the management fees imposed by their new corporate parent. Junior physicians with only small ownership shares and new physicians hired after the transaction received little from the buyout but resented the PPM firm's share of what they considered their surplus. PPM firms found themselves in the unenviable position of being the bearer of bad tidings concerning the economic realities of managed care. Most physicians looked back to double digit rates of health care cost inflation in the 1980s as the golden era of rising personal incomes and unconstrained practice styles. They viewed health plans as the cause of their problems, missing the deeper change in willingness to pay by taxpayers and employers, and often joined the PPM firms in the hopes of turning back the clock. It soon became easy for the PPMs themselves to be viewed as the source of the managed care problem, since they were the ones managing utilization patterns, cutting specialist fees, and imposing drug formularies. Clinical protocols could be interpreted as cookbook medicine imposed by a distant corporation lacking in sensitivity to local practice patterns.

The PPM firms became the victims of their own initial success. They had trumpeted to the investor community the potential gains from consolidating physician services, emphasizing the doctor's role as decision maker for a trillion-dollar industry. Investment bankers, mutual funds, pension plans, and individual investors had responded with enthusiasm, bidding up share prices in expectation of continued growth in physician affiliations and patient revenues. The ratio of stock market price to annual PPM earnings soared past 40, twice the average for all industry stocks, in reflection of investor anticipation of 40 percent annual growth rates.

High share prices provided PPM firms with a valuable currency with which to finance mergers and acquisitions, but also placed them under strong pressure to achieve their growth targets. This growth imperative created several serious problems. The PPM firms engaged in a bidding contest among themselves and with PHOs for the acquisition of particular medical groups, driving up their capital costs and making it difficult to achieve a reasonable return on investment. Indeed, the firms often had to cut costs at their newly acquired clinics rather than make good on promises to upgrade facilities and information systems. In order to continue their rate of affiliations, PPM firms were forced to acquire clinics and IPAs that were losing money. The fastest growing firms acquired medical groups that were losing money the fastest. While some losses could be stanched by better management, many were due to structural problems that would only be reversed slowly, if at all. Finally, the need to continue growing their revenue stream induced many PPM firms to accept low capitation rates from health plans in exchange for high patient volume. Financial analysts focused their attention on total revenue but lacked market-level benchmarks to interpret the adequacy of the capitation rates per enrollee. And needless to say, access to bottom-dollar payment rates was not what the physicians thought they would be getting by affiliating their practices with a PPM firm.

THE CRUCIBLE

MedPartners's rapid growth had enabled it to take advantage of numerous market opportunities but had exposed it to serious risks of overexpansion and debt. Many of the medical groups that sought PPM suitors were in difficult financial circumstances, caught between declining practice revenues and increasing practice costs. MedPartners suffered from the winner's curse, having outbid rival PPM firms to acquire the money-losing staff-model clinics of CIGNA, FHP, Aetna, and Prudential. Consolidation was most difficult in the Los Angeles market where acquisition had been most successful. MedPartners was burdened with overlapping clinics, managers, and brand names as it struggled to coordinate Mullikin Medical Centers, Friendly Hills HealthCare Network, Talbert Medical Management, Pacific Physician Services, Healthsource Medical Group, Memorial IPA, and numerous smaller groups and IPAs. Wall Street had watched the rapid expansion with caution, applauding new acquisitions but fretting over the firm's ability to integrate. As 1997 drew to a close, senior management at MedPartners came to believe that the value of the firm had peaked and that it was the moment to exit. They negotiated the sale of the firm to PhyCor for $8 billion in stock and assumption of outstanding debt.

The announcement of the PhyCor-MedPartners deal rocked the industry, since it would create a mega-company with 7,165 employed physicians, 25,282 contracting physicians, 3.3 million capitated HMO patients, several million fee-for-service patients, and annual revenues of $8.4 billion.[10] The financial markets clearly thought things had gone too far, too fast. Both PhyCor and MedPartners saw their stock prices fall by 20 percent in the days after the announcement. The PhyCor shareholders were especially concerned lest their conservatively managed company inherit a quite different set of services from an executive team that thought now was the time to get out. After two months of close examination, PhyCor management agreed with the investment analysts and pulled out of the deal. The vote of no-confidence by its erstwhile suitor could not help but damage MedPartners's image in the financial markets. The damage turned into a stampede away from its stock, however, when MedPartners was forced to announce significant losses in its California operations, illustrating the difficulties in integrating its diverse acquisitions. The MedPartners stock, which had been trading at $26 at the time of the PhyCor announcement, had fallen to a low of $2 a year later. Senior executives left the company, turnover among middle management accelerated, and the organization announced layoffs of several hundred physicians and support staff. The writing was clearly legible on the wall. No one had faith that MedPartners would recover, not the investors, not the management, and not the physicians. In November 1998 the firm announced it would be divesting all its physician units, including the multispecialty clinics, IPAs, and hospital staffing division, and refocusing on its profitable pharmaceutical services.

The difficulties confronting efforts to manage multiple medical specialties in a context of declining insurance revenues were exemplified by the PhyCor clinics in Fort Smith, Arkansas and Jacksonville, Florida.[11] The 150 physicians of the Holt-Krock Clinic in Fort Smith affiliated with PhyCor just prior to a decline in revenues as governmental and private insurers flexed their muscles. This revenue decline was accompanied by a major one-time expense in computer systems upgrading, forcing a significant decline in physician salaries. In 1997 the doctors declared that the affiliation was no longer worth the 15 percent of clinic profits that PhyCor extracted, and demanded that the corporation sell them back their clinic at a lower price than it paid for it. The local hospital recruited away many of the Holt-Krock specialists, buying out their agreements with PhyCor. The group remained intact, albeit substantially smaller than at the time of affiliation, and struggled to rebuild its relationship with the hospital where it accounted for the majority of patient admissions.

A quite different but equally difficult set of problems faced PhyCor in Jacksonville, where it had built the First Coast Medical Group from a variety of smaller practices. The Jacksonville initiative was one of several around the nation where PhyCor sought to accelerate the formation of multispecialty clinics by purchasing and consolidating formerly independent and competing small practices. But the physicians did not think of themselves as members of a unified organization, skipped meetings, referred patients to outside doctors rather than to each other, and neglected to use the group's own clinical technologies in preference over outside vendors. The local hospital competed for the affiliation of the First Coast doctors and took a hard negotiating position against the group on rates for inpatient and outpatient services. At its peak the Jacksonville group had 140 physicians. In its first year it declined to 80 and then in June of 1998 collapsed to 30. PhyCor was forced to write off its investment in Jacksonville and similar fragmented markets.

FPA was to experience the greatest difficulties, leading to complete bankruptcy, since it had relied even more heavily than MedPartners on growth through acquisition of HMO clinics and networks. FPA had paid top dollar for money-losing organizations in Sacramento, California and Tucson, Arizona, two of the most competitive markets in the nation, and had inherited physicians disenchanted after multiple ownership transitions. The Foundation Health Medical Group in Sacramento had been built without regard to cost by the parent HMO, installed in deluxe clinic settings, and then subsidized in competition with Kaiser, the Sutter hospital system, and the Hill Physicians IPA. After divesting the medical group and its related IPAs, the HMO limited the subsidies and FPA was forced to engage in stringent cost controls. The PPM firm slowed and finally simply stopped paying claims submitted by referral specialists. The situation was even more difficult in Tucson, where the Thomas-Davis multispecialty clinic had sold itself to a staff-model HMO before being divested and acquired by FPA. Many of the doctors came to see the PPM as just another profit-seeking corporate employer and themselves as just another set of exploited workers. They sought union representation and embroiled the PPM firm in an acrimonious dispute before the National Labor Relations Board.[12]

FPA sustained its financial balancing act through the last half of 1997, as it absorbed 23 Humana HMO staff clinics serving 90,000 patients in Illinois, Missouri, and Florida as well as the Orange Coast IPA serving 120,000 HMO patients in California, reaching a total of 1.4 million capitated enrollees. Its financial and operational difficulties received a full airing in 1998, however, as the company was forced to report major losses and endure a gut-wrenching stock price collapse. By March the share price was below $20, down from over $40 the previous October, and by June was below $1. In July FPA filed for bankruptcy, unable to meet interest payments on its bank loans and corporate bonds. Many HMOs terminated their contracts with the firm's IPAs, shifting patients to other physician organizations or managing the care themselves. Large FPA enrollments in New York, California, and elsewhere disappeared overnight. Some FPA clinics were purchased by competitors such as MedPartners in Dallas, Catholic Healthcare West in Sacramento, and the St. Jude Heritage Health Foundation in southern California. Some of the other clinics, such as the Thomas-Davis Medical Group, were closed outright. The firm announced it was refocusing on a much-reduced core of markets in anticipation of reemerging from bankruptcy. It was hampered by waves of adverse publicity and shareholder litigation, which only grew worse when FPA's physician executives awarded themselves multi-million-dollar raises and bonuses while the bankruptcy court protected them from claims by unpaid doctors. This was physician organization at its nadir.

GEOGRAPHIC AND PRODUCT FOCUS

The reach of the PPM firms clearly had exceeded their grasp. By the end of the decade the industry was prostrate, with the enterprises distressed, the investors disillusioned, and the physicians disgruntled. The collapse in share prices had afflicted almost every firm, leading to a 75 percent decline in the market capitalization for the industry as a whole. The environmental conditions that had spawned the PPM firms, however, continued to make increasingly strong demands for economic accountability. Governmental programs, employers, and individual consumers resisted increases in prices and premiums while insisting on access to costly new drugs and devices. Physician organizations needed to achieve economies of scale in administrative services, vendor contracting, and capitation risk spreading and economies of scope in primary, specialty, and hospital services. Capital investments were needed to transform data-poor practices into information-rich networks. If the PPM firms were to play any continuing role, however, they would need to refocus the operational strategies and reinterpret the financial assumptions that had led to their debacle.

The immediate imperative facing PPM firms was to recognize the limited economies of scope in physician services. In the long term the greatest gains will derive from the identification, codification, and transfer of best practices from leading to lagging medical groups. In the short term, however, the most important work is to be done locally, within individual communities rather than across multiple markets. Most of the benefits from consolidating administrative functions, sharing information systems, and standardizing methods of utilization management occur among group practices and IPAs that are geographically proximate to one another. Savings from volume discounting of supplies, outside specialty referrals, ambulatory surgery, and inpatient rates accrue only to organizations with concentrated local scale. Health plans make no major rate concessions in one market due to a PPM firm's penetration in another. The attempts by the PPM firms to consolidate medical groups and IPAs in distinct markets generated only modest benefits over what those groups could obtain by themselves. Yet multimarket consolidation introduced taller administrative hierarchies, competing political agendas, and divergent clinical cultures into young and fragile physician organizations.

Attempts by the leading PPM firms to coordinate the full spectrum of physician services and, in some cases, to diversify into hospital staffing, clinical trials, and more remote services embroiled them in activities where they lacked comparative advantage over the incumbent providers. Multiproduct diversification invariably sacrifices scale and focus, compared to what an equivalent expenditure of effort could achieve in one targeted domain, and is only profitable if significant economies of scope are present. As proven by the multispecialty clinics and IPAs outside the PPM context, significant advantages are to be gained by physician organizations that can coordinate primary care and specialty services, but the challenges of accomplishing this are immense. Primary care is a high volume, low margin business whose greatest financial asset derives from its influence over where patients are referred for specialty services. Specialty care is a low volume and high margin business that is dependent on referrals but is able to leverage referral volume into revenue through discretionary control over testing and procedures. Individual specialties often are quite distinct from one another. The business of oncology derives from leveraging the clinician's prescribing power over expensive drugs, while that of radiology revolves around capacity utilization of expensive machines and that of cosmetic surgery depends on direct consumer marketing and avoidance of managed care. The technology, cultures, and lifestyles of primary and specialty care are quite distinct, opening the door to invidious comparison and conflict for multispecialty organizations.

Some PPM firms responded to these difficulties by devoting their efforts to a single specialty, technology, or type of facility. Niche players proliferated with a dedication to oncology, orthopedics, or cardiology, to women's health or workers' compensation, to clinical trials or mental health. These firms could focus on the skills needed by a single clinical area without diffusing their energies over the whole of medicine. The development of clinical guidelines and protocols could take place within rather than across specialties. Most patients suffering from cancer do not need to see a cardiologist and most heart patients never visit an oncologist. Single-specialty firms could apply to relations with pri-

mary care physicians the logic that multispecialty firms applied to relations with hospitals. Just as the multispecialty firms preferred to coordinate with hospitals through contract rather than joint ownership, the
single-specialty firms preferred to coordinate with primary care through
contracts rather than through joint employment. Consolidation occurred
in the specialty PPM sector, but within rather than across particular
specialties.

A NEW CAPITAL STRATEGY

The most obvious contribution of the PPM firms was a ready supply of
equity capital. Health care does require capital, but investments need to
be made over time rather than all at once lest the rate of change in organization and technology outpace change in cultures and practice styles.
Health care is highly dependent on the motivation of individual physicians, lending itself only with difficulty and delay to the standardization
of process and product. The problems encountered by firms consolidating hospital chains and health plans pale in comparison to the challenge
facing those who would consolidate the fiercely independent small-busi-
ness community called the medical profession. The bridge loans, growth
funds, and operational investments in the physician services industry
need to be evaluated in light of the incentive distortions and diseconomies of scale they have created.

The use of Wall Street capital to buy out medical group liabilities to
their senior partners, conceptualized as a necessary step toward consolidation, proved to be an unmitigated disaster. The purchase of multispecialty clinics tended to enrich a subset of physician leaders who took
the money and left for retirement or other opportunities. Their exit deprived the local organization of the individuals with the greatest expertise in administering the day-to-day aspects of a clinical enterprise, in
managing financial risk and health care utilization, and in nurturing a
culture of cooperation among the physician membership. The dispari-
ties in payment between the senior and the junior partners inevitably
created resentments that were aggravated over time as the junior physicians realized that they would be called on to pay back through reduced
earnings the investors who funded the original buyout. The PPM firms
thus favored the senior physicians who were planning to leave and alienated the junior physicians with whom they would need to work. Yet the
true value of a medical group, and even more so of an IPA, is the accu-
mulated expertise and cultural continuity built up over many years. In

accounting terms this value is represented by the large share of total purchase price booked as goodwill, meaning the difference between price and the value of tangible physical assets. The initial overvaluation and subsequent erosion of this expertise was highlighted in the accelerated write-offs of goodwill by PPM accountants, who thereby acknowledged they would never get back what they had paid. In its new sober mood the industry developed a new purchase and accounting standard, which offered substantially lower prices to medical groups but then charged them commensurably lower management fees and amortized the value of the assets over much shorter time frames. This rebalancing of the capital partnership favored the junior over the senior partners and lightened the burden of intangible and often speculative assets on the firms' financial statements. If it cooled the ardor of senior partners to cash out on their organizations, all to the better.

The heroic era of PPM mergers and acquisitions came and went but caused little significant consolidation across markets. It culminated with an industry-wide consensus that local focus is essential and even national organizations must evaluate individual markets on a stand-alone basis. In retrospect the phenomenal rise of MedPartners and FPA were due to the sudden disillusionment among health insurance plans with the strategy of vertical integration, which led to the dumping onto the market of numerous HMO clinics and captive IPAs. The PPM firms grew so fast because so much HMO property was for sale. PhyCor prudently abstained from that feeding frenzy, recognizing the employed HMO physicians as often unmotivated and the captive IPAs as often unmanaged. Yet it found itself to be the capital partner for clinics whose democratic cultures impeded painful adjustments to constrained managed care revenues. As the supply of independent clinics diminished, PhyCor was pushed by its growth imperative to venture onto dangerous terrain, amalgamating medical groups from previously independent practices and creating joint ventures with previously competitive hospital systems. The effort to create "clinics without walls" was a failure and the joint ventures embroiled PhyCor in Byzantine hospital politics. Soon the PPM industry was in accord that all strategies going forward would be designed to reduce capital requirements.

THE WHIRLWIND

The crash in stock prices probably was inevitable given the unbalanced and unbounded growth of the PPM firms. Some positive impacts from the cataclysm were to be noted, as the weaker firms exited and the leading firms refocused on their core markets and service lines. Initial public offerings by new firms and secondary stock offerings by established firms ceased for a time, allowing the whole industry to cool off and reassess its strategies. Physicians were forced to acknowledge their status as highly skilled workers rather than as owners of some intangible asset for which unseen investors would pay huge sums. Senior partners and medical directors reinterpreted their careers as contributing to the creation of organizations that were not easily converted into cash and luxury resort condominiums. Investors were forced to recognize the difficulty in achieving above-average returns in an industry caught between constrained managed care revenues and unconstrained consumer expectations.

But the PPM firestorm did major and lasting damage to physician organization. Many once prominent medical groups and IPAs were devastated by the loss of original leadership, shotgun weddings with adjacent but incompatible groups, and subsequent turmoil from collapsing valuations and disinvestment. Many of the clinics and IPAs once owned by FPA simply vanished. MedPartners lost almost all its executive leadership and much of its local leadership, especially in its flagship California operations, before abandoning the industry altogether. The firms were besieged by litigation from shareholders accusing them of fraudulently concealing financial difficulties in order to sell stock and from physicians accusing them of fraudulently concealing information in order to buy practices. The chaos of PPM bankruptcy and near-bankruptcy drove health plans to reassess their willingness to capitate physician organizations and delegate to them the clinical responsibility for coordinating care, giving new life to arms-length utilization review and micromanagement of physician practices. State and federal regulatory agencies, corporate purchasers, and quality accreditation entities were forced to ask themselves whether physicians and physician organizations were capable of assuming a leading role in the emerging health care system. Where once the policy discussion centered on how to get the doctor back in charge of medicine, it now shifted to how to regulate physician organizations.

The most immediate beneficiary of the PPM troubles were the physician-hospital organizations, which lost their most feared competitors. PHOs pursue a strategy of product diversification but geographic focus, combining physician and hospital services while concentrating their efforts in one market. Geographic focus potentially offers lower costs through economic efficiency and higher revenues through monopoly power. Most important in the short term, PHOs offer organizational stability and consumer reputation to a physician sector in desperate need of both. Of course PHOs come with their own problems. Many hospital systems are nonprofit conglomerates all too willing to sacrifice initiative in the quest for stability, incentive in the quest for control, and entrepreneurship in the quest of harmony. Yet the turbulent events of the decade highlight the importance of the PHO virtues and the dangers of straying too far afield. The physician practice management firms had no lack of initiative, incentive, and entrepreneurship. With these they had sowed the wind but then had reaped the whirlwind.

CHAPTER 8

Physician-Hospital Organization

The hospital historically has contested with the physician for the role of coordinating medical care. The physician always held the clinical skills and the patient's trust, but lacked financial resources, managerial capabilities, and a strategic orientation. Over the course of the twentieth century hospitals have nurtured these strengths and achieved growing recognition from insurers, regulators, and purchasers as the locus of organization in this ever larger and more complex industry. Authority within the traditional hospital was split between the administration and the medical staff, and in many ways the physicians dominated the institution which observers labeled the doctor's workshop. But the leading hospitals have sustained a long-term commitment to their goals. They have merged with other hospitals and acquired nonhospital services such as ambulatory surgery, subacute care, and home health, building horizontally and vertically integrated chains that increasingly dominate regional markets. The pioneers have reconceptualized themselves from being facilities for acute inpatient care to being hubs of integrated delivery systems. An increasing number embrace global capitation and delegation of responsibility for managing care as steps toward population-based health care. All recognize that effective coordination with physicians will be the capstone of their new health care system, the culmination of a long transformation.

Many forms of organization are to be found that unify in some manner the two key pieces of the health care system. For present purposes the generic term Physician-Hospital Organization (PHO) will suffice. Even the most traditional hospital has a medical staff organization with committees and part-time medical directors. Resistance from the medical profession, as embodied most clearly in the corporate practice of medicine statutes, limited further incursion of institutional authority, and particularly hospital employment of facility-based specialists such as radiologists, anesthesiologists, and pathologists. The advent of managed care has given new impetus to integration, most commonly through loosely structured organizations that perform contracting functions but leave the physicians otherwise independent. These affiliations sometimes tighten down into a subset of the medical staff or into IPAs dominated by primary care physicians. The most serious hospital systems take the next step and begin to purchase physician practices and medical groups, circumventing the corporate practice statutes through nonprofit medical foundations and other legal fictions. These integrated delivery systems are positioned to accept an ever greater slice of the health insurance premium, moving from fee-for-service to global capitation and ultimately, perhaps, to full appropriation through ownership of a health insurance plan. Finally, as hospitals merge with one another to create regional chains and acquire multiple medical groups, the PHO comes to resemble a holding company with numerous distinct subsidiaries. We witness the advent of the health care corporate conglomerate.

CONTRIBUTIONS TO PHYSICIAN ORGANIZATION

The PHO offers itself as the financial, operational, and strategic partner to the medical group. Most hospitals begin with the premise that the physician community is inefficiently fragmented and inadequately coordinated with the other components of the health care system. Historically, hospital trustees and managers have used exhortation to advance their case for closer linkages, but through the PHO are turning to financial capital. Hospitals are purchasing physician practices, multispecialty clinics, and IPAs where they exist and are forming new groups where they do not. Capital is needed to buy out the senior partners, merge in new physicians and groups, upgrade clinic facilities and information systems, and begin improving practice patterns. Nonprofit hospital systems lack access to the stock market but obtain capital through tax-exempt bonds and through retained earnings from inpatient care and ancillary services. Even after two decades of policy efforts to constrain cost inflation, many hospitals enjoy strong profit margins on their Medicare and private insurance business. For-profit hospital systems have the advantage of publicly traded stock as a capital source, but are subject to the quarterly oversight and fickle favor of the investment community.

The most discussed contribution of the PHO to the practice of medicine lies in the domain of incentive alignment. Unified ownership between physician practices and hospital facilities creates a single organization, a single mission, and a single bottom line. PHOs can help physicians succeed under the financial stresses of capitation payment by cooperating rather than contesting efforts to substitute outpatient for inpatient care, to conservatively rather than aggressively promote testing and procedures, to install hospitalist teams that relieve the primary care physician of inpatient duties, and to speed patient discharge to subacute or home health care. The alignment of financial incentives is important to support the joint development of clinical protocols that shift patterns of utilization and hence patterns of payment. Unified ownership positions the physicians to accept capitation for both inpatient and outpatient services. While it certainly is possible for a medical group to accept global capitation by itself and then subcontract with competing hospitals, this food chain approach to hospital relationships places the physicians under great business risk if the hospitals see it in their interest to increase revenues rather than decrease costs.

The most important contribution of the PHOs to physician practice stems not from the financial capital or the day-to-day operational efficiencies they offer, but, rather, from their potential to instill a long-term strategic orientation to the system. Most medical groups and individual physicians lack strategic vision but live hand-to-mouth on whatever revenues they can seize in the moment. Business leadership and vision is sorely lacking in the profession and explains the paucity of really successful medical groups. Hospital organizations, by their very scale and complexity, must possess the rudiments of strategy, and the leading systems have much to offer to their affiliated physicians. At the most elementary level, PHO strategy involves the aggregation of individual physicians into multispecialty groups or IPAs that can accept capitation contracts, perform utilization management, and develop the data necessary for quality accountability. At a more advanced level, the PHO can bring its physician and hospital components together to define their local market, their desired role in that market, the initiatives necessary to achieve market dominance, the health plan partners they need to finance their endeavors, and the political strategies they need to coexist with the regulatory institutions.

CONTRIBUTIONS TO HOSPITAL ORGANIZATION

The contributions by the PHO to the hospital organization also may be conceptualized in terms of financial, operational, and strategic partnerships, though in ways quite different from the manner in which the integrated entity helps the physicians. The PHO's medical group ideally is the key to stable financial revenues for the hospital, fosters quality improvement throughout the system, and furthers the strategic transition of the hospital from acute inpatient services to the broader continuum of care.[1]

The hospital is a business with high fixed and low marginal costs for whom the incremental patient admission is very valuable. Hospitals are fundamentally dependent on their affiliated physicians for patients and hence for revenue, yet historically have found it difficult to cement their relationships. The duplication of capacity and technology caused by the medical arms race bears eloquent testimony to the complexity of assuring admissions during the fee-for-service era. The acquisition of physician practices is merely another facet of this effort, the acquisition of a future stream of hospital admissions. It is sometimes considered unethical or even illegal to pay a primary care physician to direct a patient admission toward a particular provider, but this channeling is the essence of the PHO. In the managed care era, hospital capacity utilization is driven increasingly by the structure of HMO contracts and, in particular, by the physician incentives to admit patients to less costly facilities. Large independent medical groups, such as those in California, were able to negotiate low payment rates to hospitals and thereby retain significant profits from capitation contracts. Purchase by the hospital of individual physician practices can forestall the development of independent medical groups, a matter of particular urgency in the context of PPM competitors intent on replicating the California squeeze on hospital revenues. Purchase by the hospital of existing physician organizations brings less immediate benefit, since the profit potentially available to the medical group will be embedded in the price at which they are willing to sell to the PHO. But these one-time costs can be amortized over the life of the organization, which in the eyes of many hospital trustees goes on in perpetuity.

The contribution by the PHO to the clinical efficiency and quality of the hospital, its subacute unit, ambulatory surgery suites, and home health agency parallels the organization's contribution to physician practice. Capitation finance and the ownership of ancillary services makes

the hospital responsible for a whole continuum of care that once lay outside its immediate purview. Under capitation, keeping hospital beds full
is no longer important if patients can be treated effectively in other settings. Medicare's prospective payment system creates an analogous imperative for the hospital to align incentives with the physicians who order tests and procedures for patients subsequent to admission and who
decide the date of discharge. The overall trend toward greater monitoring of medical processes and patient outcomes, with subsequent public
dissemination, intensifies the pressures on hospitals to foster cooperative
relationships and quality improvement initiatives with their physicians.[2]

Integration with physicians is an essential step in the transformation
of the hospital from a facility focused on acute inpatient care to a diversified organization coordinating services for a defined population of
patients. Hospital leaders have been frustrated by the impediments to
shifting from a narrow clinical to a broad public health mission. Most
determinants of health and disease occur in the community and the most
effective interventions lie in prevention and primary care. Yet by themselves hospitals respond to inadequate prenatal nutrition through neo-
natal intensive care, to childhood asthma through episodic admissions,
and to tobacco advertising through endstage chemotherapy. A shift in
strategy requires a shift in structure, with particular emphasis on the primary care physician. Capitation provides a financial basis, though not
the only one, for population-based medicine, and delegation by health
plans of utilization management provides the authority to control the
whole process of care. But only if the hospital embraces and is embraced
by the physicians will the potential be actualized. In their vision and mission statements many health care systems now are deleting the language
of hospitals, beds, and admissions while inserting the vocabulary of physicians, patients, and populations.

ST. JUDE HERITAGE HEALTH FOUNDATION

Orange County is arguably the most competitive managed care market
in the United States. Almost half the Medicare beneficiaries and two-
thirds of commercially insured residents are enrolled in HMOs that capitate medical groups for all physician and many hospital services.[3] Most
primary care physicians are affiliated with a large medical group or IPA.
The medical groups financed their growth internally through savings
from reduced inpatient utilization and prices, which exerted tremendous
pressures on the local hospital institutions. Orange County hardly seems

a propitious venue for a physician-hospital organization, yet spawned one of the largest multihospital, multiphysician systems in the nation. The St. Joseph Health System suffered through a difficult launch to its physician strategy but, by dint of sustained effort and the ill fortune of its competitors, was able to create an organization that so dominated the local market that health plans had to pay it higher prices to take on new enrollment rather than demand lower rates in exchange for this greater volume.[4]

In the early 1990s the Sisters of St. Joseph of Orange owned three prominent hospitals well distributed across the northern, central, and southern parts of the county but had no effective links to primary care physicians in an environment where contracts, patients, and revenues were shifting to capitated medical groups at the expense of solo practice and indemnity insurance. The St. Jude Medical Center in the northern part of the county was threatened by the Friendly Hills HealthCare Network, one of the largest and most innovative multispecialty clinics in California, which purchased its own hospital, flirted with a competing PHO, and then affiliated with the Caremark PPM as part of a conscious philosophical position that physicians should remain organizationally independent of hospital systems. When Caremark was acquired by Med-Partners in 1996, Friendly Hills joined forces with Mullikin Medical Centers, which also operated clinics and owned a hospital on the fringes of St. Jude's market. Then MedPartners announced a broad partnership with Tenet Healthcare, the system's primary hospital competitor. In the central portion of the county, St. Joseph Hospital invested heavily in the creation of a local IPA and primary care medical group only to see the physicians develop a management services organization and bring in venture capital funding with the explicit intention of developing a PPM firm of their own. Mission Hospital in southern Orange County faced the most serious hospital competition and was surrounded by highly entrepreneurial physician organizations such as the Bristol Park Medical Group, Monarch IPA, and Talbert Medical Management. The St. Joseph hospitals were well endowed in community reputation, philanthropic donations, and fee-for-service admissions, but the HMOs and their affiliated medical groups were preparing to extract their profits.

The St. Jude Heritage Health Foundation began inauspiciously in 1994 with the creation of a multispecialty medical group that had no HMO contracts in one of the most heavily penetrated managed care markets in the nation. It purchased a small local IPA and focused its efforts on increasing capitated business around the St. Jude hospital. By 1998 it had 68,000 HMO patients, split almost evenly between the medical group and the IPA, in addition to its fee-for-service and PPO patients. The St. Jude hospital breathed life into the Foundation by refusing to deal with nonaffiliated medical groups and IPAs, thereby using its community reputation to shift physicians and patients inside its physician network. Physicians joining the medical group or IPA agreed to admit all their patients to St. Jude rather than continuing to spread them across competing facilities.

In 1996 the Foundation acquired the Bristol Park Medical Group, which needed capital to continue growing and was attracted by a strategy of local market concentration rather than geographic market diversification. Technically the Foundation acquired Bristol Park's management services organization, with the physicians' professional corporation remaining independent but signing a long-term contractual agreement to provide clinical services. The acquisition immediately increased admissions at Mission and St. Joseph hospitals, since the medical group previously had used facilities owned by Tenet and other competitors. With financial support from the hospital system, Bristol Park opened eight new clinics and hired 40 new primary care physicians at sites up and down the Orange County coastline. It helped the Foundation negotiate the acquisition of the adjacent Yorba Park Medical Group, with 29 primary care physicians in three clinic sites. All the HMO contracts were consolidated from the medical groups to the Foundation, which by early 1998 covered 256,000 commercial and 22,000 Medicare HMO patients. The Foundation signed a single contract with each health plan for physician services covering all medical groups while the hospital system signed a single contract covering all three inpatient facilities. Most of the contracts were structured on a globally capitated and fully delegated basis, assigning all insurance risk and clinical responsibility to the system. The Foundation paid each medical group the same subcapitated rate, with total revenues for each group depending on the number of HMO enrollees who selected a primary care physician within the group.

The most sudden change of fortune occurred in the central part of the county, however, as the bankruptcy of FPA Medical Management brought financial ruin to the Orange Coast Management Services Organization, the Primary Care Doctors of California medical group, and their affiliated IPA. Orange Coast had the misfortune of being almost the last physician organization to affiliate with FPA before the firm's debts caught up with it and the whole PPM sector went into a tailspin. As the firm's bankruptcy became imminent, the HMOs terminated their contracts with FPA in Orange County and asked the St. Jude Foundation whether it would pick up the doctors and their patients. Virtually overnight the Foundation, which had very little IPA experience, gained 78,000 new patients and a broad IPA network around the St. Joseph hospital. A few months later, with the remaining FPA assets in bankruptcy court, the Foundation was able to purchase the primary care medical group, gaining another 52,000 capitated patients. A dozen of the group's physicians joined the Yorba Park Medical Group and the others decided to go back to solo or small-group practice under the IPA umbrella. The St. Jude Foundation therefore was able to pick up all the physicians and patients from the Orange Coast system at a fraction of the price it had tried unsuccessfully to buy them for a year earlier. The big losers, from a financial perspective, were the executives, venture capital partners, and physician shareholders who had been paid FPA stock that was worth $60 million at the time of the transaction but was worth zero 90 days later.[5]

By the end of 1998, therefore, the St. Joseph Health System and the St. Jude Foundation were in an admirable position, with three leading hospitals, four medical groups, and several overlapping IPAs providing services to 370,000 capitated and numerous fee-for-service patients. Its affiliated physicians now accounted for almost all admissions to the St. Jude and St. Joseph hospitals, which could refuse to deal with independent medical groups, and for a large share of admissions at Mission hospital. Its bargaining leverage with the health plans had grown substantially, since it could link negotiations for hospital, physician, and ancillary services and for HMO, PPO, and ancillary insurance products. When major health plans followed precedent in demanding rate cuts in exchange for the erstwhile FPA enrollment, the Foundation successfully countered by demanding rate increases. It faced some of the dilemmas of success, as the hospitals reached full utilization and could not find acceptable bed capacity to lease and as the Foundation worried about being able to handle the rising number of physicians seeking to shift over from the floundering MedPartners groups.

The St. Jude Heritage Health Foundation built, bought, or was given all the pieces needed for an integrated delivery system but then faced the very real challenge of integrating them. As the PPM firms had learned to their woe, growth in system capacity, utilization, and revenue is only a prelude to disaster unless it is accompanied by growth in profitability. In the very moment of achieving market dominance the Foundation experienced costs that outran its revenues and produced the worst financial year in its history. The most serious problems, ironically, stemmed from the jewel in its crown, the Bristol Park Medical Group. Flush with capital and encouragement from its hospital partners, Bristol Park had opened clinics and hired new physicians at a rate that far exceeded growth in new patient enrollment and visits. Excess capacity brought a flood of red ink since the doctors, their staffs, and the office leases needed to be paid even if the waiting rooms were not full. The Foundation felt itself obliged to narrow the traditionally large disadvantage in wages and fringe benefits suffered by employees in physician offices compared to hospital employees, which raised the operating costs of all the Bristol Park facilities. High wages and attractive benefits were key elements in the hospital's ongoing struggle to remain nonunion, whereas the primary care clinics faced no meaningful union challenge. The Foundation struggled to reduce the duplication of services between the medical group and the hospital, including human resources, marketing, physical therapy, laboratory services, claims payment, and utilization management.

Most worrisome of all was the effect of the Foundation affiliation on the productivity and entrepreneurial culture of the Bristol Park physicians. Bristol Park historically had shared the primary care physicians' skepticism of hospital dominance and the Foundation had felt the need to provide a safety net under physician earnings to convince them to go along with the sale. Income guarantees are notorious, however, for undermining the subsequent productivity of the physicians. The effects of the income guarantees were compounded by the newfound wealth of many Bristol Park physicians, who now wanted to work shorter hours and take longer vacations to enjoy their gains. In contrast to the concentrated ownership structure at some medical groups, where an inner circle of senior partners gets the lion's share of the buyout, most of the Bristol Park physicians were partners and obtained generous buyouts. To take up the slack the medical group was forced to hire new physicians who were unfamiliar with the broad scope of primary care practice pioneered at Bristol Park and were much more willing to refer challenging patients to outside specialists. Primary care medical groups always must struggle against a tendency for their physicians to rely on triage as the means to maintain large patient panels while doing few procedures themselves. Bristol Park's broad scope of primary care practice had been built up over many years but began to erode quickly. Outside specialty costs mushroomed. Changes in consumer expectations and HMO policies aggravated the problem, as patients increasing referred themselves directly to specialty consultation rather than relying on their primary care physician for services.

The St. Jude Heritage Health Foundation thus faced continuing challenges. It had acquired a broad base in primary care practices but increased clinic capacity before utilization, paid wage rates above the market norm, and undermined physician productivity through kindness and entrepreneurship through caution. The primary care medical groups that were profitable when independent began to lose money when brought into the system. For the first time the system needed to account for the value of the referrals gained by system specialists and hospitals to justify the primary care losses, and began to close clinics in outlying neighborhoods from whence it could not derive admissions. Some of these problem would decrease as the doctors and hospital managers served on enough joint committees to understand each other's needs, as rivalries attenuated and functions were regionalized, and as the hospitals leveraged access to fee-for-service patients to reduce the fees charged to the Foundation by the medical staff specialists. And over time a whole new configuration of economic forces could emerge. After a decade in which HMOs and primary care medical groups cooperated to squeeze revenues out of hospitals, a decade was dawning in which hospitals and medical groups would cooperate to squeeze higher revenues out of health plans.

MONTEFIORE MEDICAL CENTER

The densely urban and highly regulated New York environment is perhaps the antithesis of the sprawling suburban and aggressively competitive Orange County marketplace. New York historically has been a bastion of solo physician practice, fee-for-service reimbursement, and unmanaged health care utilization. University-affiliated institutions dominate the clinical and political landscape, combining federal subsidies, union jobs, and medical school faculties into an engine of specialty-driven, hospital-centered medicine. Competitive market entry by new hospitals historically has been limited by one of the nation's strongest certificate-of-need laws, for-profit hospitals have been outlawed, and until 1996 hospital rates for commercial insurers were directly regulated by state government.[6] Enrollment in HMOs was relatively high, but these plans developed very broad networks of physicians and hospitals, facilitated out-of-network referrals through point-of-service options, eschewed capitation in favor of fee-for-service, and made no serious effort to manage utilization. In Orange County these would be considered PPO insurers. HMO premiums were 17 percent higher than those in California, while rates of hospital utilization were 70 percent higher.[7] New York is an incubator of regulatory innovation, but hardly the natural environment for market-driven innovation in physician organization.

The physician practice management firms looked hungrily at the high revenues in the New York metropolitan area and established numerous beachheads on the periphery. But most of these initiatives were swept away in the industry's whirlwind of earnings disappointments, share price devaluations, and organizational retrenchments. If change in physician organization was to come to New York, the most likely sponsor would be the hospital systems, which were consolidating and linking with suburban institutions to combat rate discounting in the newly deregulated environment. Each of the major hospital systems sought to develop tighter linkages with its medical school faculty and with the voluntary physicians on their medical staffs. Some developed a third category, primary care physicians employed in ambulatory care clinics sprinkled throughout poor neighborhoods and increasingly in middle-class communities.

The most prominent hospital system in New York from the perspective of physician organization was the Montefiore Medical Center, a massive institution with two hospitals, two nursing homes, rehabilitation and psychiatric facilities, a large home health agency, and links to the Albert Einstein College of Medicine at Yeshiva University.[8] Montefiore had a distinguished history of social medicine, physician leadership, and commitment to prepaid, population-based health care.[9] The Montefiore Medical Group (MMG) was founded 50 years ago as one of the first prepaid group practices sponsored by the city of New York through the Health Insurance Plan (HIP) system. The hospital had created a network of ambulatory care clinics in response to the health needs and financial distress evident throughout the Bronx. The medical school and hospital sponsored one of the largest family practice residency programs in the nation.

The route from social medicine in the 1960s to physician-hospital organization in the 1990s was anything but direct. By the 1980s the early efforts at physician organization were in disarray, with the Montefiore Medical Group disaffiliated from HIP, the ambulatory care network struggling, the medical school hiring very few primary care faculty members, the family practice residents leaving the community after graduation, and an early IPA collapsing with the Maxicare HMO. Of greatest immediate concern to the hospital was the aging and shrinking of the voluntary medical staff, as younger physicians followed paying patients to the suburbs and abandoned the sick and the poor in the central city. In the latter part of the decade Montefiore made a renewed commitment to its medical group, building new clinics and hiring new doctors to bring primary care back into the Bronx. The MMG offices were located in the working-class and middle-class neighborhoods of the Bronx and in suburban Westchester county, remaining distinct from the ambulatory care network in the inner city. Their purpose was to generate admissions to the hospital and forestall the poaching of insured patients by institutions in Manhattan and Westchester. Initially they were reimbursed almost totally by fee-for-service insurance, but gradually the potential for capitation became evident as HMO enrollment surged in the region. Montefiore asked itself the inevitable question: how many capitated patients do we need to keep the hospital full?

A decade later the Montefiore PHO was broadly and deeply entrenched in its local market, containing a population of 1.8 million in the Bronx and southern Westchester. The Montefiore Medical Group, now merged with the ambulatory care network, had 31 clinics and 177 salaried physicians to serve the primary care needs of 140,000 patients, including 45,000 from Medicare and commercial HMOs, 30,000 from Medicaid HMOs, and the remainder from PPO and indemnity insurance. The clinics provided half a million patient visits per year and generated 10,000 of the hospital's 47,000 admissions. Specialty referrals went to the faculty practice group and to the hospital's voluntary staff. MMG and the other key components of the system, including the 720 specialists and 50 primary care physicians on the medical school faculty, the hospital's 350 active voluntary physicians, and the two hospitals, were brought under the umbrella of the Montefiore Integrated Provider Association (MIPA) for managed care purposes. MIPA contracted with almost every HMO on a globally capitated basis for primary, specialty, and hospital services after refusing to discount rates on a fee-for-service basis. The system was delegated authority for physician credentialing, claims payment, and utilization management, despite the legendary reluctance of New York carriers to outsource insurance risk and clinical responsibility.

The Montefiore PHO clearly was succeeding in achieving its initial goals. Ambulatory visits and hospital admissions were rising at Montefiore while falling elsewhere in New York. The system was well positioned to gain a lion's share of the local market's growth in HMO enrollment, with the most likely short-term gains stemming from the state's Medicaid program. MIPA established a contract management organization to perform HMO contracting, utilization management, claims payment, and data reporting. This was structured as a for-profit subsidiary to permit it to pursue management contracts with physician organizations throughout the region, to bring in outside capital investors, and potentially to become a publicly traded PPM firm. The contract management organization helped create the Montefiore North IPA in Westchester county and a mental health IPA to compete for carve-out contracts. It also explored possibilities farther afield. The lack of indigenous physician organization in the New York region created a vacuum of managed care expertise which the PPM firms had been unable to fill and which beckoned with the usual mix of risks and rewards. New York, New Jersey, and Connecticut were filled with sprawling IPAs that were specialty-dominated, paid fee-for-service, and espoused a political rather than business culture.

Despite its accomplishments and head start over competing hospital systems, the Montefiore PHO suffered from a variety of annoying and potentially serious ailments. Most obviously, the MMG clinics were hemorrhaging money. They were built with generous dimensions and attractive decor, staffed with highly paid unionized labor, and operated by salaried physicians who lacked strong incentives for productivity. They competed against independent physician practices squeezed into small offices with old equipment, nonunion staff, and doctors who knew that a penny saved was a penny earned. The system viewed them as loss leaders, an inherently money-losing activity that fulfilled a social mission and paid for themselves by feeding profitable referrals to the specialists and admissions to the hospital. The anticipated changes in physician culture and practice patterns were slow in coming due to lack of strong pressure from the HMOs or competitive rivalry from other medical groups. While MIPA was capitated for all clinical services, the individual system units did not face consistent incentives. The MMG clinics were capitated solely for primary care services, and perceived no benefit from reducing referrals and admissions. The specialist physicians in the faculty practice group and the hospital voluntary staff, on the other hand, were paid fee-for-service and hence perceived direct benefits from high primary care referrals. The manner in which the global capitation was allocated to each subunit was sufficiently arcane as to incite skepticism over the validity of subunit profit and loss statistics.

The system was so large, diverse, and complex that no one participant could disentangle the impact of his or her actions on the financial
health of the whole. The plethora of teaching, research, patient care,
safety net, public health, full employment, and prestige goals impeded
a focus on any one measure of performance. The system was far enough
ahead of its rivals to escape survival imperatives yet not far enough
ahead to turn a real profit. While 50 percent of MMG revenues were capitated, prepayment accounted for less than 10 percent of total Montefiore system income, hardly enough to sustain executive attention.
Montefiore was blessed and damned by a health insurance industry that
promised everything to everybody and prevented the PHO from developing a tight network or strong utilization management. One-fifth of
MIPA's capitation revenues leaked out of the system through referrals to
specialists and hospitals in Westchester, Manhattan, or elsewhere in the
Bronx.

The system ultimately had to struggle with the wisdom of its whole
PHO strategy, and in particular with the contribution of its promising
but costly contract management organization. The organization and its
100 employees needed a population base of 70,000 commercial and
20,000 Medicare capitated patients, far more than what was immediately within its grasp, and the system as a whole was designed for
300,000 capitated enrollees. The operational costs of the contract organization could be spread over a wider base most easily by selling services
to physician organizations outside the hospital service area, but then
Montefiore would not gain incremental admissions. If it brought in outside capital investors it could recoup its initial outlay, but would lose
control of its subsidiary. If it limited outside contracting and investment,
it would cripple the management organization and reduce its potential
contribution to physician organization in the larger region. The system
leadership was disillusioned with both horizontal hospital mergers,
which had cost so much and produced so little for its competitors, and
with vertical integration as an end in itself. The acquisition of primary
care practices was only desirable in special geographic and organizational circumstances where the hospital could capture the specialty referrals and where local economic conditions were unattractive for independent physician practices. The Montefiore Medical Center, never shy
to trumpet its accomplishments, adopted a cautious approach to its
progeny and damned with faint praise those who would build a PHO in
a more conventional suburban environment.

THREE INTERPRETATIONS OF THE PHO

Physician-hospital organizations have encountered significant problems in striving to consolidate physician practices within integrated delivery systems. From this alone one cannot conclude that the strategy of integration is flawed, since they may be merely on the steeply rising portion of the learning curve. To evaluate the future prospects of physician-hospital organization, it is necessary to consider the underlying strategy. Three images compete for our attention: the PHO as a vertically integrated firm, as a diversified conglomerate, and as a health care cartel. Each of these concepts derives from a distinct economic logic and depends for its success on different market and regulatory conditions.

Most discussions of physician-hospital organization use the language of vertical integration, evoking the process of care that takes the patient from the physician's office to the acute care setting and then on to a nursing home or home health agency. The hospital that acquires a primary care practice is integrating upstream in a sense analogous to its downstream integration through nursing home acquisitions. This process imagery is reinforced by a financial concept of vertical relationships under global capitation, where the health care premium dollar goes first to the insurer and then to the capitated physician organization. The hospital that acquires a large physician organization integrates upstream in the financial current or, to use the more colorful metaphor, moves higher in the financial food chain. From the perspective of the physician organization, the decision to join with a hospital system is an application of make-versus-buy logic. Thus to understand the PHO as a vertically integrated system one must query the advantages of unified ownership over nonexclusive, contractual relationships between physicians and hospitals, keeping in mind the general caution that vertical integration between two stages of production sacrifices economies of scale at each stage. What are the specialized physical, human, or reputational assets that impair market contracting and tip the advantage in favor of joint ownership? How can vertical integration between hospitals and physicians avoid the problems that bedeviled analogous integration between insurers and physicians and doomed the staff-model HMO?

The second commonly used concept of the physician-hospital organization is that of the cooperative enterprise, the bringing together of clinically interdependent physicians and hospitals into one organization with one set of incentives and one market reputation to uphold. The organizational independence of interdependent agents often leads to inadequate commitment, coordination, and control. The historical separation of the physician and the hospital is ascribed in this view to the autarkic culture of the physician profession, with the freestanding hospital being described as an underdeveloped or blocked organization. Unification of physicians and hospitals within the PHO opens the way to clinical as well as administrative integration, to the reduction of variable and substandard performance under the aegis of continuous quality improvement. Here the emphasis is not on vertical integration, recognizing that most primary care visits do not lead to the hospital and many hospital admissions begin in specialty clinics rather than in primary care, but on coordination across distinct services. This concept often is expanded beyond the context of the individual hospital and its medical staff to the integrated delivery system that encompasses multiple hospitals and medical groups. Organizational integration at this much broader scale not only facilitates coordination at the subunit level but potentially permits the measurement, benchmarking, and improvement of performance across hospitals and across medical groups. At this point the PHO is best conceptualized as a diversified, multiproduct conglomerate. As such, its success depends on the presence of significant economies of scope, on common physical or intellectual assets that favor a single multiproduct firm over multiple single-product firms. What is the advantage of diversification over focus in health care, given its susceptibility to attenuation of individual incentives and accentuation of internal influence politics? How does the PHO overcome the diseconomies of scope that have bedeviled conglomerate organizations in other industries?

The third prominent interpretation of the physician-hospital organization emphasizes not efficiency-enhancing features such as vertical integration or product diversification but, rather, the potential for large health care organizations to achieve monopoly profits in their local markets. Both hospitals and physicians have responded to the price discounting demanded by managed care plans by merging with erstwhile competitors to reduce competition. Horizontal integration of hospitals with hospitals or physicians with physicians clearly has the potential, if carried to the extreme, to create monopoly or at least oligopoly conditions in local health care markets. Most American communities cannot support more than a few hospitals or large medical groups, and the consolidation from three to two and from two to one organization reduces choice and competition. The risk of monopolization is more immediately apparent in the hospital than in the physician sector, since economies of scale are larger and barriers to entry are higher, and hospital mergers have attracted the lion's share of attention from federal antitrust authorities. However, the consolidation of physician practice, especially primary care practice, could generate bargaining power against the HMOs that rely on capitated medical groups and IPAs. To evaluate the PHO as an incipient health care cartel, it is necessary to ask whether the merger between hospitals and medical groups, as distinct from mergers among hospitals or among medical groups, contributes to the bargaining power of either. Vertical integration does not increase bargaining power except in very unusual circumstances, and conglomerate diversification may weaken rather than strengthen the firm's ability to extract monopoly profits in any one sector. How significant are the barriers to entry into either the hospital or physician services markets? How would health plans and purchasers respond to PHO demands for payment rates significantly above competitive levels?

THE PHO AS A VERTICALLY INTEGRATED FIRM

For some patients and some procedures the relation between primary care and hospital services does resemble a process flow that begins in the home, is diagnosed in the office, is admitted to the ward, is discharged to the subacute unit, and then returns to the home. The primary care office can be analogized as a source of consumer demand and revenue for the hospital, and hence the organizational linkage of physicians and hospitals as a form of vertical integration. The process analogy cannot, however, convincingly explain the evolution of the PHO in the managed care era. Most obviously, utilization of inpatient hospital services has declined due to the development of less invasive technologies and to the economic pressures to find lower cost settings for care. The acute care hospital is less and less central to the process of care in the modern era.[10] The technological case for the PHO suffers from a deeper liability, however, since even those aspects of care that do require close physician-hospital coordination do not demand that the physician be an employee of the hospital. As always, one must ask whether contractual alternatives exist that can perform the functions ascribed to the integrated organization. In the case of inpatient care coordination, the rise of the hospitalist specialty— the internal medicine and pulmonology teams that oversee and assume clinical authority for inpatient care—illustrates the ability of nonownership, nonemployment relationships to coordinate physicians and hospitals.[11] While the hospitalists may be employees of the hospital, they frequently are employees of the medical group, the IPA, the health insurance plan, or an independent hospitalist firm. In any case they permit the primary care physicians to remain in private practice while being assured of the care of their hospitalized patients.

Vertical integration between physicians and hospitals, if ever truly accomplished, would impose significant losses in economies of scale. Some capitated medical groups, such as Mullikin Medical Centers and Bristol Park Medical Group, did buy their own hospital facilities, and some of the most prestigious multispecialty clinics did construct hospitals in the fee-for-service era. But very few medical groups have enough patients to fill a large hospital, and the decline of inpatient utilization is aggravating this shortage. Indeed, the hospitals owned by Mullikin and Bristol Park were small facilities that lacked the size, technology, and reputation of the dominant institutions in their communities. The medical groups were only too happy to divest their hospitals when alternative mechanisms developed for coordinating care with larger facilities. Conversely, very few PHOs can aspire to owning sufficient practices to fill their beds solely with the patients from their physician employees. Even the largest integrated organizations, such as Kaiser, find it advantageous where possible to contract for the use of independent facilities or, conversely, to allow nonaffiliated physicians to use the system hospitals. Most PHOs, even prominent examples such as St. Jude in Orange County and Montefiore in New York are only partially dependent on employed physicians for their admissions. Partial vertical integration also cuts the other way, since the medical groups owned by hospital systems often find it desirable to admit some of their patients to nonsystem institutions for reasons of patient preferences and geographical convenience.

The rise of the vertically integrated PHO during the era of managed care is particularly ironic since capitation facilitates a clean financial separation between the medical group and the hospital. A large and sophisticated medical group is the only entity truly qualified to accept the insurance risk and clinical responsibility of global capitation. Ownership of or by a hospital adds little and may subtract a lot. Once the physician organization has a capitated budget for inpatient services, it can contract with multiple independent hospitals on a fee-for-service or subcapitated basis. An ownership link to any one of those hospitals is likely to interfere with efficient contracting by introducing internal influence politics, driving the medical group to favor the PHO facility even if it charges higher rates, offers lower quality, is geographically inaccessible, or otherwise is not the primary choice. A PHO that forces its physician organization to admit solely to the mother institution disadvantages it in competition with other medical groups, who can offer prospective physicians and patients a broader range of hospitals. More generally, tight linkages between particular physicians and particular hospitals run counter to the contemporary consumerist trend. Many patients have independent preferences for their primary care and their hospital, and do not want their choice of hospital to be unduly constrained by ownership linkages with their physician's medical group. The tightly structured PHO thus faces the same marketing dilemma as the tightly structured staff-model HMO.

This discussion sheds doubt on even the most elemental rationale for vertical integration, the PHO's desire to attract patient admissions. Purchase of physician practices is a costly and risky means to this end. In many communities the physicians would have admitted their patients to the system hospital even without selling their practices, since that hospital enjoys a strong reputation with the doctors and their patients. In these instances, the PHO is unnecessary. In order to obtain a decent return on its invested capital, therefore, the PHO must gain admissions that otherwise would have gone to rival institutions. In some instances this occurs. In Orange County, Bristol Park Medical Group avoided the high cost St. Jude and St. Joseph hospitals as long as the group was independent, but shifted most of its admissions to system hospitals after the acquisition. Physicians in the Montefiore Medical Group, however, would admit to the system's hospitals even if in independent practice, since the medical center has a dominant presence in the Bronx. The Montefiore system would sell the MMG clinics if it could find a willing buyer, but maintains them in the absence of alternatives since this is the only way to retain primary care in the inner city.

THE PHO AS A HEALTH CARE CONGLOMERATE

Coordination between the primary care office and the hospital facility is of great importance for the cost and the quality of care received by hospitalized patients. The decisions of whether to hospitalize or treat in an ambulatory setting, of how much testing can be done prior to admission, of how many services and procedures should be conducted after admission, and of when to schedule discharge should involve sharing of information and synchronization of effort between the primary care physician, the physician specialists, the nurses, and the administration. The organizational chasm between the physician and the hospital inevitably creates slowdowns, misunderstandings, and mistakes that a more tightly integrated system could avoid. Some nations, such as Great Britain, have resolved this dilemma by restricting hospital privileges to specialists, who are salaried employees rather than in independent practice, while focusing the primary care physician on outpatient care. Some interpretations of the PHO highlight the potential for enhanced coordination between physicians and hospitals in the actual delivery of care, as distinct from the role of the primary care physician as an upstream feeder of admissions to the hospital. When extended to integrated delivery systems with multiple hospitals and medical groups, this conceptualization is that of the PHO as a diversified health care conglomerate.

The emphasis on team coordination fits uneasily with the actual structure and strategy of the PHO. Most obviously, the benefits of coordination are likely to be greatest between hospitals and physician specialists, who actually perform most inpatient care, rather than between hospitals and primary care physicians. Yet most PHOs are focused on affiliating with primary care physicians, either through purchasing their practices or through fostering primary care IPAs. In this regard the interpretation of PHO as vertical integration bears a closer resemblance to the facts. Once the PHO expands beyond the single hospital and single physician organization into a multifacility, multigroup conglomerate, moreover, the rhetoric of clinical coordination seems even more forced. The PHO conglomerate combines numerous heterogeneous participants, each with quite distinct objectives, training, technology, and culture. Once merged into a single firm, it often becomes more rather than less difficult to monitor and motivate performance. Large and diverse firms are plagued by two principal weaknesses, the attenuation of incentives for individual participants and the growth of influence politics among subunits. These weaknesses, which account for the problems of conglomerates outside the health care sector, must be considered in the context of the PHO. Moreover, the PHO potentially suffers from two special problems that derive from the fact that the acute care hospital sector is a declining industry and that most PHOs are structured as nonprofit organizations.

The attenuation of incentives is an endemic problem in organizations which amalgamate once independent owner-managers into salaried employees without a significant ownership stake. It is a simple, albeit sobering, fact that most people work harder when they work for themselves than when they work for a larger collectivity, no matter how that collectivity presents itself as an embodiment of the common will and the common good. The medical profession is a stellar example of the general rule. Solo and small-group practice have survived for so long, despite inadequate scale and failures of coordination, since individual doctors work longer hours, see more patients per hour, and pay more attention to practice efficiency when they work for themselves than when they work for anyone else. This elementary truth has foiled numerous efforts at consolidation, limiting the growth of multispecialty medical groups, staff-model HMOs, and physician practice management firms. It certainly afflicts the PHO. The attenuation of incentives extends beyond simple productivity to encompass a decline in the entrepreneurial spirit of many physicians and medical groups once they have come within the embrace of the hospital. Physicians who spent every free moment strategizing new ways of running their practices, expanding their reach, managing utilization patterns, and contracting with payers often begin to pass these burdens to the system leadership once they sell out and sign up as employees.

The greater challenge to the PHO stems from the internal influence costs that afflict large, internally diverse organizations. Influence costs exemplify failures of agency, in which the individuals delegated authority to perform specified tasks act in their own interests rather than in those of their principals.[12] Each participant and organizational subunit can choose between devoting energy to increasing the total surplus available to the organization or, alternatively, to increasing its share of the existing surplus. This blend of cooperation and competition is not unique to the organization, of course, but characterizes contractual relationships within the market context. But the rules of economic ownership and exchange typically are much murkier and more subject to political manipulation within firms than across firms. Transactions among independent firms must generate mutual gains if they are to occur at all, whereas the reallocation of resources within organizations need not benefit all participants. Over time, of course, organizations must generate benefits for their participants sufficient to retain them as members, but may sustain considerable differences in opinion over the appropriate distribution.[13] Large organizations often are better characterized as a contested terrain of internal dissension and conflict rather than an economic commonwealth of harmony and cooperation.

The influence politics of the PHO are especially severe due to the heterogeneity of the participants.[14] The health care conglomerate often includes multiple hospitals which differ in scale and reputation, teaching status, financial stability, and even religious orientation. It includes primary care physicians and specialists, whose long-standing feuds over income and status have been aggravated by the tilt of managed care toward the historically disadvantaged generalists. Tensions among physicians can roar into civil war when some sell their practices and others remain independent, when some favor capitation while others defend fee-for-service, when some create large groups and others insist on solo practice. Tensions among hospitals and among physicians are accompanied by tensions between hospitals and physicians, who often have distrusted and disliked one another. The corporate practice of medicine statutes are merely one reminder of the profession's fear and loathing of hospital dominance. The health care conglomerate is not content with hospitals and physicians but typically includes ambulatory surgery suites, skilled nursing facilities, sports medicine clinics, home health agencies, rehabilitation centers, mental health networks, and even insurance entities. Each of these brings its own patient mix, reimbursement methodology, market imperatives, and idiosyncratic culture. Mutually hostile professions and occupations are brought into daily contact with one another, with nurse midwives and anesthetists jostling with obstetricians and anesthesiologists, chiropractors competing with orthopedists, and psychologists scowling at psychiatrists. This can be the war of all against all.

Influence costs are challenging to the PHO due to the fact that its central component, the acute inpatient hospital, is part of a declining industry. Epidemiology, technology, and economics have combined to shift an ever greater portion of health care services from the inpatient to the outpatient setting. In principle, this historic transformation could be facilitated by the incorporation of both physician and hospital activities within the same firm. In practice, however, the decline of the acute inpatient industry introduces severe tensions in the health care conglomerate. Most PHOs are dominated by trustees and executives from the hospital rather than the physician side of the enterprise. These individuals commonly see the large inpatient facility and its gleaming clinical technology as the center of the health care system, the source of pride, prestige, and, in many cases, personal income. A dramatic downsizing of the hospital in favor of outpatient services would require many changes in personnel and priorities, mostly to the disfavor of the incumbent PHO leaders. Merged hospital systems often retain excess capacity rather than close facilities and regionalize services. Many PHOs are partially but not completely unionized, which interjects a continual organized pressure for the maintenance of dues-paying union jobs, most of which are in inpatient settings, to the detriment of nonunion jobs, most of which are in outpatient settings. The decline in hospital utilization also aggravates divisions within the medical staff, since it tends to shift patients and power to primary care and away from specialty care physicians. The tradi-

tional medical staffs of PHO hospitals are dominated by specialists oriented to fee-for-service who resist changes in what they still regard as
the doctor's workshop.

The peculiar influence problems of the declining industry may explain some of the capital allocation decisions of the PHO, and in particular the decision to purchase physician practices. Firms in declining industries outside the health sector often earn above-normal profits due to
their established market dominance, but lack profitable new investment
projects. The directors and executives of publicly traded corporations in
these circumstances should reduce investment and pay out surplus profits to shareholders, who then can reinvest in other industries. The actual
tendency, however, is for firms in declining industries to retain rather
than distribute earnings and to invest in projects that offer a low rate of
return but enhance the scale, prestige, and executive compensation of the
firm.[15] Many hospital systems have been earning attractive profits on
their inpatient services under Medicare's prospective payment method
and on their fee-for-service ambulatory surgery, subacute care, and home
health activities. Some have poured these surpluses into the acquisition
of physician practices with apparent unconcern for the rate of return on
capital.

Influence costs within the PHO may be aggravated by the nonprofit
ownership and governance of these institutions. Nonprofit organizations
often suffer from a diffusion of focus and authority, compared to their
for-profit counterparts, which makes it difficult for them to act deci-
sively in competitive industries.[16] The governance of many PHOs is diffused even compared to the nonprofit norm, since they combine multiple
hospitals with different missions governed by multiple philanthropic, religious, university, and community boards. They are poorly positioned
to sustain a long-term strategy in the face of pressures from their many
internal constituencies. Nonprofit ownership is particularly problematic
in the context of a declining industry which generates economic surpluses but lacks internal investment possibilities. The unremunerative
investment of free cash flows by for-profit firms in declining industries
outside health care is the source of hostile takeovers and leveraged buyouts, as major shareholders seek to displace management and reassert
control. This market for corporate control places some limits, albeit late
and loose, on the squandering of internally generated capital.[17] Nonprofit organizations are not structured to be accountable for the use of
their capital resources, since in most cases they do not generate free cash
flows. On the contrary, nonprofit organizations typically are starved for

capital. They continually must solicit funds from philanthropists and government agencies, which instills some accountability for the ways in which that capital is to be used. The PHO may be in a unique position as a cash-rich, capital-intensive nonprofit organization and is thereby at great risk of squandering its assets on unremunerative investments in physician practice.

THE PHO AS A HEALTH CARE CARTEL

Physicians and physician organizations fight in every way they can against the tightening vise of constrained revenues and increasing costs. To the extent vertical integration and conglomerate diversification enhance efficiency, the PHO reduces costs and thereby increases the economic margin available to support physician and hospital goals. The other strategy available to health care organizations, however, is to enhance revenues by raising rates to insurers, purchasers, and consumers. In regulated environments, this revenue strategy revolves around political connections, campaign contributions, and legislative lobbying. In market environments, it focuses on monopoly power. To the extent the physician-hospital organization is able to leverage higher fee schedules and capitation rates from health plans, physicians have incentives to affiliate even if integrated organizations create no efficiency gains from scale or scope.

There is no question but that physicians, medical groups, and hospitals desire monopoly power. All economic organizations seek ways to raise their prices without suffering the penalty inflicted by competitive markets: loss of consumer patronage to lower-priced rivals. Most goods and services are sold in national or even international markets, preventing producers from gaining such a large share as to sustain prices above competitive levels. But health care is consumed locally, since few patients except those in rural areas are willing to travel long distances to visit a physician or be admitted to a hospital. The restricted scope of health care markets provides an opening for physicians and hospitals that can band together in sufficient numbers to dictate their own terms. Governmental antitrust authorities have hindered independent physicians and hospitals from colluding to set prices, but have not foreclosed the full merger of once independent providers into large integrated organizations.[18] The trend toward horizontal consolidation in medicine now is evident everywhere. Hospital chains have refocused from their erstwhile strategy of owning one facility in each of multiple cities to owning multiple facilities in a few cities. They are divesting hospitals in markets where they do not see the possibility of achieving significant penetration. Nonprofit hospitals proclaim the virtue of merging to raise prices against for-profit insurers and sometimes convince local judges that anticompetitive is not antisocial. Similarly, medical groups and IPAs seek to achieve local scale and scope so as to become indispensable components of every HMO and PPO network. The ultimate lever in rate negotiations is the threat to terminate the contract; health plans cannot make these threats to provider organizations that dominate local markets.

The physician-hospital organization is better positioned than the physician practice management firm to achieve and retain market power. The PPM firms focused their service line on physicians to the exclusion of hospitals while diversifying their geographic scope across broad regions. PHOs, in contrast, focus their geographic scope on local markets but diversify their service lines to encompass both physician and hospital activities. The PHO pursues a strategy of depth over breadth, precisely the formula for achieving monopoly power over locally produced and consumed services. PPMs certainly seek market concentration where possible, as when MedPartners consolidated multispecialty groups in Los Angeles and PhyCor targeted dominant clinics in midsized communities. But the primal urge among PPMs has been to pursue physician opportunities wherever they present themselves, since their equity investors on Wall Street use growth in gross and net revenues as the short-term index of success. Most PHOs restrict their acquisitions of physician practices and medical groups to the communities around their hospitals in the anticipation of more referrals as well as higher prices.

The pursuit of monopoly power does not guarantee that the PHO will be able to obtain higher prices for either its hospital or its physician component. If the organization controls a dominant number of the hospital beds in its community, it can raise the prices a health plan must pay for each patient day, and if it controls a dominant number of physician practices it can raise the fee schedules or capitation rates for professional services. But dominance of the market for hospital services does not leverage higher rates for physician services and dominance in the physician market does not leverage higher hospital rates. A newly merged hospital system could choose to exercise its monopoly power to raise physician fees instead of hospital rates, but it could not double whatever monopoly power it had to raise both physician and hospital rates. Vertical integration in nonhealth industries has been found not to enhance bargaining leverage except in highly unusual circumstances.[19] Similarly, multiproduct conglomerates are not able to translate market power from one product line to another. This skeptical view of PHO bargaining strategy must be tempered by the unusual circumstances of the health care industry, and in particular by the important role of governmentally fixed prices for some patients and of nonprofit ownership for many hospitals. To the extent these factors induce hospitals not to leverage their potential monopoly power into higher hospital payment rates, they may create a context in which PHOs can leverage this power into higher physician rates. The federal Medicare and many state Medicaid programs dictate hospital prices rather than allow these to be negotiated at the local level. Regardless of their market position, therefore, hospitals are price takers rather than price makers for Medicare and Medicaid patients. PHOs may feel constrained by their nonprofit governance from raising inpatient rates to commercial insurers far above those they accept from governmental insurers, while being willing to devote some of that leverage to increases in physician fees. It otherwise is hard to understand the frequent sales pitch from PHOs that hospital integration brings higher rates for physician services.

Speculation and empty promises aside, it is unlikely that PHOs have achieved significant bargaining leverage except in rural areas or small cities. Most hospital markets suffer from great excess capacity, which is growing rather than shrinking as admissions and lengths of stay continue to fall. Most PHO profits have derived from lowering their costs for Medicare fee-for-service patients rather than from raising their rates to commercial insurers. Over time, however, excess capacity may decline as aging facilities are closed and few new facilities are opened. Very low rates of inpatient utilization will lead more and more communities to support only a few hospital facilities which, if merged into one chain or PHO, would enjoy significant pricing power. Some hospital systems currently are purchasing primary care practices in the hope of moving higher in the health care food chain and increasing the rates they negotiate with health plans for inpatient services. But over time hospitals may be asked to give more than they get in bargaining leverage within their PHO structures. Indeed, the hospital of the future approximates more closely the image of the natural monopoly than does the medical group, since economies of scale are larger and barriers to entry are higher for hospital than for primary care services.

To the extent hospital systems gain market power and use it to leverage higher rates for physician services through the PHO, they could have significant impacts on the performance of medical groups and IPAs. The

short-term impact of pricing above competitive levels is to reduce somewhat the demand for the affected services, as purchasers and consumers
shift where possible to substitutes. Against these economic inefficiencies
must be balanced the potential gains from a stabilization of organizational revenues and ability to use retained earnings to invest in new
initiatives. Some of the most innovative firms and industries outside of
health care are characterized by oligopolistic market structures and possess at least some pricing power, though the direction of the causality
linkages between market structure, profitability, and innovation are
heavily disputed.[20] In the long term, however, significant monopoly
power tends to reduce the pressure on incumbent firms to improve performance, since they can take the customer for granted. This slows down
the pace of innovation. While the microeconomic evidence on competition and innovation is ambiguous, the macroeconomic record is clear.
Economies with competitive markets outperform those with protected
or monopolistic markets.[21] Organizational and clinical innovation in
health care will not be encouraged within a physician-hospital cartel.

BREAKUP OF THE HOLDING COMPANY

In principle, the integrated delivery system is a means of positioning hospital and physician organizations for an era of global capitation, clinical delegation, and direct contracting with purchasers. It is thus most
ironic that PHOs have fared so poorly in markets with the greatest degree of capitation payment. While some PHOs, such as the St. Joseph
Health System in Orange County, have prospered, most have struggled
and more than a few have disintegrated into their component pieces or
collapsed altogether.

The extreme nature of the distress suffered by physician practice
management firms such as MedPartners in markets such as Los Angeles
might lead one to believe that a locally focused, hospital-based, nonprofit
approach would have fared better. And perhaps it would have. But it is
important to note that the constituent groups in the MedPartners system
were the scarred survivors of earlier failed attempts at hospital linkages.[22]
In 1993 Mullikin Medical Centers, for example, accepted a $50 million
cash infusion from the Daughters of Charity National Health System in
exchange for 15 percent ownership representation. The Daughters of
Charity were eager to have Mullikin develop a coherent physician strategy to replace the medley of underperforming, money-losing IPAs associated with their individual facilities, while Mullikin was interested in ex-

panding from Los Angeles into the San Francisco area. Initially all went well, as the Mullikin IPA absorbed the various hospital-affiliated physician enterprises, the Daughters's hospitals were brought under Mullikin's global capitation contracts, and the system opened doors for the medical group to acquire primary care practices in northern California. It was rumored that Mullikin's senior partners offered to sell the whole enterprise to the hospital system. But then relations soured, Mullikin merged with MedPartners, the Daughters of Charity joined forces with other hospitals within Catholic Healthcare West, and each turned away from the other. CHW had the good fortune or perhaps foresight to resign its board membership and dump MedPartners' stock shortly before the price plunged.

The Friendly Hills HealthCare Network was the paragon of physician-hospital coordination after the multispecialty group purchased a small facility and tore down the financial and administrative distinctions between inpatient and outpatient care.[23] Now hospital administrators were appointed by the medical group in a determined effort to create a single culture of prepaid, physician-led, managed health care. The Friendly Hills facility was far too small for tertiary care services, however, and the medical group needed capital resources for all the usual reasons. In 1993, therefore, the medical group sold the hospital, the outpatient clinics, and all other tangible assets to the Loma Linda University hospital system, creating the first nonprofit medical foundation associated with an academic medical center.[24] With remarkable though dismaying speed, however, the legal and clinical relationship broke up, as the fee-for-service specialists on the medical school faculty disputed with the capitation-oriented primary care physicians at Friendly Hills. The medical group went searching for a white knight, and thought it found one in the Caremark PPM firm, which bought out the Loma Linda stake, reconverted the Friendly Hills hospital and clinics to for-profit status, and went in search of other physician organizations in the Los Angeles region. When Caremark encountered financial difficulties and merged with MedPartners, Friendly Hills found itself joined with its cross-town rivals at Mullikin.

MedPartners was built around Mullikin and Friendly Hills but became enmeshed in a bewildering complexity of PHO relationships and ex-relationships as it expanded further in southern California. Pacific Physicians Services, acquired by MedPartners in 1996, owned a small hospital east of Friendly Hills and also had dickered with the Loma Linda hospital system. Talbert Medical Management had been spun off from the FHP staff-model HMO, which also had owned a hospital in Orange County. FHP long had proclaimed joint ownership of insurance, hospital, and physician organizations as the key to efficiency and quality,[25] but ultimately was butchered and sold piecemeal, with the health plan going to PacifiCare, the hospital to a local nonprofit system, and the medical group to Talbert and thence to MedPartners.

The most sobering experiences of all, perhaps, were had by UniHealth America, a nonprofit hospital system that pioneered the development of HMOs and the consolidation of medical groups in the Los Angeles market.[26] In 1978 UniHealth launched what ultimately became one of the largest and most profitable health plans in the nation, PacifiCare Health Systems, as a prelude to developing a vertically integrated system modeled on Kaiser. It quickly realized, however, that PacifiCare's success depended on good relationships with non-UniHealth hospitals, which in turn depended on an arms-length relationship between the HMO and its parent organization. In 1984 the HMO was restructured as a wholly owned subsidiary, then converted to for-profit status to allow access to outside investment capital and to develop an entrepreneurial corporate culture. UniHealth owned vast blocks of PacifiCare stock but was careful not to abuse that control in charging the HMO above-market rates for hospital services or otherwise disadvantaging its prospects in the competitive struggle with other health plans. Gradually UniHealth began to sell its PacifiCare stock to finance the development of a PHO. It purchased the Harriman-Jones Medical Group and the Facey Medical Group near its hospital facilities in Long Beach and San Fernando, respectively. Under the contracts UniHealth negotiated with PacifiCare and the other HMOs, the hospital division would charge the physician division for each day of inpatient care and split with the physicians any surplus remaining in the negotiated hospital budgets. The hospital division insisted on establishing rates equal to its average costs, which were substantially in excess to the marginal cost-pricing that dominated relations between the hospitals and independent physician organizations such as Mullikin Medical Centers and HealthCare Partners Medical Group. As Harriman-Jones and Facey paid higher rates and were restricted in their choice of hospitals, they were disadvantaged relative to their medical group competitors.

The internal debate over transfer prices between the hospital and physician divisions of UniHealth came to a head as the system faced the opportunity to acquire medical groups and IPAs in communities where it owned no hospitals. Continued sale of the PacifiCare stock endowed

UniHealth with a war chest with which to compete for physician affiliations; possibilities appeared rapidly as HMOs reduced capitation rates and medical groups sought larger corporate partners. UniHealth found itself the full or partial owner of the Beaver medical group in Redlands, the Buenaventura medical group in Ventura, and the San Jose Medical Group and Redwood Empire IPA in northern California. Most importantly, it purchased the Huntington Provider Group, a dynamic IPA that soon encompassed over 400,000 HMO patients across urban and suburban Los Angeles. By 1998 UniHealth's physician services division, called UniMed, covered almost one million patients statewide.[27] But this growth came at the price of almost completely disassociating UniHealth's physician and hospital divisions. Interorganizational pricing disputes were resolved using the principle that UniMed medical groups would contract with UniHealth hospitals at the rates charged to independent groups. Internal transfer prices thus were keyed to external market prices. Furthermore, the UniMed physicians were free to admit to whichever hospital they and their patients preferred, regardless of the hospital's relationship with UniHealth. Analogous transfer pricing and consumer choice principles were applied to relations with CareAmerica, an HMO that UniHealth had launched and then restructured as a for-profit subsidiary within the holding company. Capitation rates between CareAmerica, UniMed, and UniHealth would all be set at market rates since this was the only way in which one division did not gain at the expense of the others.

The evolution of the UniHealth PHO into a holding company freed each of its divisions to pursue success in its own sector. CareAmerica followed in the footsteps of PacifiCare in growing into a well-managed and profitable HMO. UniMed added medical groups and IPAs and prepared a national launch by restructuring into a for-profit subsidiary and PPM company. The UniHealth hospitals fared less well, since excess capacity in the Los Angeles market forced hospitals to accept payment rates below their long-term average costs. Over time, however, the UniHealth corporate board began to question the logic of the conglomerate structure. If each division achieved success despite rather than because of its linkages with the others, what was the benefit of the unified organization? Did it not merely add another layer of bureaucratic oversight? Attempts to unburden the operating divisions by minimizing central management also reduced the corporate benefits and ultimately even the identity of the organization. Association with the larger entity could be as much of a liability as a value to the divisions. The UniMed physician subsidiary, for example, encountered difficulties in recruiting outside investors, who were leery of minority ownership in a for-profit physician organization that was still bound to a nonprofit hospital system.

The nonprofit conglomerate began to question whether it should continue to invest its revenues in the CareAmerica HMO, UniMed medical groups, and UniHealth hospitals or, rather, consider those operating divisions as revenue sources for other endeavors. Once the operating divisions were reconceptualized as the means to an end rather than as the end unto themselves, the writing was on the door. CareAmerica was sold to Blue Shield of California, an ironic lesson in the dangers of conglomerate hypertrophy. Blue Shield had almost been acquired as a subsidiary by UniHealth five years earlier at the height of mutual enthusiasm for vertical integration, but then had prospered by focusing on the insurance sector while UniHealth dissipated itself across the very different hospital, physician, and insurance markets. The UniMed medical groups were put up for sale to the publicly traded physician practice management firms. PhyCor almost purchased the lot but backed away after taking a close look at the organizational and financial problems. The San Jose Medical Group was sold back to its physicians. The hospitals were sold to Catholic Healthcare West, which had refocused its acquisitions strategy from vertical integration with physicians to horizontal integration with other hospitals. This was the final stage in corporate restructuring that would transform UniHealth from a fully integrated PHO into a charitable foundation unencumbered by operating divisions and free to focus its assets on disease prevention and public health for the larger community.

CHALLENGES TO THE PHYSICIAN-HOSPITAL ORGANIZATION

The physician-hospital organization offers several key advantages as the capital, operational, and strategic partner for medical groups in the era of managed care. Leading institutions possess the profits and the debt capacity to amalgamate individual practices into medical groups and to create an administrative and computer infrastructure. Coordination of physicians and hospitals can improve the operational efficiency of all, through reductions in excess capacity, streamlining of inpatient admission and discharge, and the consensual adoption of clinical protocols. The PHO can develop and implement a unified market strategy, assembling disparate pieces into a coherent organizational structure and moving from a focus on acute episodic events to an emphasis on population-based health care.

The PHO suffers, however, from often underappreciated threats to its economic efficiency and social contribution. As the acute inpatient facility moves from the center to the periphery of the clinical continuum, the technological imperative for close physician-hospital coordination weakens. The physical and human capital of health care rarely is specialized to one particular relationship, and it is relatively easy for hospitals to receive patients from multiple independent medical groups and for groups to use the services of multiple independent hospitals. Sprawling PHOs that encompass hospitals, clinics, IPAs, and ancillary services lack economies of scope sufficient to offset the inevitable erosion of individual incentives and accentuation of influence struggles. The inherent difficulties of managing a diversified, multiproduct conglomerate are magnified by the declining industry for hospital services and rising industry for physician services, which necessitate a painful recalibration of prestige and power, and by the unwieldy and overpoliticized governance structure of the nonprofit system. The concentrated geographic focus of the PHO will always tempt it to strive for monopoly power, which if successful could set the organization down the well-worn path to security, complacency, and stasis.

The PHO may offer its greatest contribution during the early phases of physician organization, when medical group capital is scarce, operational needs are great, and strategies are incoherent. Similarly, the PHO may offer its greatest benefits to the hospital system when it is struggling to move away from a cost-plus financing addiction, a clinical focus on acute episodic care, and a cultural infatuation with bricks and mortar. Unified ownership between physician and hospital organizations can facilitate a mutually beneficial sharing of what each has and the other needs. But over time, the market for medical group services is expanding. Capital, operational expertise, and strategic advice may become generically available. Physician practice management firms represent sources of finance, management, and strategy independent of hospital control, though with clear liabilities of their own. More importantly, perhaps, the capabilities needed for effective medical group management may be obtained à la carte, without the need to submit to either a PHO or a PPM firm. A growing number of banks, venture capital firms, and institutional investors are willing to invest in physician services. A growing number of management services organizations, software vendors, and professional associations offer expertise in the operational specifics of physician organization. And a growing number of medical groups, corporate consulting firms, and network partners are willing to offer strategic advice or alliances without demanding a full asset transfer. It may be that physician-hospital relationships will go through a life cycle of fragmentation, integration, and then renewed separation, as independent but interdependent firms alternatively compete and collaborate in pursuit of their partially congruent and partially conflicting goals.

CHAPTER 9

The Corporate Practice
of Medicine

The traditional health care system, dominated by the professional guild
and financed by indemnity insurance, has been shattered beyond any possibility of repair. Once complacent taxpayers and formerly paternalistic
employers have fought back against inflating costs and escalating premiums, choking back the once massive flow of subsidies for inefficient
small practices, fragmented delivery systems, and cost-unconscious consumer demand. Community-rated insurance pools have fractured as
self-interested and often self-insured purchasers pursue better value for
their health care dollar. Consumers are increasingly assertive as to their
preferences and willingness to pay for particular health benefits and
medical interventions. This diversity in demand generates a commensurate diversity in supply. Physician, hospital, and insurance organizations
now seek ever greater scale to offer ever broader scope. Niche players still
are to be found in the interstices of the health care system—in rural areas, specialized services, and unconventional therapies that do not lend
themselves to consolidation. But the dominant market strategy is full
service diversification, the production and marketing of myriad services
to match every preference and every pocketbook. Some firms are over-
reaching and overconsolidating, constructing health care conglomerates
paralyzed by weak individual incentives, internal influence politics, and
risk-averse leadership. We observe turbulent cycles of expansion and con-
traction, diversification and refocusing, mergers and divestitures. But
the system never returns to the status quo ante. The emerging organiza-

tion of medicine will resemble neither the cottage industry of professional dominance nor the vertically integrated system of managed competition. It will build on the innovations attempted and the lessons learned by multispecialty medical groups, independent practice associations, physician practice management firms, and physician-hospital organizations. The health insurance industry will build on the experiments of the PPO and network HMO, diversifying into multiple products and markets in search of new customers and higher revenue. These organizational experiments will be superseded in their turn by innovative upstarts. Patient needs and consumer preferences are varied, conflicting, and ever-changing. There is no one best solution, no enduring compromise, no form of organization, method of contracting, or system of finance that will not in turn be surpassed in the heedless rush of events.

Three powerful and conflicting forces will dominate the future trajectory of the health care system. The first and most fundamental will be the continuing pressure to adopt new cost-increasing technologies while moderating the economic burden on taxpayers, employers, and consumers. New products and procedures are in part endogenous to the health care system, since clinical experimentation occurs in many settings and the rate of diffusion is influenced by forms of organization and insurance. Changes within the health care system that promote consumer and provider cost-consciousness will attenuate the inflationary spiral. But in large part the new technologies derive from a broader accumulation of scientific and engineering knowledge, from advances in physics, pharmacology, and pathology that highlight opportunities for intervention in the mechanisms of disease, trauma, recovery, and repair. These advances do not remain under the exclusive purview of scientific or political elites but are communicated widely to the citizenry, generating strong demands for their immediate diffusion. It is now common for patients to arrive in their physicians' offices laden with articles and advertisements describing drugs and devices that a few months earlier were in the laboratory or undergoing clinical trial. Yet this enthusiastic embrace of new clinical interventions is not accompanied by a commensurate public commitment to pay for them. The increasing wealth of society permits ever-growing investments in health care and it is to be assumed that expenditures will pace the overall growth in the economy. But even the wealthiest of nations cannot continue on a trajectory that would devote 15 percent, then 20 percent, then 25 percent of total resources to health care. The limits on social willingness to pay manifest themselves in the taxpayer revolt, in labor market trade-offs between wages and fringe benefits, and in the tens of millions of citizens who lack even the most basic of insurance coverage.

The second feature of the emerging health care system, which derives from the first, is continued innovation in forms of organization, ownership, contract, finance, and governance. Given the pressure to restrain inflation, large rewards will accrue to those who pioneer cost-decreasing products and processes. Outpatient surgery, home health care, subacute facilities, nurse practitioners, inpatient hospitalist teams, practice profiling, drug formularies, and case managers for patients with chronic illness represent clinical innovations that attenuate rather than accentuate the cost of health care, compared to what the traditional hospital-centered, specialty-dominated, and indemnity-financed system would have generated. These product and process innovations do not occur in a vacuum but require organizational changes that enhance coordination and reward efficiency. Multispecialty medical groups, IPAs, practice management firms, and physician-hospital systems can be interpreted as organizational responses to the potential rewards for cost-decreasing clinical innovation. Each faces significant limitations and all are subject to continued pressure toward evolution or extinction, but they exemplify the process of organizational experimentation that has been unleashed by the transition to unmanaged competition in health care.

The corporate system of health care demonstrates daily its economic superiority over the traditional system of professional dominance and the only partially implemented systems of utility regulation and managed competition. But the long-term viability of an organizational system depends not merely on its economic prowess but also on its compatibility with the social culture and political institutions. The professional guild persisted for decades, despite changes in demography, epidemiology, and technology, due to its nostalgic appeal and financial support for legislative powerbrokers. In overturning so many traditional practices and expectations in such a short period, corporate health care has brought down upon itself the wrath of the American populist heritage that distrusts big business almost as much as it dislikes big government. The third fundamental feature of the emerging system, therefore, is continued social discontent and political backlash. There will be no reversion to utility commissions or to managed competition. But legislatures, courts, attorneys general, and administrative agencies have unleashed a torrent of hostile legislation, litigation, and regulation. Some of these impose beneficial supports for the corporate system, mandating grievance and review, financial solvency, and quality-monitoring mechanisms that enhance accountability and legitimacy. Others, however, target the very engine of innovation, impeding or prohibiting new methods of payment, utilization management, benefit design, network contracting, capital financing, and organizational affiliation.

With the dawn of the new century the fate of corporate medicine still lies in the balance. The more remarkable its economic performance, the more social friction the new system engenders and the more political resistance it faces. Corporate health care relives the history of the larger corporate system, whose economic success engendered waves of populist hostility which came to be embedded in antitrust statutes and utility commissions.[1] Through its economic dynamism, the corporate system seems to undermine the social and political basis of its own support. Historically it has been sustained less by its own efforts than by the poor economic performance and weak cultural legitimacy of its regulatory antagonists. The fate of the corporate system of health care similarly will depend on the flux of aspirations and antipathies within the American people.

THE LESSONS OF UTILITY REGULATION
AND DEREGULATION

In peering into the future of medicine we can claim no certainties and propose no panaceas. No nation has ever unleashed the forces of market competition and corporate organization on its health care system. Insights are potentially available, however, from the experiences of the transportation, communication, energy, and banking industries. For decades subject to comprehensive regulation of entry and exit, capacity and investment, price and profit, service and quality, these industries have been opened to competition and its consequences. Despite differences in physical technology, geographic concentration, and consumer demand, the experiences of the utility industries under partial and total deregulation have been broadly similar. We now have a substantial body of research from the airlines, trucking, railroad, banking, and natural gas industries, plus less comprehensive evidence from telecommunications, electric power, and cable television. The experiences from these sectors will not be replicated precisely in health care but can provide useful guideposts and standards of comparison. Indeed, the utility industries are potentially more relevant to the emerging health care system than the oft-cited experiences of health care in other nations, which evolved in different cultural contexts and under different political institutions.

The deregulation of the utility industries has been remarkable for the breadth of the industries affected and the depth of the changes effected, but also because it was so unanticipated. Scholars and industry observers have diverged widely in their assessment of the economic desirability of regulation but converged in their assessment of its political durability. Liberals often interpreted regulation as an efficiency-enhancing response to market failure and as an equity-enhancing means of subsidizing the poor; they argued that enlightened public policy would protect utility regulation as an important legacy of the New Deal era. Conservatives often denounced utility commissions as captured by the regulated industries, and hence as conducive to inefficiency and inequity. But by this very token many despaired of mobilizing a political constituency for change, since the beneficiaries of regulation are concentrated and committed while the losers are dispersed and apathetic. But over the course of the 1960s, during the era of its apparent invincibility, utility regulation was subjected to a sustained critique from both the left and the right that created an intellectual quasi-consensus and prepared the way for sweeping change in the following decades.

The new consensus, shared in diverse ways by consumer activist Ralph Nader and Nobel laureate George Stigler, by Senator Kennedy and President Reagan, was that utility regulation exacerbates rather than attenuates economic inefficiencies and social inequities. The inefficiencies stem from incentive distortions induced by particular rules and from the general climate of a protected, noncompetitive industry. Regulatory pathologies were identified in the airline industry, where price floors stimulated cost-increasing competition through amenities and flight frequency;[2] in the electric power industry, where rate-of-return limits induced a substitution of capital for labor and the construction of overly large generating facilities;[3] in the railroad industry, where restrictions on track abandonment led to excess capacity, undermaintenance, and demands for public subsidy;[4] in the banking industry, where constraints on product and market diversification limited the number and type of financial instruments and protected inefficient and poorly managed firms;[5] and in the natural gas industry, where uniform rates prevented conservation-enhancing seasonal and time-of-day pricing.[6] Barriers to market entry, product diversification, and corporate mergers protected incumbent firms against the rigors of competition, fostered managerial slack, financed above-market wages, and discouraged innovation in methods of production, supply, and marketing. The distributional impact of regulation derives from its attentiveness to mobilized political constituencies and its insulation from the larger but less vocal majority. Simplistic theories of agency capture by regulated industries failed to acknowledge the full complexity of regulatory politics, in which consumer groups, legislators, and litigators all play important roles, but did succeed in dispelling even more simplistic interpretations of regulation as a means to tax the rich and help the poor.[7] Not surprisingly, the greatest defenders of continued regulation were not the disenfranchised but the regulated firms themselves, backed by their investors, bankers, labor unions, executives, and employees.

Deregulation is not a one-time event but rather a process that unfolds in different ways across industries and geographic markets, generates instability and stress, and is threatened continually by political reaction and re-regulation. Based on the industry experiences and research evidence to date, four basic impacts can be identified.[8] Deregulation in the utility industries has stimulated productivity and performance, with significant reductions in cost and improvements in service. It has led to differentiation among product features and prices depending on the purchaser, the geographic market, the season, and other characteristics of supply and demand. The relaxation of restrictions on new entry has led to dramatic changes in market structures, organizational forms, distribution networks, and methods of purchasing. Finally, deregulation has engendered countervailing pressures to slow the pace and reverse the direction of change, to dampen the instability and impede the innovation, to cushion the blow to previously favored constituencies, and in some cases to re-regulate in whole or in part the behavior of the industry. Let us consider each of these in turn.

UTILITY DEREGULATION: COST AND QUALITY

The most visible impact of deregulation has been to lower prices and improve service to consumers.[9] After adjusting for economy-wide inflation, deregulation has reduced fares per mile traveled by 33 percent for airlines, 35 percent for less-than-truckload freight, 75 percent for full-truckload shipping, and 50 percent for railroads. Natural gas prices have fallen 30 percent for both residential and industrial users. Service frequency has increased substantially in air transportation, due to lower fares and higher demand; service times have declined substantially for less-than-truckload and full-truckload shipping; both the mean and standard deviation of railroad transit times have fallen by approximately 20 percent; banking is more convenient due to longer hours, automatic tellers, and no restrictions on branching; natural gas service is more reliable as shortages have been eliminated.

Higher value to the consumer has derived from improved industry productivity, capacity utilization, and network configurations and from a virtuous cycle of lower costs, lower prices, increased demand, and further reductions in costs. The hub-and-spoke route configuration developed by the deregulated airline industry has raised rates of seat occupancy from 52 percent to 62 percent and thereby lowered costs per mile flown by 25 percent. Fare wars have driven down air fares, dramatically increased business and leisure air travel, and permitted ever more frequent flights.[10] The trucking industry has increased the percentage of full truckloads and reduced the number of empty return miles, thereby permitting price reductions that have attracted additional business from nontrucking firms that previously shipped on their own vehicles to avoid the costs of trucking regulation. Railroads have abandoned approximately one-third of their trackage, reduced operating costs, improved profitability, and thereby escaped from the regulation-induced death spiral of mandated excess capacity, high operating costs, high prices, declining demand, and need for ever greater subsidy. Banks have lowered their operating costs through extended electronic and branch banking, raised interest rates above regulatory ceilings, and developed new financial products that better balance risk and return. Natural gas firms have restructured their transmission and distribution networks and improved pipeline capacity utilization, reducing overall operating and maintenance expenses by 35 percent.

UTILITY DEREGULATION: PRICE
AND PRODUCT DIFFERENTIATION

A common characteristic of utility regulation was uniformity in products and prices in the face of great variability in consumer preferences and the actual costs of providing service. This one-size-fits-all approach led to services that were of excessive cost for some consumers and insufficient quality for others, impeded the use of price flexibility to enhance capacity utilization, and juxtaposed overcapacity and low load factors in some industries with undercapacity and shortages elsewhere. It generated cross-subsidies from consumers for whom the cost of service was low to consumers for whom the cost of service was high. Shippers on heavily traveled routes subsidized shippers on remote routes; vacation airplane travelers with flexible schedules subsidized business travelers with last-minute schedules; long-distance telephone users sub-sidized local callers.

Deregulation has spurred an outpouring of new services that incur different costs and impose different prices, permitting a better match be-tween supply and demand. Air travelers can obtain substantial discounts if they purchase tickets in advance and stay for the weekend, but must pay the full cost of standby capacity if they want to delay their decisions to the last minute. Shippers can obtain low rates if they allow their freight to be combined with others' and be routed over less direct but more heavily traveled corridors, or can choose to pay the full cost of less-than-truckload delivery. The increased variability in price and service results in part from the deregulation of contracting between buyers and sellers. Rail and road regulation, for example, often prohibited shippers from negotiating with transporters for volume discounts, flexibility factors, multimarket or multiyear agreements, or other variations from uniform price and service standards. Now half of rail freight moves at specially contracted rates, allowing better track utilization for the railroads and better coordination of production, inventory, and distribution for the shippers. The adoption by American manufacturers of Japanese "just-in-time" inventory and assembly methods would not be possible with-out the ability to negotiate precise volumes and times of delivery. Deregu-lation permits the contractual flexibility that allows buyers and sellers to explore potential gains from new electronic and information technolo-gies, thereby accelerating the adoption and diffusion of innovation.

Pricing has become highly variegated by time of day, time of year, and time of delivery to accommodate fluctuations in capacity utilization. Telephone users obtain lower rates if they call on evenings or weekends; natural gas is shipped at lower prices at off-peak hours and seasons; fre-quent travelers are awarded mileage bonuses that help airlines fill seats that otherwise would have gone empty. Deregulated prices now more closely accord with the variable cost of providing service to particular customers in particular markets. University endowments and mutual funds obtain volume discounts through lower brokerage fees than small investors; shippers with regular and predictable volume obtain lower prices than those with irregular and unpredictable demand; travelers us-ing small aircraft to fly between rural communities pay more than trav-elers using wide-bodied aircraft on trunk routes. Changes in relative pricing to reflect relative costs have sharply reduced the cross-subsidies among consumers and communities that prevailed under regulation. For some products and customers prices have increased, frequency has decreased, and service has deteriorated despite the industry-wide improvements in cost and quality. Deregulation also has hurt producer and provider interests that benefited from restrictions on new entry and price competition. The unequal distribution of costs and benefits under regulation was rendered invisible through long familiarity, while the new configuration of costs and benefits is highly visible.

UTILITY DEREGULATON: MARKET AND ORGANIZATIONAL STRUCTURES

Deregulation stimulates competitive entry into previously protected industries and local markets. Start-ups challenged the most prominent firms in airlines, trucking, electric power, and telecommunications and even have appeared in specialized niches of the railroad industry. After an initial turbulent phase, however, deregulated industries undergo a process of concentration through merger, acquisition, market exit, and bankruptcy. Airlines, railroads, and banking firms are almost all larger now than prior to deregulation, and we witness an apparently similar wave of consolidation in the electric power and telecommunications sectors. Deregulation has spurred exit from particular product and geographic markets as firms have pulled out, sold out, or gone under in the face of new entry. Much of this was overdue, since regulation protected incumbents from more efficient and innovative outsiders. Large scale is not incompatible with the most intense competition, as much growth has occurred through product and market diversification. Measured at the national level, the number of firms is smaller and the size of firms is larger, but measured at the local market level the number of potential competitors is larger and the intensity of competition is fiercer.

Some firms have grown by developing broader networks that better fit the needs and preferences of customers. Airlines have thickened their regional nets by servicing more communities around their hubs and have developed joint venture and contractual arrangements to service global demand. Railroads have merged end-to-end to more efficiently link ports to mines to manufacturing centers, and have purchased or developed contractual affiliations with maritime shipping firms and trucking companies to offer intermodal transport services. Many mergers and acquisitions are designed to penetrate new geographic markets, as in branch banking and local service telecommunications, or to penetrate new product markets, as in linkages between commercial banks, investment banks, and stock brokerages. Substitution stimulates rivalry for traditional services and their producers. Mutual funds, corporate lenders, life insurers, and other financial intermediaries now compete with savings and loan institutions for deposits. Of course some consolidation is designed to reduce rather than increase competition. While end-to-end mergers increase rivalry in the railroad industry, parallel mergers decrease it. Airlines dominant at particular hubs can exploit the shortage in airport capacity to exclude rivals and raise rates. But all in all the utility industries have become increasingly competitive as the deregulatory process has unfolded, even in what were formerly considered natural monopolies such as electric power and telecommunications. The strategy of full-service diversification, driven by the heterogeneity of preferences, technology, and geography within particular industries, leads to the creation of large firms competing fiercely across many products and many markets.

UTILITY DEREGULATION: POLITICAL BACKLASH

Deregulation has exerted a major impact on the political climate of the utility industries, in some cases stimulating a backlash that finds sympathetic ears in legislatures and the courts. Formerly subsidized consumers deplore market-level price and quality. Airline pilots, unionized teamsters, stock brokers charging fixed commissions, employees of power companies with cost-plus rate structures, and domestic crews on U.S.-owned ships all have experienced the reduction in industry costs as a reduction in personal incomes. Americans as a whole are winners, with more choices, better service, and lower prices, but significant subgroups find themselves to be losers. Everyone appreciates price decreases and quality increases in services where regulation offered neither subsidy nor shelter. We lament, however, similar effects in industries where we were protected and pampered. The political backlash has been weak in industries where winners are organized while losers are dispersed. But the controversy festers where winners are dispersed and losers are mobilized. Here are heard the most insistent denunciations of competition and the most strident demands for renewed regulation.

The consumer and producer backlash against utility deregulation has found sympathetic ears in Congress, state legislatures, and executive agencies due to the structure of political incentives and institutions. Legislators look not to the aggregate social impacts of deregulation but to the costs and benefits accruing to their local constituents. They seek to slow, stop, and reverse adverse impacts, such as the abandonment of little-used railroad trackage, competitive threats to hometown truckers, and the transfer of jobs to distant communities. Elected politicians and appointed administrators are concerned with short-run rather than long-run effects and are uncomfortable with the instability created as deregulation opens long-protected industries to entry and innovation. All three branches of government are under continual pressure to do no direct harm, to minimize adverse impacts on the visible and vocal at the expense of the invisible and inarticulate, thereby upholding perceived standards of due process while rewarding the politically most powerful interests.

The process of deregulation has generated considerable friction but has not been reversed, with partial exceptions in the cable television and electric power sectors, due to large short-run benefits that have diffused the pressures for re-regulation. Indeed, the deregulatory process has spread to previously untouched industries and previously unconvinced nations, as local phone service sees the first glimmerings of competition, global maritime and airline regulations are loosened, and European nations reexamine their internal telecommunications and transportation policies. Over time, moreover, deregulation creates a constituency in its own support, as producers, consumers, and communities advantaged by the changes mobilize against re-regulatory initiatives. Nevertheless, the process is fragile and always endangered. Utility deregulation depends on the political as well as the economic marketplace, on the temporal and geographic incidence of costs and benefits, on the comparative salience of winners and losers, and on the likelihood that demagogues will find in the turbulence of change the opportunity to pursue other agendas.

COMPARING HEALTH CARE
WITH THE UTILITY INDUSTRIES

No exact analogies can be drawn between the changes sweeping through health care and the revolutionary transformations spurred by deregulation in the transportation, communication, energy, and finance industries. Health care was never subjected in such an explicit and comprehensive fashion to the dictates of a utility commission. A few states imposed rate regulations affecting all hospital patients, many experimented with price controls covering a subset of insurers, and all imposed certificate-of-need entry barriers for at least some services and facilities. The Medicare program imposed a uniformly administered hospital pricing system for its patients, and many states imposed Medicaid payment rates that were based on budgetary politics rather than any reasonable analysis of the true cost of care. But the performance of the traditional health care system so closely resembled a regulated utility, and health care competition has affected performance in ways so similar to utility deregulation, that significant commonalties must be acknowledged and important lessons can be learned.

The traditional system of health care exhibited many of the telltale signs of utility regulation: barriers to entry and exit, absence of price competition, vigorous nonprice rivalry, excess investment and overcapacity in some sectors, capital shortage and undercapacity in others. These pathologies stemmed in large part from the very visible hand of federal and state government in the financing, mandating, and monitoring of care. Public payers account for half of industry revenues and until recently frowned on principles of market contracting in favor of administered prices and performance. Health plans and providers that reduced their costs could not obtain the usual market reward of greater demand from price-sensitive purchasers. Public policy embraced the indemnity structure of traditional health insurance, subsidizing it in the private sector through the uncapped tax exclusion and imposing it in the public sector through the fee-for-service structure of Medicare and Medicaid. Indemnity insurance imposes a 100 percent tax on cost-reducing innovation but rewards cost-increasing innovations and amenities by reimbursing every new product and procedure with a new payment. State legislatures strived to impose a uniformly high cost, high coverage standard on insurance benefits by mandating the coverage of whichever services, facilities, and devices could muster a potent political lobby. Barriers to entry and exit derived not merely from explicit certificate-of-need statutes but from legislated bans on for-profit hospitals, prepaid group practices, limited provider networks, and other organizational challenges to the status quo. The medical profession was for decades exempt from oversight by the antitrust agencies, and local judges still wink at anticompetitive hospital activities under the dubious theory that nonprofit monopolies will not exploit bargaining leverage to finance their vision of the social good. All in all, the utility ethos was pervasive in traditional health care. Whatever moved was to be taxed, whatever moved quickly was to be regulated, and whatever did not move was to be bailed out.

HEALTH CARE: COST AND QUALITY

Market competition and corporate organization already have demonstrated a remarkable ability to moderate the inflationary trajectory.[11]

The development of medical groups, health care systems, multiproduct insurers, capitation contracting, and utilization management during the 1990s held the growth in health care costs to the lowest levels in 50 years, confounding the skeptics and contributing to the strong economic performance of the decade. It is difficult to ascertain the influence of corporate organization on health care quality, due to the inherent difficulties in measuring outcomes and to the lack of preexisting baselines for comparison. The overall quality of care is improving, but this is due primarily to longer trends in laboratory and clinical research, physician training, and technology diffusion than to recent changes in markets and organization. The record on customer service is decidedly mixed. Cost pressures have led to a shortening of physician visits and oversight of utilization patterns that patients resent, while the new emphasis on satisfaction surveys and enhancement has induced providers to offer longer office hours, 24-hour telephone advice, and other consumer conveniences.

The short-term success against health care cost inflation does not imply that the long-term battle for stable expenditures has been won. On the contrary, Americans are poised to enjoy the clinical benefits but rue the budgetary implications of an outpouring of new drugs, devices, tests, and treatments that prevent infection, dispel uncertainty, enhance functional ability, and generally contribute to a healthier and more long-lived citizenry. This technological dynamic opens diagnostic and therapeutic opportunities that are hard to ignore, but is less important perhaps than the revolution of rising expectations. It is clear that as the population gets healthier it demands more, not less, from its medical care system. We embrace treatments for old ailments that once were merely suffered, from childhood viruses and rashes through migraine headaches and springtime allergies to the impotence and arthritis of our golden years. We open our hearts and our wallets to medical breakthroughs that offer life and dignity to victims of the great scourges of our time, from childhood cancer through AIDS to Alzheimer's. We take gains in longevity for granted, expect that full physical, social, and intellectual functioning will continue to the now more distant end, and insist that these advances are for all to share.

The corporate system does not seek to stop the development of quality-increasing technology or to quell the revolution of consumer expectations, both of which inevitably accompany the growing wealth of society. It does, however, create significant changes in economic incentives and organizational structures that will temper the rate of inflation and enhance the overall value of health care services in a manner analogous to the gains in efficiency and quality in the deregulated utility industries. Four dimensions are particularly worthy of note.

The shift from the professional guild to integrated organization, from indemnity insurance to managed care, and from nonprice rivalry to price competition creates strong economic rewards for the diffusion of cost-decreasing clinical innovations. The medical arms race rewarded the development of technologies that raised quality, real or perceived, but not ones that reduced costs. Now firms and individuals at every point along the health care value chain, from bench scientists to clinical researchers, pharmaceutical manufacturers, hospital managers, multispecialty medical groups, single-specialty networks, and primary care physicians can increase their status and income if they discover, develop, or adopt interventions that reduce the overall expense of care. Market competition and corporate organization in nonhealth industries stimulate innovations that are productivity-enhancing and hence cost-reducing. This same dynamic will appear in medicine. These efficiency-enhancing innovations will lower the costs of some forms of medical care and thereby make it easier for the nation to finance the adoption of other innovations that raise costs as a byproduct of raising quality.

The corporate system rapidly is restoring the normal economic relationship between supply and demand, between market disequilibrium and price changes in health care. The United States has inherited an excess supply of acute care hospitals and physician specialists, analogous to the excess capacity generated by entry and exit regulation in many utility industries. In the now passing system of guild organization and indemnity insurance, excess capacity stimulated cost-increasing nonprice competition analogous to that experienced by the rate-regulated airline industry. Health services researchers delighted in discovering ever new economic pathologies, from Roemer's Law that a built bed is a filled bed, to the medical arms race of duplicative clinical technology, to supplier-induced demand in response to physician fee reductions. Henceforth facilities and services that are in excess supply will receive lower, rather than higher, prices than otherwise comparable facilities and services that enjoy excess demand. The painful recalibration of relative incomes within the profession and across the industry will continue, redirecting investments and career choices toward areas of need rather than areas of excess.

The original demand placed on the corporate system by public and private purchasers was to reduce the cost of care, not to improve quality and service, and the system responded accordingly. The greatest emphasis in the early years has been on methods of payment, network contracting, utilization management, benefit design, and organizational structure that promise to restrain the inflationary spiral. Considerable success has been achieved in this endeavor. But the American question remains: what have you done for me lately? Patients are worried lest the emphasis on cost control reduce the quality of the care they receive. Consumers are annoyed with every obstacle to obtaining what they want when they want it. The corporate system is shifting its emphasis to developing methods for measuring and improving service, in a manner analogous to the process pursued in the utility industries after deregulation. For the first time, the health care industry is being subjected to systematic monitoring of quality and service levels, with the intent of promoting clinical comparisons and quality-conscious consumer choice. The road to be traveled is a difficult one, since almost all the monitoring tools need to be invented. A salient feature of the professional guild was reliance on unmonitored trust and opposition to quantitative, validated measures of performance. Purchasers, plans, and provider organizations now experiment with satisfaction surveys, indicators of preventive services utilization, tracers for appropriate clinical processes, and risk-adjusted measures of patient outcomes. This process is unfolding according to the etiquette of the corporate system, with considerable duplication, turbulence, and controversy. Critics can point to yet another form of administrative waste and argue that a fully regulated system would impose a uniform method for monitoring quality. But the erstwhile professional system, whether regulated or unregulated, imposed no systematic quality measurement of any kind. The new monitoring mechanisms hold great potential to enhance as well as simply measure the quality of care, since statistical and epidemiological methods always outperform bad-apple approaches to quality improvement. The conceptual framework and empirical methods of continuous quality improvement have diffused from their Japanese pioneers to American manufacturing and ultimately will take hold in American medicine.

Deregulation has not universally improved quality and service in the utility industries. We all bemoan the paucity of empty seats on the airlines or the ubiquity of small fees for banking services that once were offered free. Some forms of regulation imposed a uniformly high cost, high quality style of service by forbidding firms from developing economy options. Without the ability to attract customers through lower prices, airlines added flights that they knew would be half-empty and financial institutions offered white-glove service to those customers who could come in during bankers' hours. Deregulation in these contexts led initially to a reduction in service as a byproduct of an even greater reduction in price. But the value offered to the customer, defined as including both service and price, increased. Most of us are willing to put up with strangers in adjacent seats in order to obtain economy fares and, for those who are not, the airlines offer business class service. Similarly, the corporate system of health care will experiment with different combinations of price and service to find the mix that offers best value in the mind of the consumer. There are trade-offs to be made between broad and narrow provider networks, stringent and loose utilization management, thick and thin benefit coverage, high deductible and first-dollar cost sharing, and, of course, between connoisseur class and economy prices. The trade-offs are more controversial in health care than in the utility industries since the benefits of elite service accrue to the patient while the benefits of low cost often accrue to the employer or taxpayer. But in every case, for every self-paid insurance package, employer-paid fringe benefit, or tax-paid entitlement program, the corporate system will seek the best value in service and price, since that is the only sustainable method for retaining the customer.

HEALTH CARE: PRICE AND PRODUCT DIFFERENTIATION

Generations of reformers have sought to overcome the variability in health care demand and supply through uniform benefits, premiums, and prices that do not vary according to incomes, preferences, health, location, employment, or other characteristics of consumers and producers. In the absence of strong governmental controls, however, the heterogeneity among consumers in what they are willing to buy and among providers in what they are willing to sell is driving a thoroughgoing price and product differentiation in health care. Benefit coverage and network design, premiums and prices, and method of marketing and distribution now are highly variegated and promise to become ever more so.

The defeat of President Clinton's Health Security Act spelled the demise of the uniform benefit package as the foundation of health care policy in the United States. Simply put, those who currently enjoy rich benefits and low premiums, due to good subsidies, good health, or good luck, are unwilling to sacrifice anything so that the less endowed, healthy, or fortunate can come up to their level. A uniform benefit package sufficiently rich to be politically acceptable to the voter would be economically unacceptable to the taxpayer. The unstandardized marketplace is responding to the diversity in incomes and preferences through a wide variety of benefit packages, cost-sharing provisions, network configurations, and methods of utilization management. Self-employed individuals and small firms now can shop from a long menu of options, with inclusion, exclusion, or partial coverage for prescription drugs, mental health services, rehabilitation therapy, and complementary medicine, with different levels of cost sharing, and with combinations of deductibles and copayments for particular services. Large public and private purchasers demand idiosyncratic benefit configurations, reminding the health plans and providers that those who pay the piper call the tune. Network designs are proliferating at an equally astonishing rate, mixing and matching PPO and HMO components, gatekeepers and self-referral, prior authorization and retrospective profiling, out-of-network wraparounds and out-of-area expansions. The three-letter acronyms that once anchored our understanding of health insurance alternatives are rapidly becoming untethered as the industry crafts hybrid strains in a dizzying display of product engineering.

Premiums and prices have lost whatever uniformity they once possessed, with community-rating and standard methods of capitation and fee-for-service being swept aside by the market imperative to vary prices according to underlying variations in costs. Consumers choosing rich benefit packages, loose network designs, and patrician physician practices find themselves paying substantially more than those content with thinner benefits, more tightly managed access, and community-based practitioners. Public and private sponsors are continuing their slow and painful transition from defined benefits to defined contributions, paying a fixed dollar amount rather than encouraging costly choices through higher subsidies. In a competitive market each product must be priced to be self-supporting, since cross-subsidies invite new entry that appeals to the overcharged customers. The diverse options in benefit and network design are reflected in actuarially sound, and hence diverse, price levels. Insurance premiums and provider payments will increasingly reflect the health status and cost of care required by the individual enrollee and patient. Risk-adjusted prices are desirable since they remove incentives to cherry-pick the healthy and avoid the ill. They are essential for the continued economic viability of safety-net providers who attract the sickest patients due to their geographic location or open-door policy. In the absence of risk-adjusted subsidies, market competition will shift the economic burden of illness onto the ill while allowing the healthy to pay for only their modest medical needs. The United States currently maintains a tattered fabric of risk-adjusted subsidies, with employer-paid benefits, government entitlement programs, and the health insurance tax deduction allocating greater sums for sick than for healthy citizens. But the system has many loopholes and exceptions. Competitive markets and corporate organizations in health care would benefit from a well-designed and well-financed system of risk subsidies, since this would eliminate the pressure to deny coverage and would convert charity cases into paying customers. But steps in this direction are difficult since they would violate the ban on new taxes, which is one manifestation of the "do no direct harm" principle in contemporary politics.

The marketing of health care is becoming quite differentiated and methods of branding, distributing, and selling are becoming key competitive skills for health plans and provider organizations. It is increasingly hard to imagine that all Americans one day will pick up their health insurance at the local Social Security office or be channeled through a corporate open enrollment process. Consumers obtain their information and options through brokers and agents, private and public employers, state insurance pools and Medicaid agencies, federal Medicare and military programs, and myriad other options. The industry is pioneering ever new ways of connecting buyers and sellers, including print and electronic media, direct mail and the Internet, community organizations and consumer cooperatives. Through it all the American consumer reigns sovereign over a complete menu of choices, chaos of opportunities, and cacophony of sales pitches promising a product as unique as the individual and as affordable as the alternative.

HEALTH CARE: MARKET AND ORGANIZATIONAL STRUCTURES

We are witnessing massive changes in the structure of health care markets and organizations. Many of today's most prominent organizational forms, such as independent practice associations and physician-hospital organizations, were difficult to find 20 years ago. Multispecialty medical groups have a long and illustrious history in some communities but have been thoroughly transformed by the marketplace shift toward managed care. Preferred provider insurance displaced indemnity and the network HMOs displaced their staff-model progenitors only in the 1990s. Forms of contracting are in a state of ferment, with payment methods that borrow from both capitation and fee-for-service and methods of utilization management that compromise between arms-length review and full delegation. Organizations are becoming larger and more complex through merger, acquisition, and product diversification. But increased scale is stimulating competition rather than cartels as local barriers fail to impede entry by multiproduct, multimarket firms.

The most visible feature of the corporate system of health care is ceaseless acquisition and divestiture, integration and outsourcing, combination and recombination. Medical groups, hospital systems, and health plans are coming together and then coming apart, substituting contract for joint ownership, creating diversified conglomerates and refocused facilities, and experimenting with ever new structures of ownership, finance, governance, and management. After decades in which medicine was frozen into a cottage industry of solo physician practices, freestanding community hospitals, and single-state Blue Cross insurers, incumbents and upstarts are pushing boundaries in ways once not merely infeasible but unthinkable. They are exploring potential economies of scale, the advantages offered by large size in insurance risk bearing, administrative efficiencies, and vendor contracting, but also the diseconomies that accompany the attenuation of individual incentives and accentuation of influence politics. Firms are exploring the economies and diseconomies of scope, the trade-offs between conglomerate versus staff-and-line organization, broad-spectrum versus niche positioning, transfer versus market pricing, diversification versus product focus, coordination versus clinical specialization. They seek some middle ground between the extremes of vertical integration and spot contracting, some balance of coordinated and autonomous adaptation in the face of ever new challenges.

This process of trial and error is generating a diversity rather than uniformity of organizations and contracts. The heterogeneity of regional providers and purchasers, technologies and transactions, economics and demographics, popular cultures and political institutions supports an enduring variety in the health care marketplace. We observe striking cross-market and within-market differences in methods of payment, medical management, data reporting, and quality accountability. Some physician communities are characterized by multispecialty medical groups, others by more loosely structured IPAs, and others by a continuing diaspora of unaffiliated practices. For-profit hospital chains hold a strong position in some communities, while others are dominated by large nonprofit systems and the remainder cling to hometown facilities. Different

regions favor different mixes of HMO, PPO, and hybrid insurance products. This heterogeneity stems both from enduring regional characteristics and from transient differences in each community's place on the
health care learning curve, as experiments that succeed in one locality
are copied in others.

The structure and performance of local health care markets oscillates
between the most vigorous competition and the incipient cartel. Medical groups, hospital systems, and health plans want to avoid the rigors
of competition by acquiring or merging with their rivals, seeking oligopoly and ultimately monopoly power to dictate prices and protect profits.
But accomplishment seems ever to lag behind aspiration, as purchasers,
suppliers, substitute services, and entrepreneurial outsiders compete for
their share of those potential monopoly profits. The organizational diversification of health plans and providers has created a ravenous crowd
of well-financed and battle-hardened competitors able to jump into new
products and new markets when revenue opportunities arise. Entry barriers are lower, not higher, than in the bygone era when the professional
guild boycotted group practices, fixed prices, restricted advertising, enforced any-willing-provider laws, and banned the corporate practice of
medicine. The cottage industry structure of yesteryear lent itself well to
the most thoroughgoing anticompetitive practices, while the large corporate organizations, consolidated industry structures, and complex
contractual relationships of today lend themselves to the most vigorous
competition ever observed in health care.

HEALTH CARE: POLITICAL BACKLASH

The political backlash against competitive markets and corporate organization in health care has far exceeded the reaction against deregulation in the utility industries. The success against cost inflation has produced large savings for employers and governmental programs but little
visible benefit to individual employees and taxpayers. Had the rate of
inflation that prevailed in the five years prior to the defeat of President
Clinton's Health Security Act continued for the five years following that
landmark event, health care costs and premiums at the end of the decade
would have been twice their actual levels, creating dire personal hard-
ships, acrimonious tax politics, and conflictual labor relations. But the
transition to a market-driven health care system coincided with an acceleration of trends away from paternalistic employment policies and
welfare state politics. Many employees experienced the stabilization or

decline in overall premiums as an increase in their paycheck deductions and compared unfavorably the network restrictions and utilization oversight of managed care with the halcyon days of first-dollar indemnity insurance.

Consumer concerns have been accompanied and encouraged by an even stronger producer backlash against the changing market and organizational structures in health care. Hospital employees and their labor unions are dismayed to note the shift in jobs from unionized inpatient settings to often nonunion ambulatory, subacute, and home health settings. Medical specialists resent the new tilt in status and income toward primary care. Physician earnings have continued to rise but at a slower pace and in a much more uneven pattern than in the era of cost-unconscious consumer demand. Medical groups and hospital systems impose a degree of administrative oversight, peer review, and public accountability that feels foreign and uncomfortable to clinical miracle-workers. Caregivers resent the budgetary constraints necessary for financial solvency as unwarranted incursions on their clinical autonomy. Specialty societies, labor unions, manufacturers of medical devices, and all the other constituents of the medical-industrial complex have mobilized in defense of their economic self-interest, naturally explaining their behavior as a defense of patient rights and the quality of care.

The number of uninsured and underinsured Americans grew during the 1990s, despite the moderation in premiums and prices. The savings from private sector cost control accrued first to employers and thence to employees through higher wages and to consumers through lower prices. Public sector cost savings accrued first to governmental programs and thence to taxpayers through budgetary surpluses and forgone tax increases. Health care cost control contributed to the macroeconomic prosperity of the era, with buoyant consumer demand, strong private investment, and expansionary fiscal policy. But the savings were not gathered together and channeled into health insurance for the uninsured, despite modest efforts targeted at children and other especially deserving groups. The lack of universal insurance coverage is a major blemish on the American polity and the Achilles' heel of the corporate system of health care. Its manifest inequities and inefficiencies provide continuing fuel for populist sentiments that interpret large organizations and competitive markets as somehow responsible for the callous disregard by many citizens for their less fortunate compatriots. Inadequate insurance fosters the non sequitor that since governmental mechanisms are necessary to subsidize insurance for the poor then governmental mechanisms are necessary to command and control the day-to-day operations of the health care delivery system.

The consumer and producer backlash against the health care equivalent of utility deregulation threatens to do much mischief but also may foster the checks and balances necessary for the sustained viability of the new system. Rules are needed for every game; some form of oversight is needed for every market. Utility commissions and statutory compulsions were not replaced by laissez faire in the transportation, communications, and finance industries but by a mix of disclosure mandates, safety standards, financial reserve requirements, and other safeguards that protect the public interest with a hand somewhat less visible than before. By analogy, mechanisms of oversight and accountability are beneficial and indeed essential for the corporate system of health care.

A salient characteristic of medicine is the clinical uncertainty of each individual's diagnosis and appropriate treatment. It is essential that administratively efficient and socially acceptable mechanisms be developed for reviewing, adjudicating, and appealing differences concerning benefit coverage, experimental treatment, and medical necessity. These mechanisms must be sufficiently close to the clinical interface to produce informed and timely outcomes but be sufficiently independent to claim a broader legitimacy. The system will need to grope to some workable mix of mediation, arbitration, and litigation to resolve differences in what is an inherently stressful and complex decision-making arena.

Health insurance involves the collecting of premiums and subsequent paying of claims in a manner that invariably raises the possibility of overextension and insolvency. State insurance departments traditionally regulated indemnity, Blue Cross, and HMO carriers but have been outstripped by the geographic expansion, product diversification, and capitation contracting of the industry. The locus of administrative control and the incidence of risk is no longer clear in health plans that operate in multiple states, offer multiple network designs, and sell every form of insurance, partial insurance, and reinsurance. Private employers and public agencies with self-insured fringe benefits programs escape state regulatory oversight altogether. Medical groups, physician practice management firms, and physician-hospital systems cover capitated populations larger than the enrollments in some insurance companies yet are often exempt from formal insurance regulation. The emerging system needs to revisit the nuts and bolts of tangible net equity, liquidity ratios, and other means for ensuring that the money paid at the beginning of the year is still available to cover the stream of claims that trickle in at the end.

The emerging health care system has pioneered new methods for the collection, dissemination, and comparison of data on customer service and clinical quality. The progress to date has been frustratingly slow but has laid the foundation for more specific, severity-adjusted, and outcomes-oriented measures in the future. This is an arena with important roles for public agencies that can mandate participation, for nonprofit organizations that can develop the instruments, and for health plans and providers who can cooperate on data collection and compete on quality results. The proliferation of print, television, and Internet avenues for the dissemination of quality and service data repeats the experience of the deregulated utility industries, where the rise of choice and competition created a new demand and thereby spurred a new supply of information to consumers.

Competition appears to be replacing collusion as the modus operandi of the emerging health care marketplace. But caution is necessary lest the ever present urge to merge not create cartels in local physician, hospital, or insurance markets. Antitrust law constitutes a form of regulation subject to its own excesses and abuses but nevertheless serves as an important support for a competitive economy. It is particularly important in health care. The long record of landmark antitrust cases bears ample witness to the anticompetitive and anticonsumer proclivities of medical societies, nonprofit hospitals, Blue Cross insurers, and other purportedly beneficent entities as well as the more usual cast of for-profit suspects. The tendency to consolidate into local cartels will grow as the pressure on health care revenues intensifies and is already perceptible in the behavior of some medical groups and many physician-hospital organizations. Vigilant oversight and vigorous enforcement by the antitrust agencies will be necessary at times to dissuade would-be monopolies from pursuing their dreams.

THE CORPORATE PRACTICE OF MEDICINE

The corporate health care system has adopted forms of organization, ownership, and contracting from the most dynamic sectors of the larger economy and applied them to the technology, culture, and institutions of medicine. Its foundations lie in the multispecialty and network medical groups that realign economic incentives and redesign clinical practice at the grassroots level. Medical groups offer a balance of competition and cooperation that accommodates the social needs for efficiency, adaptation, and innovation. The now passing guild of autonomous physician practices and informal referral networks offered only a cost-increasing form of service competition and impeded clinical cooperation among fragmented community caregivers. The joining of physicians in medical groups, either multispecialty clinics or IPAs, opens possibilities for informal consultation, evidence-based accountability, and a new professional culture of peer review. Affiliation with practice management firms and physician-hospital organizations broadens the scope of clinical coordination but heightens the risk of incentive attenuation and bureaucratic hypertrophy. Competition among health care organizations is conducive to ever-improving medical standards in the same way that competition among sporting teams is conducive to ever-improving athletic standards.

Health plans have adjusted to the heterogeneity of consumer demand by marketing multiple networks, methods of managing utilization, and benefit packages priced with multiple premiums, deductibles, and coinsurance provisions. Product diversification is accompanied by geographic expansion, as plans and providers reduce their dependence on any one region and leverage skills gained in one local market into competitive advantages in others. These multistate, multiproduct firms are consolidating through mergers and acquisitions, leaving most metropolitan markets dominated by a small number of large organizations. But entry barriers are lower, not higher, than in the era of professional dominance, rewarding competition and undermining cartels. Vertical disintegration is the norm, permitting health plans, medical groups, and hospital systems to focus on those services they perform best while coordinating with other services through contractual relationships. Innovation in organizational structures is accompanied by innovation in contractual structures, as plans and providers experiment with new methods of payment, medical management, and quality measurement.

The corporate system of health care has produced ever stronger organizations and ever more intense performance competition among them. But its sustainability as an economic system has not thereby been assured. The very dynamism of the corporate system disrupts established social norms and disadvantages powerful political constituencies. American health care will never go back to professional dominance, which lost its political power as well as its organizational basis in the transition to managed care. It will not proceed to the complete consolidation, the full vertical and horizontal integration embodied in the principles of managed competition. But corporate health care is threatened by a new form of regulation. This will not be the entry barriers and rate setting of the utility commission, but will come through myriad small rules, requirements, and judicial precedents designed to protect the purportedly helpless consumer against the hazards of choice and competition. Individually, each new regulation will limit only modestly the discretion of health care purchasers and providers. Cumulatively, however, they could strap down the corporate Gulliver through a thousand small impediments on innovation, taxes on efficiency, and litigious disputes over clinical uncertainties.

Despite the serious challenges facing the emerging health care system, it is possible to conclude on a cautiously optimistic note.[12] Political backlash followed the growth of large diversified firms in the American economy but did not reverse its course due to the remarkable gains in efficiency and quality generated by market competition and corporate organization. Capacity investment, market entry, product price, and service specifications have been opened to competition in the transportation, communication, energy, and finance industries after decades of utility regulation. The competitive corporate system has been sustained because it proposes not incremental improvements in cost or quality for the preexisting set of goods and services but, rather, revolutionary changes in the basic organizational and market structures of the economy. Similarly, the corporate system does not offer incremental reforms to the framework of professional dominance in medicine but has swept it away completely, along with fragmented physician practice, arms-length indemnity insurance, and cost-unconscious consumer demand. In the final analysis it is not incremental improvement in price and quality that counts, but rather the radical competition from the entirely new product and service, the new technology, the new source of supply, and the new type of organization, competition that strikes not at the margins of the profits and the outputs of the existing organizations but at their foundations and their very lives. This is the corporate practice of medicine.

Notes

CHAPTER 1. INTRODUCTION

1. K. R. Levit, C. Cowan, B. Braden et al., "National Health Expenditures in 1997: More Slow Growth," *Health Affairs* 17, no. 6 (1998): 99–110.

2. E. Freidson, *Professional Dominance: The Social Structure of Medical Care* (New York: Atherton Press, 1970).

3. J. E. Wennberg, J. L. Freeman, R. M. Shelton, and T. A. Bubloz, "Hospital Use and Mortality among Medicare Beneficiaries in Boston and New Haven," *New England Journal of Medicine* 321, no. 17 (1989): 1168–1173.

4. W. P. Welch, M. E. Miller, H. G. Welch et al., "Geographic Variation in Expenditures for Physicians' Services in the United States," *New England Journal of Medicine* 328 (1993): 621–627.

CHAPTER 2. UNREGULATED PROFESSIONALISM

1. In 1965, 89 percent of the 268,000 American physicians still practiced alone or with only one partner. As late as 1995, 66 percent of the now greatly expanded supply of 613,000 physicians were still in solo practice or two-physician partnerships. By that year, however, 94,000 physicians were members of groups with between 3 and 15 physicians, while 117,000 physicians, accounting for 15 percent of the total, practiced in larger organizations. P. L. Havlicek, *Medical Groups in the US: A Survey of Practice Characteristics* (Chicago: American Medical Association, Department of Data Survey and Planning, 1996).

2. T. Parsons, *The Social System* (London: Tavisock Publications, 1952), chap. 10. K. J. Arrow, "Uncertainty and the Welfare Economics of Medical Care," *American Economic Review* 53, no. 5 (1963): 941–973. R. Stevens, *American Medicine and the Public Interest* (New Haven: Yale University Press,

1971). E. Freidson, *Professional Dominance: The Social Structure of Medical Care* (New York: Atherton Press, 1970). E. Freidson, *Profession of Medicine* (New York: Harper and Row, 1970).

3. R. Stevens, *In Sickness and Wealth: American Hospitals in the Twentieth Century* (New York: Basic Books, 1989). C. Rosenberg, *The Care of Strangers: The Rise of America's Hospital System* (New York: Basic Books, 1987). P. Starr, *The Social Transformation of American Medicine,* (New York: Basic Books, 1982).

4. Hospital administrators had long decried the independence of the practicing physician from hierarchical control. D. F. Drake, *Reforming the Health Care Market: An Interpretative Economic History* (Washington, D.C.: Georgetown University Press, 1994). M. I. Roemer and J. W. Friedman, *Doctors in Hospitals: Medical Staff Organization and Hospital Performance* (Baltimore: Johns Hopkins University Press, 1971).

5. M. V. Pauly and M. Redisch, "The Not-for-Profit Hospital as a Physicians' Cooperative," *American Economic Review* 63 (1973): 87–99. M. V. Pauly, *Doctors and their Workshops* (Chicago: University of Chicago Press, 1980).

6. C. D. Weller, "Free Choice as a Restraint of Trade in American Health Care Delivery and Insurance," *Iowa Law Review* 69 (1984): 1351–1392.

7. H. M. Somers and A. R. Somers, "Private Health Insurance: Problems, Pressures, and Prospects," *California Law Review* 46 (1958): 376–410, 508–557. S. A. Law, *Blue Cross: What Went Wrong?* (New Haven: Yale University Press, 1975). Starr, *Social Transformation*. R. Cunningham and R. M. Cunningham, *The Blues: A History of the Blue Cross and Blue Shield System* (De Kalb: Northern Illinois University Press, 1997).

8. T. L. Delbanco, K. C. Meyers, and E. A. Segal, "Paying the Physician's Fee: Blue Shield and the Reasonable Charge," *New England Journal of Medicine* 301 (1979): 1314–1320.

9. M. S. Feldstein, "The Medical Economy," *Scientific American* 229 (1973): 151–160. M. S. Feldstein and B. Friedman, "Tax Subsidies, the Rational Demand for Insurance, and the Health Care Crisis," *Journal of Public Economics* 7 (1977): 155–178.

10. A. C. Enthoven, "A New Proposal to Reform the Tax Treatment of Health Insurance," *Health Affairs* 3, no. 1 (1984): 21–39.

11. T. R. Marmor, *The Politics of Medicare* (Chicago: Aldine, 1973). R. Fein, *Medical Care, Medical Costs: The Search for a Health Insurance Policy* (Cambridge, Mass.: Harvard University Press, 1986).

12. Marmor, *Politics of Medicare*.

13. M. I. Roemer, "Hospital Utilization and the Supply of Physicians," *Journal of the American Medical Association* 178, no. 10 (1961): 989–993. M. I. Roemer, "Bed Supply and Hospital Utilization: A Natural Experiment," *Hospitals* 35, no. 21 (1961): 36–42.

14. M. R. Chassin, R. H. Brook, R. E. Park et al., "Variations in the Use of Medical and Surgical Services in the Medicare Population," *New England Journal of Medicine* 314, no. 5 (1986): 285–290. C. M. Winslow, J. B. Kosecoff, M. R. Chassin et al., "The Appropriateness of Performing Coronary Artery Bypass Surgery," *New England Journal of Medicine* 260, no. 4 (1988): 505–509.

J. E. Wennberg, J. L. Freeman, R. M. Shelton, and T. A. Bubloz, "Hospital Use and Mortality among Medicare Beneficiaries in Boston and New Haven," *New England Journal of Medicine* 321, no. 17 (1989): 1168–1173.

15. H. S. Luft, J. C. Robinson, D. W. Garnick et al., "The Role of Specialized Clinical Services in Competition among Hospitals," *Inquiry* 23 (1986): 83–94. J. C. Robinson, D. W. Garnick, and S. J. McPhee, "Market and Regulatory Influences on the Availability of Coronary Angioplasty and Bypass Surgery in U.S. Hospitals," *New England Journal of Medicine* 317 (1987): 85–90.

16. P. Joskow. "The Effects of Competition and Regulation on Hospital Bed Supply and the Reservation Quality of the Hospital," *Bell Journal of Economics* 11 (1980): 421–447. J. C. Robinson, H. S. Luft, S. J. McPhee et al., "Hospital Competition and Surgical Length of Stay," *Journal of the American Medical Association* 259 (1988): 696–700.

17. J. C. Robinson and H. S. Luft, "Competition and the Cost of Hospital Care, 1972–1982," *Journal of the American Medical Association* 257 (1987): 3241–3245.

18. D. Dranove, M. Shanley, and W. D. White, "Price and Concentration in Hospital Markets: The Switch from Patient-Driven to Payer-Driven Competition," *Journal of Law and Economics* 36 (1993): 179–204.

19. M. S. Feldstein, "The Medical Economy," *Scientific American* 229, no. 3 (1973): 151–160. M. S. Feldstein and B. Friedman, "Tax Subsidies, the Rational Demand for Insurance, and the Health Care Crisis," *Journal of Public Economics* 7 (1977): 155–178.

20. Molière, "The Physician in Spite of Himself," *Eight Plays by Molière,* trans. M. Bishop (New York: Modern Library, 1957). G. B. Shaw, "The Doctor's Dilemma," *Six Plays by Bernard Shaw* (New York: Dodd, Mead, 1941).

21. R. Dubos, *The Mirage of Health: Utopian Progress and Biological Change* (New York: Anchor Books, 1959). R. Carlson, *The End of Medicine* (New York: Wiley Interscience, 1975). I. Illich, *Medical Nemesis* (New York: Bantam Books, 1976). R. C. Fox, "The Medicalization and Demedicalization of American Society," *Daedalus* 106, no. 1 (1977): 9–22.

22. Dubos, *Mirage of Health.* J. H. Knowles, "The Responsibility of the Individual," *Daedalus* 106, no. 1 (1977): 57–80.

23. T. Szasz, *The Myth of Mental Illness* (New York: Dell, 1961). E. Goffman, *Asylums: Essays on the Social Situation of Mental Patients and Other Inmates* (Garden City, N.J.: Anchor Books, 1961). K. Kesey, *One Flew Over the Cuckoo's Nest* (New York: New American Library, 1962). M. Foucault, *Madness and Civilization: A History of Insanity in the Age of Reason* (New York: Vintage Books, 1965).

24. Only Illich, in his *Medical Nemesis,* went that far. P. Starr, "The Politics of Therapeutic Nihilism," *Working Papers for a New Society* 4, no. 2 (1976): 48–55.

25. D. R. Hyde and P. Wolff, "The American Medical Association: Power, Purpose, and Politics in Organized Medicine," *Yale Law Journal* 63, no. 7 (1954): 937–1022. R. A. Kessel, "Price Discrimination in Medicine," *Journal of Law and Economics* 1 (1958): 20–53. C. D. Weller, "Free Choice as a Restraint of Trade in American Health Care Delivery and Insurance," *Iowa Law Review*

69 (1984): 1351–1392. M. Friedman, *Capitalism and Freedom* (Chicago: University of Chicago Press, 1962).

26. M. Friedman and S. Kuznets, *Income from Independent Practice* (New York: National Bureau of Economic Research, 1945). R. A. Kessel, "The AMA and the Supply of Physicians," *Law and Contemporary Problems* 35 (1970): 267–283. E. Rayback, *Professional Power and American Medicine: The Economics of the American Medical Association* (Cleveland: World Publishing, 1967).

27. Freidson, *Professional Dominance,* and Freidson, *Profession of Medicine.*

28. M. L. Millenson, *Demanding Medical Excellence: Doctors and Accountability in the Information Age* (Chicago: University of Chicago Press, 1998).

29. Hyde and Wolff, "The American Medical Association: Power, Purpose, and Politics in Organized Medicine." Weller, "Free Choice as a Restraint of Trade in American Health Care Delivery and Insurance." J. G. Smillie, *Can Physicians Manage the Cost and Quality of Health Care? The Story of the Permanente Medical Group* (New York: McGraw-Hill, 1991).

30. Hyde and Wolff, "The American Medical Association: Power, Purpose, and Politics in Organized Medicine."

31. C. C. Havighurst, "Antitrust Enforcement in the Medical Services Industry: What Does It All Mean?" *Milbank Memorial Fund Quarterly* 58, no. 1 (1980): 89–124. A. N. Lerner, "Federal Trade Commission Antitrust Activities in the Health Services Field," *The Antitrust Bulletin* (Summer 1984): 205–224.

32. Havighurst, "Antitrust Enforcement in the Medical Services Industry."

33. W. R. Glaser, *Health Insurance in Practice: Institutional Variations in Financing, Benefits, and Problems* (San Francisco: Jossey-Bass, 1991).

34. A. E. Kahn, *The Economics of Regulation: Principles and Institutions* (New York: John Wiley, 1971). A. E. Kahn, "Deregulation: Looking Backward and Looking Forward," *Yale Journal on Regulation* 7 (1990): 325–354. P. L. Joskow and R. C. Noll, "Regulation in Theory and Practice: An Overview," in *Studies in Public Regulation,* ed. G. Fromm (Cambridge, Mass.: MIT Press, 1981).

35. Kahn, *Economics of Regulation,* and Kahn, "Deregulation."

36. G. J. Stigler, "The Theory of Economic Regulation," *Bell Journal of Economics and Management Science* 2 (1971): 22–50. S. Pelzman, "Toward a More General Theory of Regulation," *Journal of Law and Economics* 19 (1976): 211–240. G. Becker, "A Theory of Competition among Pressure Groups for Political Influence," *Quarterly Journal of Economics* 98 (1983): 371–400. S. Pelzman, "The Economic Theory of Regulation after a Decade of Deregulation," *Brookings Papers: Microeconomics* 1989 (1989): 1–41.

37. D. M. Fox, "Sharing Governmental Authority: Blue Cross and Hospital Planning in New York City," *Journal of Health Politics, Policy, and Law* 16, no. 4 (1991): 719–746.

38. American Hospital Association, *Hospital Regulation: Report of the Special Committee on the Regulatory Process* (Chicago: American Hospital Association, 1977).

39. J. E. McDonough, *Interests, Ideas, and Deregulation: The Fate of Hospital Rate Setting* (Ann Arbor: University of Michigan Press, 1997).

40. H. Averch and L. Johnson, "Behavior of the Firm under Regulatory Con-

straint," *American Economic Review* 52 (1962): 1052–1069. G. J. Stigler and C. Friedland, "What Can Regulators Regulate? The Case of Electricity," *Journal of Law and Economics* 5 (1962): 1–16. Stigler, "Theory of Economic Regulation." G. W. Douglass and J. C. Miller, "Quality Competition, Industry Equilibrium, and Efficiency in the Price-Constrained Airline Market," *American Economic Review* 64 (1974): 657–669.

41. C. Winston, "U.S. Industry Adjustment to Economic Deregulation," *Journal of Economic Perspectives* 3 (1998): 89–110. C. Winston, T. M. Corsi, C. M. Grimm et al., *The Economic Effects of Surface Freight Deregulation* (Washington, D.C.: Brookings Institution, 1990). R. W. Crandall, *After the Breakup: U.S. Telecommunications in a More Competitive Era* (Washington, D.C.: Brookings Institution, 1991). A. N. Berger, A. K. Kashyap, and J. M. Scalise, "The Transformation of the U.S. Banking Industry: What a Long Strange Trip It's Been," *Brookings Papers on Economic Activity* 2 (1995): 55–218. S. A. Morrison and C. Winston, *The Evolution of the Airline Industry* (Washington, D.C.: Brookings Institution, 1995).

42. C. C. Havighurst, *Deregulating the Health Care Industry: Planning for Competition* (Cambridge, Mass.: Ballinger, 1982).

43. D. Cohodes and C. Eby, "What Do We Know about Rate Setting?" *Journal of Health Politics, Policy, and Law* 10 (1985): 299–327. J. C. Robinson and H. S. Luft, "Competition, Regulation, and Hospital Costs, 1982 to 1986," *Journal of the American Medical Association* 260 (1988): 2676–2681. D. Crozier, "State Rate Setting: A Status Report," *Health Affairs* 1 (Summer 1982): 66–83. F. A. Sloan, "Rate Regulation as a Strategy for Hospital Cost Control: Evidence from the Last Decade," *Milbank Memorial Fund Quarterly* 61, no. 2 (1983): 195–217.

44. G. F. Anderson, "All-Payer Ratesetting: Down but Not Out," *Health Care Financing Review* (1991; Annual Supplement): 35–41. J. E. McDonough, "Tracking the Demise of State Hospital Rate Setting," *Health Affairs* 16, no. 1 (1997): 142–149. McDonough, *Interests, Ideas, and Deregulation: The Fate of Hospital Rate Setting*.

45. M. McClellan, "Hospital Reimbursement Incentives: An Empirical Analysis," *Journal of Economics and Management Strategy* 6, no. 1 (1997): 91–128. M. A. Morrisey, F. A. Sloan, and J. Valvona, "Shifting Medicare Patients Out of the Hospital," *Health Affairs* 7, no. 5 (1988): 52–64.

46. W. B. Schwartz and D. M. Mendelson, "Hospital Cost Containment in the 1980s: Hard Lessons Learned and Prospects for the 1990s," *New England Journal of Medicine* 324, no. 15 (1991): 1037–1042.

47. A. S. Detsky, S. R. Stacey, and C. Bombardier, "The Effectiveness of a Regulatory Strategy in Containing Hospital Costs," *New England Journal of Medicine* 309, no. 3 (1983): 151–159. R. G. Evans, J. Lomas, M. L. Barer et al., "Controlling Health Expenditures: the Canadian Reality," *New England Journal of Medicine* 320, no. 9 (1989): 571–577. V. R. Fuchs and J. S. Hahn, "A Comparison of Expenditures for Physician Services in the United States and Canada," *New England Journal of Medicine* 323, no. 13 (1990): 884–890.

48. Needless to say, free choice of provider and treatment were circumscribed by the upstream rationing of physician, hospital, and technological supply.

49. D. U. Himmelstein, S. Woolhandler et al., "A National Health Program for the United States: A Physicians' Proposal," *New England Journal of Medicine* 320, no. 2 (1989): 102–108.

CHAPTER 3.   UNMANAGED COMPETITION

1. P. M. Ellwood, N. N. Anderson, J. E. Billings et al., "Health Maintenance Strategy," *Medical Care* 9, no. 3 (1971): 291–298.

2. L. D. Brown, *Politics and Health Care Organization: HMOs as Federal Policy* (Washington, D.C.: Brookings Institution, 1983). P. Starr, *The Social Transformation of American Medicine* (New York: Basic Books, 1982).

3. A. C. Enthoven, "Consumer Choice Health Plan," *New England Journal of Medicine* 298 (1978): 650–658, 709–720.

4. C. D. Weller, "Free Choice as a Restraint of Trade in American Health Care Delivery and Insurance," *Iowa Law Review* 69 (1984): 1351–1392.

5. A. C. Enthoven, *Theory and Practice of Managed Competition in Health Care Finance* (Amsterdam: North Holland, 1988).

6. S. B. Jones, "Multiple Choice Health Insurance: The Lessons and Challenge to Private Insurers," *Inquiry* 29, no. 2 (1990): 161–166. J. P. Newhouse, W. B. Schwartz, A. P. Williams et al., "Are Fee-for-Service Costs Increasing Faster than HMO Costs?" *Medical Care* 23, no. 8 (1985): 960–966.

7. C. G. McLaughlin, "Market Responses to HMOs: Price Competition or Rivalry?" *Inquiry* 25 (1988): 207–218.

8. G. R. Wilensky and L. F. Rossiter, "Patient Self-Selection in HMOs," *Health Affairs* 5 (1986): 66–80. F. J. Hellinger, "Selection Bias in Health Maintenance Organizations: Analysis of Recent Evidence," *Health Care Financing Review* 9 (1987): 55–63. H. S. Luft and R. H. Miller, "Patient Selection in a Competitive Health Care System," *Health Affairs* 7 (1988): 97–119. M. Giacomini, H. S. Luft, and J. C. Robinson, "Risk-Adjusting Community-Rated Health Plan Premiums: A Survey of Risk Assessment Literature and Policy Applications," *Annual Review of Public Health* 16 (1995): 401–430.

9. A. C. Enthoven and R. Kronick, "A Consumer-Choice Health Plan for the 1990s," *New England Journal of Medicine* 320 (1989): 29–37, 94–101.

10. A. C. Enthoven, "Management of Competition in the FEHBP," *Health Affairs* 8 (1989): 33–50. S. B. Butler and R. E. Moffit, "The FEHBP as a Model for a New Medicare Program," *Health Affairs* 14 (1995): 47–61. U.S. General Accounting Office, *Health Insurance: California Public Employees Alliance Has Reduced Recent Premium Growth,* GAO/HRD-94-40 (Washington, D.C.: U.S. Government Printing Office, November 1993).

11. J. C. Robinson, "Health Care Purchasing and Market Change in California," *Health Affairs* 14, no. 4 (1995): 117–130. H. H. Schauffler and T. Rodriquez, "Exercising Purchasing Power for Preventive Care," *Health Affairs* 15, no. 1 (1996): 73–85. U.S. General Accounting Office, *Health Insurance: Management Strategies Used by Large Employers to Control Costs,* GAO/HEHS-97-71 (Washington, D.C.: U.S. Government Printing Office, May 1997).

12. U.S. General Accounting Office, *Private Health Insurance: Problems*

Caused by a Segmented Market, GAO/HRD-91-114 (Washington, D.C.: U.S. Government Printing Office, July 1991).

13. P. M. Ellwood, A. C. Enthoven, and L. Etheredge, "The Jackson Hole Initiatives for a Twenty-First Century American Health Care System," *Health Economics* 1 (1992): 149–168.

14. W. A. Zelman, "The Rationale Behind the Clinton Health Reform Plan," *Health Affairs* 13, no. 1 (1994): 9–29. P. Starr, "The Framework of Health Care Reform," *New England Journal of Medicine* 329, no. 22 (1993): 1666–1672. A. M. Epstein, "Changes in Delivery of Care under Comprehensive Health Care Reform," *New England Journal of Medicine* 329, no. 22 (1993): 1672–1676.

15. A. C. Enthoven and S. J. Singer, "A Single-Payer System in Jackson Hole Clothing," *Health Affairs* 13, no. 1 (1994): 81–95.

16. W. A. Zelman, "Who Should Govern the Purchasing Cooperative?" *Health Affairs* 12 (1993, Supplement): 49–57. R. Kronick, "A Helping Hand for the Invisible Hand," *Health Affairs* 13, no. 1 (1994): 96–101.

17. P. D. Wellstone and E. R. Schaffer, "The American Health Security Act—A Single-Payer Proposal," *New England Journal of Medicine* 328, no. 20 (1993): 1489–1493.

18. W. A. Zelman and L. D. Brown, "Looking Back on Health Care Reform: No Easy Choices," *Health Affairs* 17, no. 6 (1998): 61–68.

19. T. Skocpol, "The Rise and Resounding Demise of the Clinton Plan," *Health Affairs* 14, no. 1 (1995): 66–85. R. J. Blendon, M. Brodie, and J. Benson, "What Happened to Americans' Support for the Clinton Health Plan?" *Health Affairs* 14, no. 2 (1995): 7–23.

20. Ellwood, Enthoven, and Etheredge, "Jackson Hole Initiatives."

21. Zelman, "Who Should Govern the Purchasing Cooperative?"

22. The small-firm purchasing alliance in California pioneered a method for risk-adjusting premiums to competing plans based on incidence of rare but exceptionally high cost diagnoses. S. Shewry, S. Hunt, J. Ramey, and J. Bertko, "Risk Adjustment: The Missing Piece of Market Competition," *Health Affairs* 15, no. 1 (1996): 171–181. T. C. Buchmueller, "Managed Competition in California's Small-Group Insurance Market," *Health Affairs* 16, no. 2 (1997): 218–228.

23. U.S. General Accounting Office, *Private Health Insurance: Problems Caused by a Segmented Market,* GAO/HRD-91-114 (Washington, D.C.: U.S. Government Printing Office, 1991), Table 1.1.

24. J. M. Yegian, T. C. Buchmueller, J. C. Robinson et al., *Health Insurance Purchasing Alliances for Small Firms: Lessons from the California Experience* (Oakland: California Healthcare Foundation, 1998).

25. Robinson, "Health Care Purchasing and Market Changes in California. H. H. Schauffler and T. Rodriquez, "Exercising Purchasing Power for Preventive Health," *Health Affairs* 15, no. 1 (1996): 73–85.

26. On the role of inefficiency by design in political institutions and bureaucracies, see T. M. Moe, "Political Institutions: The Neglected Side of the Story," *Journal of Law, Economics, and Organization* 6 (1990, Special Issue): 213–253.

27. *Health Care Financing Review, Medicare and Medicaid Statistical Sup-*

plement, 1997, Table 1: Personal Health Expenditures, by Source of Funds (Baltimore: U.S. Department of Health and Human Services, 1997).

CHAPTER 4. VIRTUAL INTEGRATION

1. Even indemnity insurance adopts an implicit network structure, rate structure, and method of utilization review. It limits coverage to services provided by licensed physicians while excluding many ancillary providers; caps payments according to its fee schedule or determination of usual, customary, and reasonable rates; requires that the services be medically necessary rather than cosmetic; and excludes experimental procedures.

2. A. L. Siu, A. Leibowitz, W. H. Rodgers et al., "Use of the Hospital in a Randomized Trial of Prepaid Care," *Journal of the American Medical Association* 259, no. 9 (1988): 1343–1346.

3. C. C. Havighurst and G. M. Hackbarth, "Private Cost Containment," *New England Journal of Medicine* 300, no. 23 (1979): 1298–1305. P. J. Feldstein, T. M. Wickizer, and J. Wheeler, "Private Cost Containment: The Effects of Utilization Review on Health Care Use and Expenditures," *New England Journal of Medicine* 318, no. 20 (1988): 1310–1314. G. W. Grumet, "Health Care Rationing through Inconvenience: The Third Party's Secret Weapon," *New England Journal of Medicine* 321, no. 9 (1989): 607–611.

4. HMO enrollment percentages include point-of-service products. J. Gabel, D. Liston, G. Jensen, and J. Marsteller, "The Health Insurance Picture in 1993: Some Rare Good News," *Health Affairs* 13 (Spring 1994): 327–336.

5. E. W. Hoy, R. E. Curtis, and T. Rice, "Change and Growth in Managed Care," *Health Affairs* 10, no. 4 (1991): 18–36.

6. G. A. Jensen, M. A. Morrisey, S. Gaffney, and D. K. Liston, "The New Dominance of Managed Care: Insurance Trends in the 1990s," *Health Affairs* 16, no. 1 (1997): 125–136.

7. I. R. Macneil, "Contracts: Adjustments of Long-term Economic Relations under Classical, Neoclassical, and Relational Contract Law," *Northwestern University Law Review* 72 (1978): 854–906. O. E. Williamson, *The Economic Institutions of Capitalism* (New York: Free Press, 1985).

8. P. L. Joskow, "Vertical Integration and Long-term Contracts: The Case of Coal-burning Electric Generating Plants," *Journal of Law, Economics, and Organization* 1 (1985): 33–80.

9. B. Klein and K. B. Leffler, "The Role of Market Forces in Assuring Contractual Performance," *Journal of Political Economy* 89 (1981): 615–641.

10. For an introduction to the history of prepaid group practice, see P. Starr, *The Social Transformation of American Medicine* (New York: Basic Books, 1982) and M. Shadid, *A Doctor for the People* (New York: Vanguard Press, 1939).

11. H. S. Luft, *Health Maintenance Organizations: Dimensions of Performance* (New York: John Wiley, 1981). W. G. Manning, A. Leibowitz, G. A. Goldberg et al., "A Controlled Trial of the Effect of a Prepaid Group Practice on Use of Services," *New England Journal of Medicine* 310, no. 23 (1984): 1505–1510.

Siu, Leibowitz, Rodgers et al., "Use of the Hospital in a Randomized Trial of Prepaid Care."

12. A. R. Somers, *The Kaiser-Permanente Medical Care Program* (New York: Commonwealth Fund, 1971). J. G. Smillie, *Can Physicians Manage the Quality and Costs of Medical Care? The Story of the Permanente Medical Group* (New York: McGraw-Hill, 1991).

13. K. Pavitt, "Sectoral Patterns of Technical Change: Towards a Taxonomy and a Theory," *Research Policy* 13 (1984): 343–373. G. P. Pisano, "The R&D Boundaries of the Firm: An Empirical Analysis," *Administrative Science Quarterly* 35 (1990): 153–176. D. J. Teece, "Profiting from Technological Innovation: Implications for Integration, Collaboration, Licensing, and Public Policy," *Research Policy* 15 (1986): 285–305. G. Dosi, "Sources, Procedures, and Microeconomic Effects of Innovation," *Journal of Economic Literature* 26 (1988): 1120–1171.

14. A. Saxanian, *Regional Advantage: Culture and Competition in Silicon Valley and Route 128* (Cambridge, Mass.: Harvard University Press, 1994).

15. O. E. Williamson, *The Economic Institutions of Capitalism* (New York: Free Press, 1985). B. Klein, R. G. Crawford, and A. A. Alchian, "Vertical Integration, Appropriable Rents, and the Competitive Contracting Process," *Journal of Law and Economics* 21 (1978): 297–326.

16. G. J. Stigler, "The Division of Labor Is Limited by the Extent of the Market," *Journal of Political Economy* 59 (1951): 185–193. A. D. Chandler, *Scale and Scope: The Dynamics of Industrial Capitalism* (Cambridge, Mass.: Harvard University Press, 1990).

CHAPTER 5.   THE MULTISPECIALTY MEDICAL GROUP

1. Information on HealthCare Partners Medical Group was obtained from the trade press and company documents, and from interviews with physician and administrative leaders of the medical group and from leaders of other physician organizations, hospital systems, and health insurance plans. See also J. C. Robinson and L. P. Casalino, "The Growth of Medical Groups Paid through Capitation in California," *New England Journal of Medicine* 333 (1995): 1684–1687. B. S. Bader, "HealthCare Partners Medical Group," *Health System Leader* 6, no. 1 (1994): 14–22. M. Moser, "The Growth of Multispecialty Medical Groups 1982–1989," *Journal of Ambulatory Care Management* 14, no. 3 (1991): 9–13. L. P. Casalino and J. C. Robinson, *The Evolution of Medical Groups and Capitation in California* (Oakland: California HealthCare Foundation, 1997). R. Thompson and R. Brown, *Medicare Beneficiaries and HMOs: A Case Study of the Los Angeles Market* (Menlo Park, Calif.: Kaiser Family Foundation, 1998).

2. Unified Medical Group Association, *Annual Report 1995–96* (Seal Beach, Calif.: Unified Medical Group Association, 1996). Casalino and Robinson, *The Evolution of Medical Groups and Capitation in California.*

3. Information on the Nalle Clinic was obtained from the trade press and company documents, and from discussions with physician and administrative

leaders at the clinic, at PhyCor, at other physician organizations, and at health insurance plans.

4. Information on the Summit Medical Group was obtained from the trade press and from discussions with physician and administrative leaders at the medical group and at other physician organizations, hospital systems, and health insurance plans. See also J. C. Robinson, "Consolidation of Medical Groups into Physician Practice Management Organizations," *Journal of the American Medical Association* 279, no. 2 (1998): 144–148. For information on the New York and New Jersey managed care markets see L. T. Kohn, P. Kemper, R. J. Baxter et al., *Health System Change in Twelve Communities* (Washington, D.C.: Center for Studying Health System Change, 1997). A. Aizer, M. Gold, and R. Brown, *Medicare Beneficiaries and HMOs: A Case Study of the New York City Market* (Menlo Park, Calif.: Kaiser Family Foundation, 1998).

5. J. E. Wennberg, *The Dartmouth Atlas of Health Care* (Chicago: American Hospital Association, 1996).

6. Robinson and Casalino, "The Growth of Medical Groups Paid through Capitation in California."

7. J. C. Robinson and C. D. Damberg, "Contractual Relations between Large Medical Groups and Health Maintenance Organizations in California, Oregon, and Washington" (unpublished manuscript, Pacific Business Group on Health and University of California, Berkeley, 1997).

8. P. J. Feldstein, T. M. Wickizer, and J. Wheeler, "Private Cost Containment: The Effects of Utilization Review Programs on Health Care Use and Expenditures," *New England Journal of Medicine* 318, no. 20 (1988): 1310–1314.

9. E. A. Kerr, B. S. Mittman, R. D. Hays et al., "Managed Care and Capitation in California: How Do Physicians at Financial Risk Control Their Own Utilization?"

10. Kerr, Mittman, Hays et al., "Managed Care and Capitation in California: How Do Physicians at Financial Risk Control their Own Utilization?"

11. Casalino and Robinson, *Evolution of Medical Groups and Capitation in California.*

12. Hoechst Marion Roussel, *HMO-PPO Digest, 1996* (Kansas City, Mo.: Hoechst Marion Roussel, 1995). U.S. Department of Health and Human Services, Public Health Service, *National Hospital Discharge Summary, 1993,* Vital and Health Statistics, series 13, no. 121 (August 1995), Table B.

13. Robinson and Casalino, "Growth of Medical Groups Paid through Capitation in California."

14. Hoechst Marion Roussel, *HMO-PPO Digest, 1996.* Medicare and Medicaid Statistical Supplement, *Health Care Financing Review* (Baltimore: U.S. Department of Health and Human Services, Health Care Financing Administration, 1995).

15. These capacity and utilization statistics refer to nonfederal community hospitals. American Hospital Association, *Hospital Statistics, 1995–96 Edition* (Chicago: American Hospital Association, 1996).

16. HMO penetration and cost growth was measured for the decade between 1983 and 1993. J. C. Robinson, "Decline in Hospital Utilization and Cost Inflation under Managed Care in California," *Journal of the American Medical*

Association 276, no. 13 (1996): 1060–1064.

17. Robinson and Damberg, "Contractual Relations between Large Medical Groups and Health Maintenance Organizations."

18. M. L. Berk, A. C. Monheit, and M. M. Hagan, "How the U.S. Spent its Health Care Dollar, 1929–1980," *Health Affairs* 7, no. 4 (1988): 46–60. M. L. Berk and A. C. Monheit, "The Concentration of Health Expenditures: An Update," *Health Affairs* 11, no. 4 (1992): 145–149.

19. R. M. Wachter and L. Goldman, "The Emerging Role of Hospitalists in the American Health Care System," *New England Journal of Medicine* 335 (1996): 514–517.

20. E. A. Kerr, B. S. Mittman, R. D. Hays et al., "Quality Assurance in Capitated Physician Groups: Where is the Emphasis?" *Journal of the American Medical Association* 276 (1996): 1236–1239.

21. D. M. Berwick, "Continuous Improvement as an Ideal in Health Care," *New England Journal of Medicine* 320, no. 1 (1989): 53–56.

22. J. K. Iglehart, "The National Commission on Quality Assurance," *New England Journal of Medicine* 335 (1996): 995–999.

23. J. W. Thompson, J. Bost, F. Ahmed et al., "The NCQA's Quality Compass: Evaluating Managed Care in the United States," *Health Affairs* 17, no. 1 (1998): 152–158. D. M. Eddy, "Performance Measurement: Problems and Solutions," *Health Affairs* 17, no. 4 (1998): 7–25.

24. J. C. Shiely, M. S. Balyliss, S. D. Keller et al. *SF-36 Health Survey Annotated Bibliography: First Edition, 1988–1995* (Boston: The Health Institute, New England Medical Center, 1997).

25. California Cooperative Healthcare Reporting Initiative, *California Health Plan Performance Results: 1997 Report on Quality* (San Francisco: Pacific Business Group on Health, 1997).

26. Pacific Business Group on Health, "PBGH Releases Results from First-of-its-Kind Physician Value Check Survey," *Pacific Currents* 3 (Fall 1997): 4–7.

27. The most comprehensive data to date have been posted at *www.healthscope.org,* maintained by the Pacific Business Group on Health. Some health plans have developed their own medical group quality indicators; see *www.pacificare.com.* The Buyers Health Care Action Group in Minneapolis has developed quality data on provider organizations in that market, posted at *www.choiceplus.org.*

CHAPTER 6.   THE INDEPENDENT PRACTICE
ASSOCIATION

1. P. L. Havelicek, *Medical Groups in the US: A Survey of Practice Characteristics* (Chicago: American Medical Association, Division of Survey and Data Resources, 1996).

2. Many IPAs evaluate contracts with PPO insurers on behalf of their members, but typically the insurer then signs an individual agreement with each physician, pays that physician directly rather than via the IPA organization, and retains authority for utilization management within the plan rather than

delegating it to the IPA.

3. The Federal Trade Commission and U.S. Department of Justice have maintained a skeptical and watchful eye on IPAs, striving to develop standards by which to distinguish organizations that generally promote efficiency from organizations that principally seek market power. U.S. Department of Justice and Federal Trade Commission, *Statements of Antitrust Enforcement Policy in Health Care* (Washington, D.C.: Federal Trade Commission, August 1996).

4. For case study and survey information on IPAs, see B. Schenkin, "The Independent Practice Association in Theory and Practice," *Journal of the American Medical Association* 273, no. 24 (1995): 1937–1942. K. Grumbach, J. Coffman, K. Vranizan et al., "Independent Practice Association Physician Groups in California," *Health Affairs* 17, no. 3 (1998): 227–237.

5. R. Gumbiner, *FHP: The Evolution of a Managed Care Health Maintenance Organization, 1955–1992* (Berkeley: University of California Press, 1995). L. P. Casalino, "Medical Groups and the Transition to Managed Care in California" (Ph.D. dissertation, University of California, 1997).

6. H. S. Luft, *Health Maintenance Organizations: Dimensions of Performance* (New York: John Wiley and Sons, 1981).

7. When it launched its HMO TakeCare in 1978, Blue Cross of Northern California initially followed the lead of its southern California counterpart in contracting with multispecialty clinics. It quickly discovered the limits of trying to market a network composed only of a few groups, and turned to the hospital-based IPAs. Subsequent HMOs followed its lead, and the multispecialty model never spread significantly beyond the Palo Alto, San Jose, Gould, Bay Valley, MedClinic, and Sunnyvale groups.

8. Information on Hill Physicians was obtained from the trade press and from discussions with physician and administrative leaders of the group and of other physician organizations, hospital systems, and health insurance plans.

9. T. Fourkas, *The Evolution of Managed Care in the Sacramento Region* (Sacramento: Sierra Health Foundation, 1997). V. Schmitz and R. C. Dobler, "The Mercy Medical Foundation," in *Hospital-Physician Integration: Strategies for Success* (Chicago: American Hospital Association, 1994). R. H. Miller, H. L. Lipton, and A. K. Duke, *Health System Change in the Greater Sacramento Area* (Sacramento: Sierra Health Foundation, 1997).

10. Hill Physicians Medical Group, *1997 Annual Report* (San Ramon, Calif.: Hill Physicians Medical Group, 1998).

11. Information on Brown and Toland was obtained from the trade press and from discussions with physician and administrative leaders of the group and of other physician organizations, hospital systems, and health insurance plans.

12. This interpretation of IPA payment incentives was developed through discussions at Brown and Toland, Hill Physicians, FPA Medical Management, North American Medical Management, East Bay Medical Network, Monarch IPA, Huntington Provider Group, Orange Coast Managed Care Services, Adesso Specialty Services Organization, Redwood Empire Medical Group, Alta Bates Medical Group, the Marin IPA, and Mullikin IPA.

13. Referral-based or contact capitation was pioneered in the large IPAs in

southern California. Insights into the incentives were obtained through discussions at Huntington Provider Group, Monarch HealthCare, and St. Joseph Medical Corporation. Also see The Governance Committee, *To the Greater Good: Recovering the American Physician Enterprise* (Washington, D.C.: Advisory Board Co., 1995).

CHAPTER 7. PHYSICIAN PRACTICE MANAGEMENT

1. J. C. Robinson and L. P. Casalino, "The Growth of Medical Groups Paid through Capitation in California," *New England Journal of Medicine* 333 (1995): 1684–1687. Hoechst Marion Roussel, *Managed Care Digest Series 1997: HMO-PPO/Medicare-Medicaid Digest* (Kansas City, Mo.: Hoechst Marion Rossell, 1997).

2. E. A. Kerr, B. S. Mittman, R. D. Hays et al., "Managed Care and Capitation in California: How Do Physicians at Financial Risk Control their Own Utilization?" *Annals of Internal Medicine* 123 (1995): 500–504. D. M. Berwick, "Payment by Capitation and the Quality of Care," *New England Journal of Medicine* 335, no. 16 (1996): 1227–1231.

3. L. C. Marsh and A. Feinstein, *Of Minds and Men: Changing Behavior in the New Physician Enterprise* (New York: Salomon Brothers, March 1997). American Medical Association, *Physician Practice Management Companies: What You Need to Know* (Chicago: American Medical Association, 1997). B. G. O'Neil and T. B. Manderfeld, *Physician Practice Management: Searching for Value* (Minneapolis: Piper Jaffray, August 1997).

4. J. E. Wennberg et al., *The Dartmouth Atlas of Health Care in the United States* (Chicago: American Hospital Publishing, 1996).

5. J. A. Schumpeter, *Capitalism, Socialism, and Democracy* (New York: Harper and Row, 1942). A. D. Chandler, *Scale and Scope: The Dynamics of Industrial Capitalism* (Cambridge, Mass.: Harvard University Press, 1990). R. R. Nelson, "Capitalism as an Engine of Progress," *Research Policy* 19 (1990): 193–214.

6. Information on PhyCor was obtained from the trade press and from discussions with management and clinical leaders at PhyCor, competitor PPMs, hospital systems, health insurance plans, investment banking firms, and industry observers.

7. J. D. Ederer and J. M. Rosenbluth, *PhyCor, Inc.* (San Francisco: Volpe Brown Whelan and Co., June 1997). O'Neil and Manderfeld, *Physician Practice Management*. Marsh and Feinstein. *Of Minds and Men*. E. H. Kerns and N. T. Ockers, *PhyCor, Inc.: Leading Physician Practice Management Company* (Baltimore: Alex Brown, March 1997). J. D. France, R. M. Willoughby, and A. G. Ballou, *PhyCor Inc.* (New York: Credit Suisse First Boston Equity Research Americas, July 1997). NASDAQ, *The Nasdaq Stock Market Corporate Record: PhyCor Inc.* (New York: NASDAQ, 1997). L. C. Marsh and A. T. Feinstein, *PhyCor, Inc.* (New York: Salomon Smith Barney, June 3, 1998).

8. J. C. Robinson, "Consolidation of Medical Groups into Physician Practice Management Companies," *Journal of the American Medical Association* 279, no. 2, 1998): 144–149. This interpretation of FPA was developed from dis-

cussions with and documents from physician and administrative leaders at FPA, other PPM firms, hospital systems, investment banks, and health insurance plans.

9. This interpretation was developed through discussions with and documents from physician and administrative leaders at MedPartners, its affiliated medical groups, competing organizations, hospital systems, health insurance plans, and investment banking firms.

10. MedPartners, Inc., "PhyCor Announces Agreement to Acquire Med-Partners, Combining Nation's Leading Physician Management Organizations" (press release, October 29, 1997). C. A. Hewitt and K. S. Abramowitz, *PhyCor to Acquire MedPartners' Capitation Expertise and Market Position* (New York: Bernstein Research, November 7, 1997). L. C. Marsh and A. T. Feinstein, *MedPartners, Inc.* (New York: Salomon Smith Barney, May 21, 1998).

11. A. Sharpe, "PhyCor Tries to Mesh Doctor Practices, Finds It Like Herding Cats," *Wall Street Journal* (May 4, 1998): p. A1. M. C. Jacklevic, "Sparks Flies with PhyCor Docs," *Modern Healthcare* (September 21, 1998): 30.

12. M. Haglund, "Rocket Men," *California Medicine* (February 1998): 31–37.

CHAPTER 8.   PHYSICIAN-HOSPITAL ORGANIZATION

1. The Advisory Board, Governance Committee, *The Grand Alliance: Vertical Integration Strategies for Physicians and Health Systems* (Washington, D.C.: Advisory Board, 1993). S. M. Shortell, R. R. Gilles, and D. A. Anderson, "The New World of Managed Care: Creating Organized Delivery Systems," *Health Affairs* 13, no. 5 (1994): 46–64. M. A. Morrissey, J. Alexander, L. R. Burns, and V. Johnson, "Managed Care and Physician-Hospital Integration," *Health Affairs* 15, no. 4 (1996): 62–73.

2. M. L. Millenson, *Demanding Medical Excellence: Doctors and Accountability in the Information Age* (Chicago: University of Chicago Press, 1997).

3. For an overview of the Orange County health care market, see P. B. Ginsburg and N. J. Fasciano, eds., *The Community Snapshots Project: Capturing Health System Change* (Washington, D.C.: Center for Studying Health System Change, 1994).

4. This interpretation of the St. Jude system is derived from the trade press and company documents, and from discussions with physician and administrative leaders at St. Jude, Bristol Park Medical Group, other physician organizations, hospital systems, and health insurance plans.

5. As is frequently the case in similar transactions, recipients were not permitted to sell the FPA stock within 90 days of the transaction. The Orange Coast shareholders reportedly rejected a cash-only payment in exchange for the all-stock payment since the latter had a higher value at the time of the negotiations.

6. J. E. McDonough, *Interests, Ideas, and Deregulation: The Fate of Hospital Rate Setting* (Ann Arbor: University of Michigan Press, 1997).

7. Hoechst Marion Roussel, *Managed Care Digest Series 1997: HMO-PPO/Medicare-Medicaid Digest* (Kansas City, Mo.: Hoechst Marion Roussel, 1997).

8. This interpretation of the Montefiore PHO is based on the trade press and

discussions with physician and administrative leaders with the organization, with other physician and hospital organizations, and with health insurance plans.

9. The early history of Montefiore hospital is recorded in D. Levenson, *Montefiore: The Hospital as Social Instrument, 1884–1984* (New York: Farrar, Straus, and Giroux, 1984).

10. J. C. Robinson, " The Changing Boundaries of the American Hospital," *Milbank Quarterly* 72, no. 2 (1994): 259–275. J. C. Robinson, "Decline of Hospital Utilization and Cost Inflation under Managed Care in California," *Journal of the American Medical Association* 276, no. 13 (1996): 1060–1064.

11. R. M. Wachter and L. Goldman, "The Emerging Role of Hospitalists in the American Health Care System," *New England Journal of Medicine* 335 (1996): 514–517.

12. K. J. Arrow, "The Economics of Agency," in *Principals and Agents: The Structure of Business,* ed. J. W. Pratt and R. J. Zeckhauser (Boston: Harvard Business School Press, 1985). M. C. Jensen and W. H. Meckling, "Theory of the Firm: Managerial Behavior, Agency Costs, and Ownership Structure," *Journal of Financial Economics* 3 (1976): 305–360.

13. C. Barnard, *The Functions of the Executive* (Cambridge, Mass.: Harvard University Press, 1939). A. Alchian and H. Demsetz, "Production, Information Costs, and Economic Organization," *American Economic Review* 62 (1972): 777–795.

14. J. C. Goldsmith, "Driving the Nitroglycerin Truck," *Healthcare Forum Journal* (March/April 1993): 36–44.

15. M. J. Jensen, "Agency Costs of Free Cash Flows, Corporate Finance, and Takeovers," *American Economic Review* 76, no. 2 (1986): 323–329. M. J. Jensen, "Eclipse of the Public Corporation," *Harvard Business Review* (September–October, 1989): 61–74.

16. H. B. Hansmann, "The Role of Nonprofit Enterprise," *Yale Law Journal* 89 (1980): 835–898. H. B. Hansmann, *The Ownership of Enterprise* (Cambridge, Mass.: Harvard University Press, 1996).

17. Jensen, "Agency Costs of Free Cash Flow, Corporate Finance, and Takeovers." A. Shleifer and R. W. Vishny, "A Survey of Corporate Governance," *Journal of Finance* 52, no. 2 (1997): 737–783.

18. Antitrust is relatively clear and effective in its opposition to collusion by independent physicians and hospitals to raise prices, but must adopt a more complex balancing approach to evaluating full asset mergers. See *Statement of Antitrust Enforcement Policy in Health Care,* issued by the U.S. Department of Justice and the Federal Trade Commission, August 1998. For an overview of hospital horizontal merger law and economics, see J. B. Baker, "The Antitrust Analysis of Hospital Mergers and the Transformation of the Hospital Industry," *Law and Contemporary Problems* 51, no. 2 (1989): 93–164.

19. For an introduction to the literature on antitrust implications of vertical integration, see the papers by M. K. Perry, "Vertical Integration: Determinants and Effects," and M. L. Katz, "Vertical Contractual Relations," both in *Handbook of Industrial Organization,* ed. R. Schmalensee and R. D. Willig (Amsterdam: Elsevier Science Publishers, 1989).

20. There is a substantial economic literature on market structure and performance, and in particular on the Schumpetrian hypothesis that concentrated market power is conducive to technological innovation due to ability to internally finance projects with uncertain and long-term profitability. For an overview of related issues, see W. M. Cohen, "Empirical Studies of Innovation and Market Structure," in *Handbook of Industrial Organization.* Also see G. Dosi, "Sources, Procedures, and Microeconomic Effects of Innovation," *Journal of Economic Literature* 26 (1988): 1120–1171.

21. The economic evidence on this point is massive and compelling, as is the experience of noncompetitive economies under state socialism and state capitalism. For recent contributions, see M. E. Porter, *The Competitive Advantage of Nations* (New York: Free Press, 1990) and D. Yergin and J. Stanislaw, *The Commanding Heights* (New York: Simon and Schuster, 1998).

22. The evolution of the Mullikin physician organization, including its relations with the Daughters of Charity, are chronicled in various issues of the *Integrated Healthcare Report,* an industry newsletter. This interpretation of events was based on the trade press, discussions with Mullikin leaders and members, and discussions with individuals in unaffiliated organizations.

23. This interpretation of the evolution at Friendly Hills is derived from the trade press and company documents, and from discussions with physician and administrative leaders in the organization and in other physician organizations, hospital systems, and health insurance plans. Further information on Friendly Hills can be obtained through L. P. Casalino and J. C. Robinson, *The Evolution of Medical Groups and Capitation in California* (Oakland: California Health-Care Foundation, 1997).

24. A. E. Barnett, "Building a Vertical Provider System," *Physician Executive* (November–December 1993).

25. R. Gumbiner, *FHP: The Evolution of a Managed Care Health Maintenance Organization, 1955–1992* (Berkeley: University of California Press, 1995).

26. This interpretation of the UniHealth experience was based on the trade press, company documents, and discussions with physician and administrative leaders at the system, its affiliated medical groups, competing organizations, and health insurance plans.

27. For information on UniMed, see J. C. Robinson, "Consolidation of Medical Groups into Physician Practice Management Organizations," *Journal of the American Medical Association* 279 (1998): 144–149.

CHAPTER 9.   THE CORPORATE PRACTICE OF MEDICINE

1. R. H. Wiebe, *The Search for Order 1877–1920* (New York: Farrar, Straus and Giroux, 1967). E. W. Hawley, *The New Deal and the Problem of Monopoly* (Princeton: Princeton University Press, 1966). L. Galambos, *The Public Image of Big Business in America 1880–1990* (Baltimore: Johns Hopkins University Press, 1975).

2. D. W. Douglass and J. C. Miller, "Quality Competition, Industry Equilibrium, and Efficiency in the Price-Constrained Airline Market," *American Economic Review* 64 (1974): 657–669. E. E. Bailey, D. R. Graham, and D. P.

Kaplan, *Deregulating the Airlines* (Cambridge, Mass.: MIT Press, 1985). The classic paper on the cost-increasing effects of competition in the presence of rate regulation is G. J. Stigler, "Price and Non-Price Competition," *Journal of Political Economy* 76 (1968): 149–54. R. H. K. Vietor, *Contrived Competition: Regulation and Deregulation in America* (Cambridge, Mass.: Harvard University Press, 1994).

3. H. Averch and L. Johnson, "Behavior of the Firm under Regulatory Constraint," *American Economic Review* 52 (1962): 1052–1069. P. L. Joskow and R. Schmalensee, "Incentive Regulation for Electric Utilities," *Yale Journal on Regulation* 4, no. 1 (1986): 1–49. P. L. Joskow, "Regulatory Failure, Regulatory Reform, and Structural Change in the Electric Power Industry, *Brookings Papers: Microeconomics* 1989 (1989): 125–199.

4. A. F. Friedlander and R. H. Spady, *Freight Transport Regulation: Equity, Efficiency, and Competition in the Rail and Trucking Industries* (Cambridge, Mass.: MIT Press, 1981). T. E. Keeler, *Railroads, Freight, and Public Policy* (Washington, D.C.: Brookings Institution, 1983). A. F. Friedlander, E. R. Berndt, and G. McCullough, "Governance Structure, Managerial Characteristics, and Firm Performance in the Deregulated Rail Industry," *Brookings Papers: Microeconomics 1992* (1992): 95–183.

5. A. N. Berger, A. K. Sashyap, and J. M. Scalise, "The Transformation of the U.S. Banking Industry: What a Long Strange Trip It's Been," *Brookings Papers on Economic Activity 1995*, no. 2 (1995): 55–218.

6. A. DeVany and W. D. Walls, "Natural Gas Industry Transformation, Competitive Institutions, and the Role of Regulation," *Energy Policy* 22, no. 9 (1994): 755–763. K. W. Costello and D. J. Duann, "Turning Up the Heat in the Natural Gas Industry," *Regulation 1996*, no. 1 (1996): 52–59. Vietor, *Contrived Competition.*

7. G. J. Stigler, "The Theory of Economic Regulation," *Bell Journal of Economics and Management Science* 2 (1971): 22–50. S. Pelzman, "Toward a More General Theory of Regulation," *Journal of Law and Economics* 19 (1976): 211–240. G. Becker, "A Theory of Competition among Pressure Groups for Political Influence," *Quarterly Journal of Economics* 98 (1983): 371–400. S. Pelzman, "The Economic Theory of Regulation after a Decade of Deregulation," *Brookings Papers: Microeconomics 1989* (1989): 1–41. A. E. Kahn, *The Economics of Regulation: Principles and Institutions* (New York: John Wiley, 1971; 2nd ed., 1988). P. L. Joskow and R. C. Noll, "Regulation in Theory and Practice: An Overview," in *Studies in Public Regulation,* ed. G. Fromm (Cambridge, Mass.: MIT Press, 1981). M. W. White, "Power Struggles: Explaining Deregulatory Reforms in Electricity Markets," *Brookings Papers: Microeconomics 1996* (1996): 201–267.

8. A. E. Kahn, "Deregulation: Looking Backward and Looking Forward," *Yale Journal on Regulation* 7 (1990): 325–354. C. Winston, "Economic Deregulation: Days of Reckoning for Microeconomists," *Journal of Economic Literature* 31 (1993): 1263–1289. J. R. Meyer and W. B. Tye, "Toward Achieving Workable Competition in Industries Undergoing a Transition to Deregulation: A Contractual Equilibrium Approach," *Yale Journal on Regulation* 5 (1988): 273–297. Vietor, *Contrived Competition.*

9. These quantitative estimates are derived from the literature survey in C. Winston, "U.S. Industry Adjustment to Economic Deregulation," *Journal of Economic Perspectives* 12, no. 3 (1998): 89–110.

10. Fare ceilings imposed by Civil Aeronautics Board had stimulated non-price competition through more frequent flights, reducing occupancy rates and raising average costs per passenger mile, and it was anticipated that deregulation would reduce frequency by stimulating price competition. But the increase in demand stimulated by the lower prices more than compensated for the frequency-reducing impact of higher seat occupancy rates.

11. K. Levit, C. Cowan, B. Braden et al., "National Health Expenditures in 1997: More Slow Growth," *Health Affairs* 17, no. 6 (1998): 99–110.

12. The cognoscenti will recognize the debt of this paragraph and, indeed, this entire book to J. A. Schumpeter, *Capitalism, Socialism, and Democracy* (New York: Harper and Row, 1942).

Index

Design: Steve Renick
Composition: G&S Typesetters, Inc.
Printing and binding: Haddon Craftsmen
Index: Beaver Wood Associates